501 TV-free Science Experiments for Kids

HB

HINKLER
BOOKS

Authors: Melanie McLennan, Lis Schoenborn, Andrea Eales, Owen Eales, Sarah Macdonald,
Francesca Ciavola, Bianca Iavazzo and Pete Kavadias
Cover Design: Sam Grimmer
Cover Photography: Ned Meldrum
Editor: Susannah Burgess
Illustrator: Simon Sherry, Palmer Higgs
Text Design: William Ainger, Palmer Higgs
Typesetting: Palmer Higgs, Box Hill, Vic Australia

501 Science Experiments
Published in 2005 by Hinkler Books Pty Ltd
17–23 Redwood Drive
Dingley VIC 3172 Australia
www.hinklerbooks.com

ISBN 1 7412 1952 3
Printed and bound in Australia

Contents

An ALPHABETICAL INDEX follows the final experiment

How to use this book

As you know, learning is always best when it's shared. While these experiments have been designed to be fun, easy and child-friendly, to get the best results for your child we recommend that you work as a team. As teachers, we use hands-on activities because they engage and inspire children to learn, and by talking about the activity it reinforces understanding. Just a note, we have provided you with experiments that can be performed with instant results, and some that encourage patience and observation skills.

While an age range is given, this is a guide only. Most experiments will be suitable for all children, with varying degrees of adult supervision needed.

All materials listed are cheap and easy to find around the average house and/or garden.

The 'Did You Know?' section gives a brief explanation of the science that happened, or gives an interesting fact relating to the experiment.

Have fun!

Guide to symbols

This simple legend of symbols gives a quick visual reference to the basic elements present in each experiment.

Adult supervision for all ages:

This symbol indicates that adult supervision is recommended for all ages, as equipment such as matches are used.

Adult supervision for younger children:

This symbol indicates that adult supervision is recommended for young children, as equipment such as scissors are used.

No adult supervision needed:

This symbol indicates that adult supervision is not required for children of any age.

Outdoor experiment:

This symbol indicates an experiment can be performed outside.

Indoor experiment:

This symbol indicates an experiment can be performed inside.

Note: If both symbols are ticked, the experiment can be performed both outdoors and indoors.

Tools required:

This experiment requires tools of some type. This could be anything from a simple bowl and vegetable peeler to balloons and craft materials. All these activities have been designed with the basic everyday items in the home such as cereal boxes etc. Some activities may require items to be purchased from a shop but should be inexpensive or alternatives can be found.

The symbols indicated in this book are a guide only. It is the responsibility of all adults to determine the appropriate experiments for each child and the skills they possess. The use of tools requires adult supervision.

How to use the workbook

On the opposite page is a blank template of a science workbook. Use this template as a basis for your child to create their own science workbook, where they can record the results of their experiments.

There is space provided for your child to record their observations, either in the form of simple text or as a simple picture of what they noticed, or both. This encourages good scientific practice, and is a useful opportunity for your child to reflect on the experiment.

Your child might like to keep the pages in a loose leaf binder or paste them into a scrapbook, which they can decorate and personalise in any way they like.

NAME OF EXPERIMENT

WHAT I FOUND OUT:

_____

_____

_____

_____

_____

_____

_____

_____

MY PICTURE:

About the authors

Melanie McLennan is a grade 5/6 teacher at an inner city school in Melbourne, Victoria, Australia. She has just completed her Master of Education and she was the Victorian Graduate Teacher of The Year in 2001.

Lis Schoenborn teaches science to grades prep to 6 at an inner city school in Melbourne. Before she became a teacher, Lis was a research scientist at Melbourne University finding out which bacteria live in soil.

Andrea Eales is a grade 5/6 teacher at an inner city school in Melbourne. She was the Victorian Novice Teacher of The Year in 2002. Andrea has a keen interest in mathematics and science.

Owen Eales currently teaches adult education at the Melbourne CAE (Centre for Adult Education). He has a passion for the classics and investigating our ancient world.

Sarah Macdonald is a prep teacher at an inner city Melbourne school. She graduated with honours from the Bachelor of Education at the University of Melbourne. Sarah was part of a team who produced a CD-ROM for teachers on the teaching of decimals and is very interested in the teaching of mathematics and science in primary schools.

Francesca Ciavola is a grade 3/4 teacher at a primary school in Melbourne. Francesca has a keen interest in science and believes that it is a very important aspect of all children's education.

Bianca Iavazzo is a junior school teacher at a Melbourne primary school. Bianca enjoys all areas of science, especially hands on experiments.

Pete Kavadias is currently completing his Bachelor of Education (Secondary) and his disciplines are science and physical education.

Astronomy

Jar Compass

AIM

To see the attraction of Earth's magnetic field.

MATERIALS

- needle
- magnet
- scissors
- small piece of card
- jar
- thread
- pencil

Did You Know?

The needle is free to turn on its own and will always align itself so that it points north and south. The needle acts as a magnet and is attracted to Earth's magnetic force.

STEPS

1. Stroke the needle with the magnet to magnetise it.

2. Tie one end of your string to the small piece of card and the other end to the pencil.

3. Push the needle through your piece of card.

4. Suspend the piece of card inside the jar by laying the pencil across the mouth of the jar so the string is dangling. Do not allow the card to touch the bottom.

5. The needle should lie horizontally. You should try to get the middle of the needle to rest in the middle of the card.

6. Leave to stand freely and the needle should act as a compass for you.

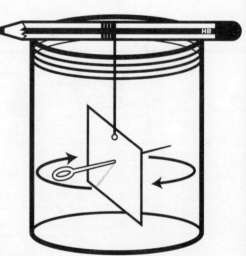

Travel to the Moon

AIM

To experience how difficult it is to reach a moving target.

MATERIALS

- string
- ruler
- scissors
- sticky tape
- metal washer
- books
- small pieces of paper scrunched into balls

Did You Know?

Plotting a course through space is hard – both the spacecraft and the Moon or planet are moving. To save fuel rockets are aimed at where the Moon or planet will be when the rocket is ready to land.

STEPS

1. Measure and cut a piece of string about 60 cm (24 in) long.
2. Stick one end of the string to the ruler.
3. Tie a washer to the other end of the string.
4. Place the ruler on the edge of a table so that the string is hanging over.
5. Keep the ruler in place by putting a heavy book on top.
6. Try to hit the washer with the pieces of paper.
7. Swing the washer and try to hit it with the paper.

EXPERIMENT
2

Rocket Launch

AIM

To experience a rocket launching.

MATERIALS

- cardboard
- pen
- ruler
- scissors
- plastic bottle
- sticky tape
- funnel
- jug of water
- cork
- bradawl (corkscrew)
- air valve
- plastic tubing
- bicycle pump

Did You Know?

The force of a rocket comes from the amount of propellant it shoots out. The water in the bottle is the propellant. Compressed air above the water provides the energy that makes the thrust.
Warning: *Launch your rocket in an open space away from buildings and trees.*

STEPS

1. Rockets have fins to help them fly. Cut out four 20 cm (8 in) long fin shaped pieces of cardboard, e.g.

2. Fold over the flap of the fin and with sticky tape attach to the bottle.

3. Use the funnel to half fill the bottle with water.

4. Use the bradawl (corkscrew) to carefully drill a hole through the cork.

5. Push the wide end of the valve into the tubing.

6. Push the valve through the hole in the cork.

7. Push the cork and the valve into the top of the plastic bottle. Make sure it fits firmly.

8. Attach the other end of the plastic tubing to bicycle pump.

9. Turn your rocket the right way up – so that the cork is on the ground.

10. Pump the bicycle pump.

EXPERIMENT
3

Rocork Launch!

SUPERVISED

ACTIVITY

AIM

To experience a mini rocket launching.

MATERIALS

- teaspoon of bicarbonate of soda (baking soda)
- paper towel about 10 cm × 20 cm (4 in × 8 in)
- $\frac{1}{2}$ cup of water
- $\frac{1}{2}$ cup of vinegar
- paper streamers or ribbons
- drawing pin
- cork
- plastic bottle

Did You Know?

A chemical reaction between the vinegar (liquid oxygen) and the baking soda (fuel) produces carbon dioxide gas. The pressure inside the bottle pushes against the cork. In real rockets the gas is jetted out of the actual spacecraft, propelling it forward!
Warning: *When the rocork is about to launch make sure you are a safe distance away.*

STEPS

1. Place the baking soda on the middle of the paper towel.
2. Roll up the towel and twist the ends to keep the baking soda inside.
3. Pour the water and vinegar into the bottle.
4. Cut out some streamers or ribbons and with a drawing pin attach them to the cork.
5. Drop the paper towel into the bottle and very quickly push the cork into the bottle.
6. Place the bottle in an outside area that is away from windows etc.
7. Stand well away and watch.

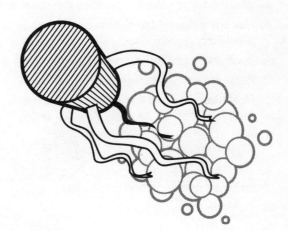

Escaping Gravity

AIM

To experience how gravity can be escaped so spacecraft can leave Earth.

MATERIALS

- cardboard
- PVA glue
- ruler
- 10 cm × 5 cm piece of plastic
- scissors
- baking tray
- magnetic strip
- Blu-Tak
- sticky tape
- ball bearings
- plasticine

Did You Know?

To orbit Earth a rocket must reach at least 28,500 km/h (17,700 mph). To escape Earth's gravity and travel further into space a spacecraft must reach 40,200 km/h (25,000 mph). The magnet represents the pull of Earth's gravity while the trough is the path of the rocket as it soars into orbit. At first the ball bearing sticks to the magnet because the velocity is not fast enough to escape the magnet's pull. When the trough is raised the speed of the ball bearing is increased and like a rocket entering space the magnet's force is not strong enough.

STEPS

1. Cut out a piece of cardboard 30 cm × 10 cm (12 in × 4 in).
2. Fold the strip of cardboard lengthways four times to form a trough in the shape of an M.
3. Cut the magnetic strips into about five pieces and stick them to the piece of plastic with Blu-Tak.
4. Stick the magnet at the end of the baking tray in the centre.
5. Place the trough over the magnet and attach with sticky tape.
6. Roll the plasticine into a ball. Place it under the other end of the trough, raising it slightly.
7. Place a ball bearing at the end of the trough and let it roll down.
8. Raise the trough and try again.
9. Continue until the ball bearing rolls past the magnet.

EXPERIMENT

5

Balloon Rocket

 ✓

 ✓

🏠

✂ ✓

AIM

To view the stages of a rocket launch.

MATERIALS

- 2 paper or plastic drinking cups
- scissors
- sticky tape
- long balloon
- round balloon

Did You Know?

Rockets transport humans to the Moon. The Moon and Earth are the only two places in our solar system that humans have been to.

STEPS

1. Carefully cut out the bottoms of two paper or plastic cups and sit one of the cups inside the other.

2. Partly blow up the long balloon. Do not tie.

3. Slide the drinking cups over the untied end of the balloon.

4. Fold the untied end of the balloon over the side of the cup and sticky tape it down firmly so air cannot escape.

5. Place the round balloon inside the cups and blow up the balloon.

6. Hold the untied end of the round balloon. Do not tie.

7. Hold the rocket so it is facing the sky.

8. Unstick the long balloon's end.

9. Let go of the round balloon.

EXPERIMENT

6

Working in Space

AIM

To experience how astronauts feel working in space.

MATERIALS

- nuts and bolts
- rubber gloves
- big bowl
- water

STEPS

1. Place the nuts and bolts onto a table and try picking them up and screwing them together.

2. Put on a pair of rubber gloves (these represent spacesuit gloves) and try to do the same.

3. Fill the bowl with water.

4. Add the nuts and bolts.

5. Try to pick up the nuts and bolts and screw them together.

Did You Know?

Bulky spacesuits make it very hard for astronauts to work in space. Heavy and stiff spacesuits tire out astronauts quickly and prevent them from feeling things properly.

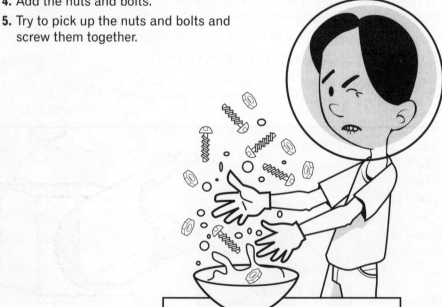

EXPERIMENT

7

Robot Arms

SUPERVISED

ACTIVITY

AIM

To become an astronaut and work a robot arm.

MATERIALS

- cardboard
- scissors
- ruler
- bradawl (corkscrew)
- 2 split pins
- dowelling
- picture hook
- 2 paper clips
- plasticine

Did You Know?

If satellites break down, astronauts are required to fix them. Robot arms are used by astronauts to rebuild and fix these satellites.

STEPS

1. Measure out three cardboard strips about 30 cm × 5 cm (12 in × 2 in).
2. Cut them out.
3. Use the bradawl (corkscrew) to make a hole about 2 cm ($^3/_4$ in) from both ends of each strip.
4. Join the strips with split pins.
5. Bend one of the paper clips into an 's' shape and slide it through the hole at the end of the arm.
6. Take the hook and screw it into the end of the dowelling.
7. Pass the hook on the dowelling through the hole in the end of the cardboard. Move the dowelling to move the robot arm.
8. Make a ball out of the plasticine and gently push in the second paper clip.
9. Try to pick up the plasticine ball with the robot arm.

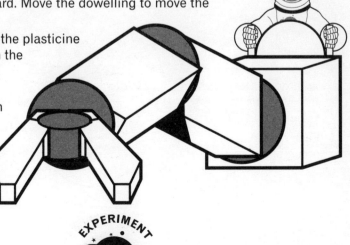

EXPERIMENT
8

Aliens in the Night

SUPERVISED

ACTIVITY

AIM

To use shadows to produce an alien play.

MATERIALS

- coloured pens/pencils
- white sheet
- scissors
- string
- cardboard
- pegs
- sticky tape
- chairs
- bendy straws
- torch or lamp

Did You Know?

So far the only place in the Universe known to have life is Earth. Many astronomers believe that life most probably exists on one or many of the billions of planets that we do not know about.

STEPS

1. Draw a large alien shape on the cardboard.
2. Cut out the alien figure.
3. Make as many alien characters as you like.
4. Bend the straw and stick the shorter end to the back of the alien.
5. Push one straw into the other to make a longer handle.
6. Place two chairs about one metre (3 ft) apart.
7. Tie string between the two chairs.
8. Peg the sheet onto the string as the curtain.
9. Place the torch or lamp behind the curtain and the puppet.
10. Perform a play about aliens.

EXPERIMENT

9

Eating in Space

 ✓

SUPERVISED

 ✓
 ✓

ACTIVITY

AIM

To experience what astronauts would eat in space.

MATERIALS

- baby food or puréed vegetables
- microwave oven
- plastic bag

STEPS

1. Puree the vegetables.
2. Place pureed vegetables or baby food into a plastic bag.
3. Freeze.
4. Place the plastic bag into the microwave and heat.
5. Eat!

Did You Know?

Space crews eat three meals a day. They can choose from about 70 different meals. These meals are decided on and planned before the mission begins.

EXPERIMENT

10

Meteor Burnout

SUPERVISED ✓

ACTIVITY ✓ ✓

AIM

To view how a meteor burns up as it enters Earth's atmosphere.

MATERIALS

- plastic bottle
- water
- ½ seltzer tablet

STEPS

1. Fill up the plastic bottle with water.
2. Drop the tablet into the water.
3. Observe.

Did You Know?

Meteors are small rock-like chunks that are probably broken pieces of comets or asteroids that travel around in outer space. They burn up as they enter and pass through Earth's atmosphere.

EXPERIMENT

11

Astronaut Suits

✓

SUPERVISED

 ✓

 ✓

ACTIVITY

AIM

To experience how an astronaut would feel in a spacesuit.

MATERIALS

- 2 large pairs of overalls
- newspaper
- ski gloves
- ski boots or gum boots
- motorcycle or bicycle helmet
- backpack
- books

Did You Know?

Space suits protect the astronauts from the airless vacuum of space. Without the suits the astronauts' blood would boil and they would die within seconds. Spacesuits are like their own spacecraft, giving astronauts help with cooling, oxygen and power.

STEPS

1. Put on both pairs of overalls.

2. Stuff scrunched up newspaper in between the two overalls.

3. Put on the ski gloves, ski boots and helmet.

4. Place some books into a backpack and put the backpack onto your back.

5. Slowly walk around the house. Take note of how you feel and move.

6. Now try to pick up items in your house, e.g. books, a drinking glass etc.

Shadow Lines

✓

 ✓
 ✓
 ✓

AIM

To experiment with the relationship between the angle of light and a shadow's length.

MATERIALS

- toothpick
- glue
- cardboard
- scissors
- torch
- natural sunlight

Did You Know?

The Sun is our oldest time machine. The position of the Sun in the sky changes as Earth rotates. This change in position changes the shape and size of shadows on Earth.

STEPS

1. Cut a small rectangular piece out of the cardboard approximately 2 cm × 10 cm (¾ in × 4 in).

2. Push a toothpick into the centre of the small piece of cardboard.

3. Put this piece of cardboard on top of a larger piece of cardboard about 20 cm × 20 cm (8 in × 8 in).

4. Shine the torch on the toothpick to create a shadow line.

5. Try different ways of making the shadow line by changing the direction the torch shines.

6. Now use natural sunlight to create a shadow with the toothpick.

7. Note any differences.

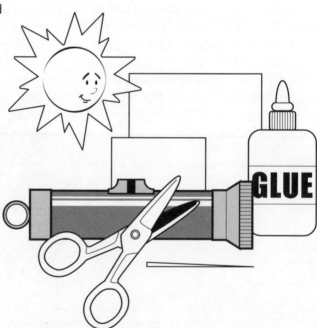

EXPERIMENT
13

Star Tracker

AIM

To track the wavelengths coming from the Sun.

MATERIALS

- sheet of paper
- drinking glass
- water

Did You Know?

Light from the Sun shows many colours. Astronomers can tell what different types of gases make up a star by studying the bands, or spectrums, of light it gives off.

STEPS

1. Find a sunny spot.
2. Place the sheet of paper on the table or ground.
3. Half fill the glass with water.
4. Hold the glass between your thumb and finger about 7 or 8 cm (2½ or 3 in) above the sheet of paper.
5. Slowly move the glass up and down and slightly onto an angle.

SUPERVISED

ACTIVITY

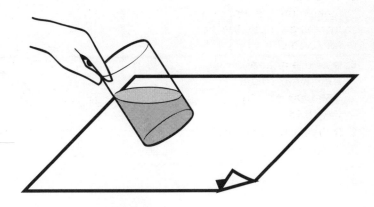

EXPERIMENT
14

Starry Night Sky

5–12
AGES

 ✓

SUPERVISED

 ✓
 ✓

ACTIVITY

AIM

To view your very own night sky.

MATERIALS

- shoe box
- torch
- sharp pencil
- scissors

Did You Know?

The oldest stars in the Milky Way are packed together in giant balls called globular clusters. One such cluster is the Omega Centauri, which contains several million stars.

STEPS

1. Copy the pattern of your favourite cluster of stars or constellation (for example, the Southern Cross – or design your own!) onto the side of a shoe box.

2. With a sharp pencil poke through the cardboard of the shoe box to create small holes.

3. On the opposite side of the shoe box trace around the head of the torch.

4. Cut it out and fit the torch into the box.

5. In a dark room point the torch to the roof or a wall.

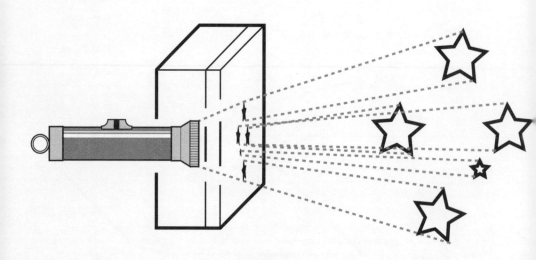

How Old Are You Really?

 ✓

SUPERVISED

 ✓

ACTIVITY ✓

AIM

To find out your age according to the length of another planet's year.

MATERIALS

- paper
- pen
- calculator

STEPS

1. The first thing you need to do is put your own age into the calculator.

2. Now you need to press divide on the calculator and then press in the planet's period of revolution. (For example, if you want to work out how old you would be on Mars you would press 12 ÷ 1.88 = 6.38 years old!)

3. Now you know how old you would be if you lived on another planet! Alternatively, you don't have to use a calculator, you could try working it out by yourself!

Planet	Period of Revolution (compared to Earth)
Mercury	0.241 Earth years (87.9 Earth days)
Venus	0.615 Earth years (224.7 Earth days)
Earth	1.0 Earth year
Mars	1.88 Earth years (686.9 Earth days)
Jupiter	11.9 Earth years
Saturn	29.5 Earth years
Uranus	84.0 Earth years
Neptune	164.8 Earth years
Pluto	248.5 Earth years

Did You Know?

There are nine planets in our solar system and Saturn is the second biggest planet, but did you know it is also the lightest planet? It is also the only planet in our solar system that could float in water.

EARTH YEARS = 12   JUPITER YEARS = 1!

Potato Asteroids

SUPERVISED

ACTIVITY

AIM

To make and bake asteroids.

MATERIALS

- baking tray
- potato
- oven
- oven mitt or pot holders
- mixing bowl and large spoon
- 4 to 8 cups of mashed potatoes
- ¼ cup (½ stick) of butter or margarine
- pot
- potato masher

Did You Know?

Asteroids are chunks of rock that never quite made it to fully-fledged planet-hood when our solar system formed. Most of them orbit the Sun in a 'belt' between Mars (the fourth planet) and Jupiter (the fifth planet). But some asteroids have orbits that cross or come close to Earth's orbit.

STEPS

1. Turn on your oven to 190°C (375°F). Ask an adult to help.

2. Take a little slice of the butter or margarine and rub it evenly on the baking tray.

3. Make the mashed potatoes (a lot – eight cups or a little – four cups).

4. Add butter or margarine, salt and pepper to the potatoes and mix well. The mixture should stick together. If it's too dry, add a little milk.

5. Take a handful of potatoes (about ½ cup or more) and shape it into your own idea of an interesting asteroid shape. Use your fingers to poke dents in it for craters.

6. Set the asteroid on the greased baking tray.

7. Put the tray full of asteroids in the hot oven for about 20 to 25 minutes, or until they are brown.

8. Using the pot holders or oven mitt, remove the tray from the oven, and using the large spoon, transfer the asteroids to a serving plate.

9. Enjoy your asteroids!

MMM ... asteroids - straight from the oven!

EXPERIMENT

17

Meteorites and Craters

SUPERVISED

ACTIVITY

AIM

To investigate how the size, angle and speed of a meteorite's impact affects the properties of a crater.

MATERIALS

- 2 shallow basins (cat litter boxes work well)
- ruler
- 2 bags of unbleached flour
- pencil
- box of instant cocoa
- newspaper
- several pebbles, various sizes
- chair

> **Did You Know?**
>
> All craters that we have seen on the Moon and Earth are pretty much circular. The reason is that an explosion occurs on impact and the forces associated with an explosion are always spherically symmetrical.

STEPS

1. Fill one of the basins with flour about 3–4 cm deep (1–1½ in). Spread the newspaper out and place the basin on top.
2. Sprinkle a little cocoa on the surface.
3. Pick out one of the smallest pebbles, stand on a chair and drop (not throw) the pebble into the basin.
4. Observe and try to predict the appearance of a crater formed by a larger pebble dropped from the same height.
5. Repeat step 3, but this time with a medium-sized pebble. What is different?
6. Repeat step 3, again, but this time with the largest pebble.
7. Repeat steps 3 to 5 but this time vary the height. Smooth the flour and sprinkle on more cocoa. Throw a medium-sized pebble with moderate force vertically into the basin.
8. Throw the same-sized pebble at about the same speed, but at a slight angle. Observe the shape of the new crater and predict how the shape will change as the angle increases.
9. Continue throwing pebbles into the basin, taking care to throw the same-sized rocks at the same speed, but at varying angles.

Equinox

 ✓

 ✓

 ✓

AIM

To experiment with the different locations of the Sun at specific times of the year.

MATERIALS

- square shaped piece of cardboard
- wooden stick about 15 cm to 25 cm (6 in to 10 in)
- glue

Did You Know?

The cause of the change in the shadow's location (i.e. the location of the Sun) is the tilt of Earth's axis. This causes Earth to face the Sun at an angle of 23 degrees. Where Earth is located in its orbit around the Sun determines the length of the day. Since Earth's location around the Sun is changing continuously, so is the length of the days.
The only two days where the Sun's location matches at any time are March 21 (Vernal Equinox) and September 21 (Autumnal Equinox).

STEPS

1. Glue the wooden stick to the cardboard so that it stands upright.

2. Once the glue has dried and the stick can stand by itself, place the cardboard square on a flat surface where it will be exposed to the Sun. Take note of the time of day.

3. Mark the point on the board where the tip of the shadow is located and write the date.

4. Repeat this daily, or weekly, at the exact same time each day. Be very careful to place the board in exactly the same spot.

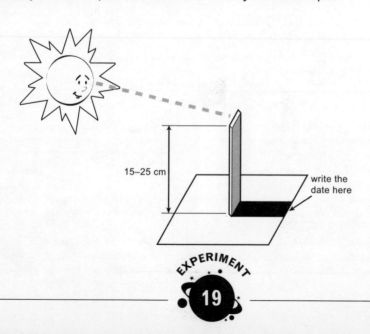

15–25 cm

write the date here

Pole Gravity

AIM

To see the forces of gravity.

MATERIALS

- pole

STEPS

1. Stand up straight and balance the pole in the palm of your hand vertically.

2. Move to a spot a few feet away and try to keep the pole upright vertically. The pole should change position.

3. When you stand still again the pole will change position also.

Did You Know?

In this experiment downward gravity and forward motion are working against one another. When you are standing still only one of these forces is working, but when you take steps forward both of the forces are working. Can you work out which?

Spinning on an Axis

 ✓

SUPERVISED

 ✓
 ✓

ACTIVITY

AIM

To imitate how Earth spins on its axis.

MATERIALS

- 2 pins
- new coin (20 cent piece is best)

STEPS

1. Place the two pinpoints at opposite ends of the coin. Now pick it up, without slipping, only using the pins.

2. Don't get discouraged, keep trying.

3. Once you have picked up the coin, gently blow on the top of it.

Did You Know?

An object that is spinning revolves around a line. This line is called the object's axis. Earth also revolves on an axis but, unlike in this experiment, you cannot see anything supporting it.

Angled Light

SUPERVISED

ACTIVITY

AIM

To see angled light.

MATERIALS

- torch
- white paper

STEPS

1. Turn the lights off in a room.
2. Put your piece of white paper on a table and aim the torch straight down at the paper. Note what you see.
3. Now tilt your torch a little and aim it at the paper. Note what you now see.

Did You Know?

When the sun shines on Earth at the equator it is more intense, just like the torch facing straight down. When you move away from the equator the climate cools down because the light is on an angle.

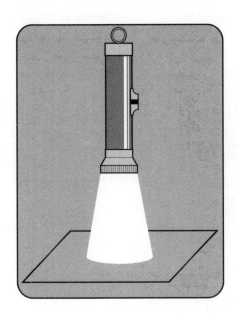
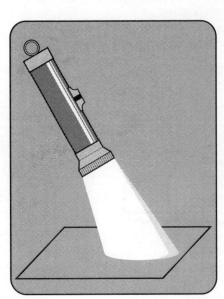

Shrinking Sun

SUPERVISED

ACTIVITY

AIM
To follow the movements of the Sun.

MATERIALS
- nearby tree
- sunglasses
- far-away object

STEPS

1. Find a place that faces east or west and that contains your nearby tree and far-away object.

2. You need to line up your tree and your far-away object. You need to do this so that you are looking at the same spot each day.

3. At dawn or dusk each day make a note of where the Sun appears in relation to your object.

4. Do this for a week or two and you should start to see some changes.

Did You Know?
By tracking the Sun's movements, astronomers were able to see that it passed through 12 constellations. These constellations became known as the zodiac, and gave us the star signs which we relate to our birth.

Shadow Dances

AIM

To make a shadow dance.

MATERIALS

- glue or tape
- cardboard
- styrofoam
- toothpick
- torch

Did You Know?

The differences in the light sources happen because the sun is further away and therefore the angles of the shadow may not have been noticeably different.

STEPS

1. Cut a small strip from the styrofoam and push the toothpick into it. Put this strip onto the piece of cardboard.

2. Shine your torch on the toothpick to make a shadow.

3. Move the torch to change what the shadow looks like. Do not move the toothpick. How have you changed it and what did you do?

4. Now move the toothpick but do not move the torch. What happens to your shadow now?

5. You can move your shadow using just the sun and the toothpick.

6. Note any changes in the shadow when you use the torch and the sunlight.

EXPERIMENT
24

E.T. Rocks

AIM

To collect and observe extra-terrestrial rocks.

MATERIALS

- white paper (large piece)
- magnet
- magnifying glass

Did You Know?

Every day tonnes of these particles fall to Earth from meteorites. You will not feel them, or see them, unless you look very carefully because they are miniscule.

STEPS

1. Go outside on a sunny day and secure your large piece of paper to an area that is not covered by trees.

2. Leave the paper there for 4–6 hours. Do not leave it out in the rain.

3. Collect the paper gently. Make sure you gather it so that anything you have collected rolls into the middle of the paper.

4. Hold your magnet under the paper and lightly shake off the material gathered. The material not attracted to your magnet will just fall off.

5. Collect the material that did not fall off and look at it through a magnifying glass.

6. Extra-terrestrial rocks usually have dark round particles with pitted surfaces.

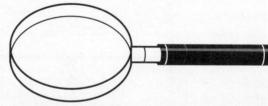

Greenhouse Effect

SUPERVISED

ACTIVITY

AIM

To create the greenhouse effect felt on Venus.

MATERIALS

- outdoor thermometer
- glass jar with a lid
- sunlight

Did You Know?

Strong rays of light hit the surface of Venus and heat it up, but the clouds and carbon dioxide in the air do not allow the strong heat to escape. This means that Venus never cools down because the hot air is trapped there.

STEPS

1. Put the jar outside in the sun with the lid off and place the thermometer inside with the bulb facing the bottom of the jar.

2. Wait for a couple of minutes for the temperature to stabilise and then record the temperature.

3. Put the thermometer inside the jar with the bulb facing the sky. Put the lid on and place it in the sun with the lid facing down.

4. Wait for the temperature to stop moving and then record it.

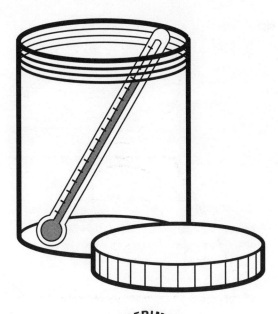

Making a Parallax

AIM

To create a parallax (a parallax is how astronomers measure the distance to stars).

MATERIALS

- pencil
- bookshelf

STEPS

Did You Know?

Astronomers measure the distance to nearby stars by measuring their parallax. They do this six months apart, when Earth moves from one side of the Sun to the other. The parallax occurs in the middle of the two points.

1. Hold your pencil in front of you as far as your arm will stretch and focus your eyes on the bookshelf.

2. Close your left eye and make a note of where you see the pencil on your bookshelf.

3. Do not change your position at all, but just swap your eyes by closing your right eye instead of your left.

4. What do you notice about the position of the pencil?

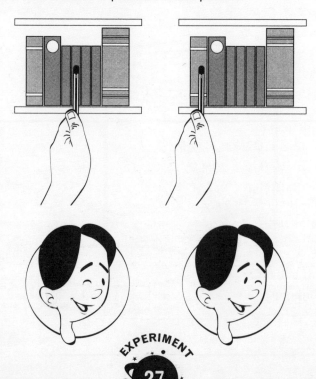

Stars in the Day

SUPERVISED

ACTIVITY

AIM

To see daytime stars.

MATERIALS

- paper
- hole punch
- card
- white envelope
- lamp

Did You Know?

You can see the stars better in the country than in the city. In the city the sky has a lot of pollution and streetlights, making it difficult to see faint lights in the sky.

STEPS

1. Use your hole punch to make holes in the card. These holes will represent stars.

2. Put the piece of card inside a white envelope.

3. Turn the lights out in a room and shine a lamp onto the front of the envelope. The envelope reflects the light so you cannot see the stars inside.

4. Try shining the light from behind the envelope.

Bubble Rocket

 ✓

SUPERVISED
 ✓

 ✓
ACTIVITY

AIM

To build a bubble powered rocket.

MATERIALS

- paper
- photo film canister
- tape
- scissors
- antacid tablet
- paper towels
- water
- sunglasses

Did You Know?

A real rocket works the same way that yours does, but instead of using an antacid tablet, it uses rocket fuel. The antacid tablet releases bubbles and when the air escapes from the bubbles it pushes the sides of the canister. The canister cannot expand so it pops its lid and the rocket takes off!

STEPS

1. Cut your paper to make a rocket shape (your rocket can be long, short, wide or skinny).

2. Insert your film canister inside the rocket and attach it with tape. Make sure the lid of the canister is facing down.

3. Cut out a circle shape. Roll it into a cone and attach it to the top of your rocket.

4. Put on your sunglasses.

5. Turn the rocket upside down and take off the film canister lid.

6. Fill the canister one third full of water and drop the antacid tablet in (you must do these steps quickly).

7. Put the lid back on and place your rocket the right way up on your driveway or any piece of concrete.

8. Stand back and watch it blast off.

Centrifugal Force

 ✓

 ✓
 ✓

AIM

To see the effect of centrifugal force.

MATERIALS

- string
- carrot with the leaves still attached
- large spool
- small spool

STEPS

1. Tie the string to the top of the carrot with the leaves.

2. Slip the other end of the string through the large spool and then attach it to the small spool by tying it up.

3. Hold the large spool and begin making circles with your hand. The small spool should lift in the air.

4. Watch the carrot to see what happens.

Did You Know?

The force of the rotation acts as a pulling force. This pulling force is what causes the carrot to move. Centrifugal force is the force that pulls away from the centre circle.

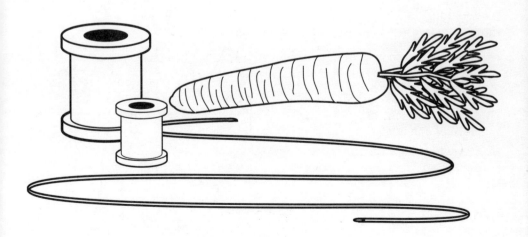

EXPERIMENT
30

Falling Paper

SUPERVISED

ACTIVITY

AIM

To see how things move through the air.

MATERIALS

- 2 pieces of paper
- plastic bag
- string
- paper clip
- tape
- scissors

Did You Know?

Leonardo da Vinci designed the first parachutes. He was also a very famous painter.

STEPS

1. Keep one piece of paper flat and crumple the other one up.

2. Hold both sheets of paper out in front of you and drop them to the floor at the same time.

3. Cut the bag into a square and attach the string to each corner. Gather all the strings together at the bottom and attach them to a paper clip to act as a weight.

4. Open the chute and let it fall from the same height as you did the paper.

5. Cut slits into the bag and repeat the previous steps.

Gazing at Stars

AIM

To see how galaxies are drifting away.

MATERIALS

- balloon
- waterproof marker

STEPS

1. Blow up your balloon to half its capacity but do not tie it.
2. With your marker draw small specks all over the balloon.
3. Blow more air into the balloon and then note the position of the specks.
4. Keep blowing and observing the specks. What do you notice?

Did You Know?

Scientists think that the Universe is growing in size just like your balloon did. This means that the galaxies are moving away from each other leaving big distances between them.

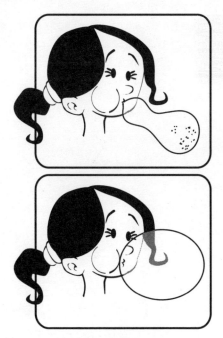

Making Meridians

AIM

To see how Earth is divided.

MATERIALS

- large orange
- string
- ruler
- felt marker
- torch

Did You Know?

Long ago Earth was divided into 24 sections called meridians. On one part of Earth it is daytime while on the other side of Earth it is night-time. The meridian lines cannot be seen as they are imaginary lines.

STEPS

1. Measure around the middle of the orange by holding the string around it and then laying the string against your ruler.

2. With your marker make a small mark every 12 mm (½ in) around the middle of the orange. You should end up with 24 marks.

3. Make a line from the top of the orange through one of the marks in the middle all the way to the bottom of the orange.

4. You must repeat this step for every mark on your orange.

5. Shine your torch straight at the orange, turn the orange and note what you see.

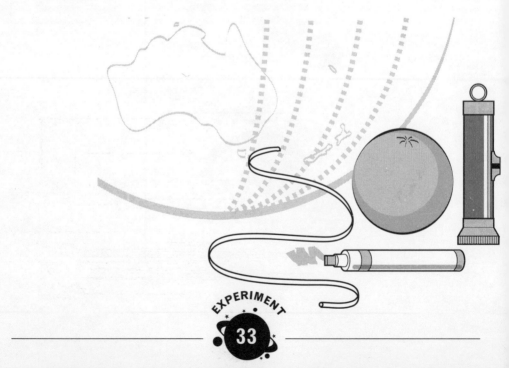

See Inside a Box

SUPERVISED

ACTIVITY

AIM

To see inside a closed box without taking the lid off.

MATERIALS

- a large box with a lid
- an object (teddy, drink bottle)
- knitting needle or skewer
- a piece of paper

Did You Know?

Scientists use radars to look at Earth's surface when clouds cover it. Radars use light energy but we can't see it. The radar bounces off surfaces and makes echo noises that the radar antenna hears.

STEPS

1. Put the object inside the box and close the lid.

2. Stick the piece of paper to the top of the lid.

3. Use your skewer to gently poke through the lid of the box.

4. You will need to measure how far your knitting needle goes into the box before it hits something. Measure the knitting needle and use a different colour for each measurement, then record this on the paper on top of the box.

5. When you have done this across the whole lid of the box you will see a shape start to emerge.

6. Using the heights you have recorded you will be able to get a 3D idea of the object.

EXPERIMENT

34

Seeing Ions in Action

5–12
AGES

SUPERVISED ✓

ACTIVITY

 ✓
✓

AIM

To make pieces of paper stick to a balloon.

MATERIALS

- balloon
- paper
- hole punch

Did You Know?

An ion is a group of atoms that get an electric charge by gaining or losing an electron. Have you heard that opposites attract? Your balloon has stolen electrons from your hair and this gives it a negative charge. The paper has lost electrons so it has a positive charge. When they meet they are attracted to each other!

STEPS

1. Blow up your balloon to a size that will still fit in your hand. Tie it.

2. Use the hole punch to cut a small circle in your paper.

3. Rub the balloon on your hair 12 times. Don't press too hard and make sure that your hair is clean.

4. Hold the balloon close to the paper and see what happens.

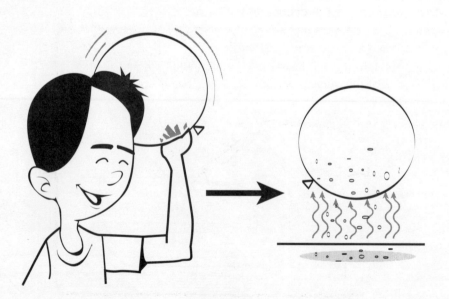

Simulating Satellites

AIM

To simulate radio waves received by satellites.

MATERIALS

- flashlight
- mirror

STEPS

1. Position three people so that they make a large triangle.

2. Give each person a job: the caller, the receiver and the satellite.

3. Give the caller a flashlight, the satellite a mirror and get the receiver to stand (the satellite can stand on a chair to appear more realistic).

4. Turn the light off and get the caller to shine their flashlight on the mirror. The person holding the mirror will shine the light onto the receiver.

Did You Know?

Satellites are able to send information just like you have done in this experiment. Satellites can send their information from one side of Earth to the other.

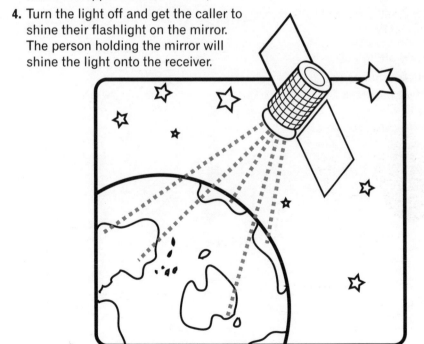

EXPERIMENT
36

Spacecraft Material

SUPERVISED

ACTIVITY

AIM

To test materials to see if they are suitable for space.

MATERIALS

- empty soft drink can (the new material)
- balloon
- fat rubber band
- boiling water
- scissors

Did You Know?

The temperatures in space are either very hot or very cold. There is little gravity and there is radiation. You could not wear the clothes you wear at home into space as they would not protect your body sufficiently.

STEPS

1. Cut the top off your balloon.

2. Twist the pop top off the can and pour the boiling water into it (ask an adult to help you).

3. Stretch the balloon over the top of the can and attach the balloon with a rubber band. If you don't do this the balloon might pop off or leak.

4. Record what happens first, when the water cools and when it is cold.

Star Motion

AIM

To familiarise yourself with the motions of stars.

MATERIALS

- torch
- Blu-Tak
- small round paper (from a hole punch)
- paper
- star map
- pins

Did You Know?

What you have just observed is how the stars would appear to move at the North Pole.

STEPS

1. Trace your star map onto a piece of paper and push a pin through all the points of the paper that have a star.

2. Ask someone to hold your paper and shine a torch from the bottom so that the holes made by the pins are seen on your ceiling.

3. Use your Blu-Tak to stick a small piece of paper where each pin prick appears on the ceiling.

4. Use your map to help you locate Polaris and the Big Dipper. You can ask an adult for help if you need it.

5. When you have located Polaris stand directly underneath it and slowly turn yourself in an anticlockwise direction.

Super Hearing

 ✓
 ✓
 ✓

AIM

To have super hearing like a satellite.

MATERIALS

- large piece of poster cardboard
- clear tape

STEPS

1. Roll the paper into a cone shape but make sure you leave a small hole at the pointy end. Leave the large hole as big as you can.

2. Put tape on the cone to hold it in place.

3. Place the small end of the cone near your ear and go outside.

4. Take note of the sounds you hear. Are noises louder or softer?

Did You Know?

A satellite dish has a cone shape stuck to its surface. The small end points to the sky and the large end is stuck to the dish. This means that people in space can send messages to the satellite dish because they have the small end of the cone.

The Shape of Earth

AIM

To replicate the shape of Earth.

MATERIALS

- balloon
- water
- string
- hand drill
- screw eye

Did You Know?

The shape you have just made is an oblate spheroid. Earth also has this shape, although not quite as extreme as your balloon's shape.

STEPS

1. Fill the balloon with water and tie the balloon with your string.

2. Put a screw eye into your hand drill where the drill bit normally goes.

3. Tie the balloon to the screw eye using the other end of the string.

4. Go outside or to a sink and start to turn the handle of the drill.

5. Add more speed gradually.

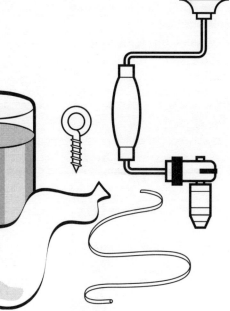

Flying in Space

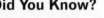

AIM
To create a gliding machine.

MATERIALS
- scissors
- plastic lid from a container
- squirt top from a dishwashing liquid bottle
- glue
- balloon

Did You Know?
An air cushion is created when you let the balloon's air out of the squirt lid. It is this air cushion that allows your glider to lift up.

STEPS
1. Cut a little hole in the middle of the lid.
2. Put the squirt top over the hole and glue it to the lid making sure that no air can escape from the hole. Make sure the writing on top of the lid is facing up.
3. Blow up the balloon and slip the opening over the squirt top. Make sure the squirt top is closed.
4. Place the lid on a smooth table and lift the squirt top opening and see what happens.

SUPERVISED

ACTIVITY

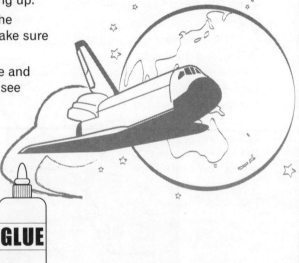

GLUE

PADDOCK · GHEE
MARGARINE

EXPERIMENT

Creating an Eclipse

 ✓

 ✓
 ✓

AIM

To create an eclipse.

MATERIALS

- tennis ball
- ping pong or table tennis ball
- torch
- table (with a table cloth)

Did You Know?

Long ago Chinese people used to think that a solar eclipse was a dragon swallowing the Sun. They would make noise by banging on drums and yelling to try and scare the dragon away. Of course, because solar eclipses are only temporary the Sun would always return.

STEPS

1. In a dark room place the tennis ball about 60 cm (24 in) from the torch and the ping pong ball between them (so the ping pong ball should be about 30 cm (12 in) from each object).

2. Shine the torch onto the tennis ball and move the ping pong ball around the tennis ball.

3. The tennis ball is Earth, the ping pong ball is the Moon and the torch is the Sun.

4. See what happens when the ping pong ball moves between the torch and the tennis ball and when it moves behind the tennis ball.

Black Holes

SUPERVISED

ACTIVITY

AIM

To simulate what astronomers see when a black hole moves in front of a distant object.

MATERIALS

- magnifying glass
- newspaper

STEPS

1. Hold your magnifying glass just above the newspaper print.

2. Move it back and forth slowly.

3. What you see is what astronomers see.

Did You Know?

Because black holes suck in light astronomers can't see them. They have to look for gravity swirling around the hole just as water does around a bathtub plughole.

Day and Night

AIM

To view day and night.

MATERIALS

- piece of string
- balloon
- paper and pen
- scissors

STEPS

Did You Know?

Earth is like a giant ball spinning in the darkness of space. Earth is always moving and takes 24 hours to spin on its axis. When one side of Earth is facing the Sun it is experiencing daytime, while on the other side it is experiencing night time.

1. Draw the shape of Australia with the pen on the paper. Cut it out and place it onto the balloon in its global position.

2. Tie the balloon so it is free hanging.

3. Shine the torch onto one side of the balloon.

4. Slowly turn the balloon.

5. Try holding the balloon to show these times:
   - midnight
   - sunrise
   - midday
   - sunset

Seasons

ACTIVITY

AIM

To view how Earth experiences the different seasons.

MATERIALS

- balloon with a line drawn around the middle (Earth and its equator)
- bowl (to rest Earth on)
- torch (the Sun)
- books (to rest the torch on)

> ### Did You Know?
>
> Light from the Sun does not fall evenly onto Earth because our planet is round. The equator is the hottest part of our planet because it is closest to the Sun and therefore it is where the Sun's light and heat is the strongest.

STEPS

1. Slowly spin Earth around.

2. Sit Earth onto the bowl so the line of the equator is slightly sloping.

3. Rest the torch onto the books so it is shining just above the equator. Where the Sun's light is brightest, the countries will be experiencing summer. Where the Sun's light is furthest away, the countries will be experiencing winter.

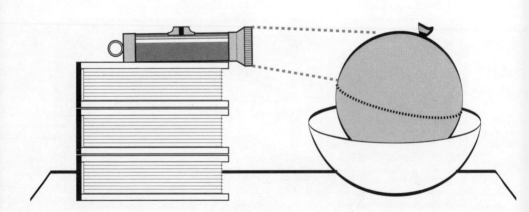

Phases of the Moon

AIM

To view the different phases of the Moon.

MATERIALS

- ball or balloon wrapped in tinfoil (the Moon)
- torch (the Sun)
- darkened room
- friend

Did You Know?

The Moon is our closest neighbour in space. It is about a quarter of the size of Earth, measuring 3476 km (2172 miles) across. The Moon circles around Earth about once a month and travels 385,000 km (240,625 miles). We call these phases of the Moon quarter Moon, full Moon and crescent Moon.

STEPS

1. Place a ball or a balloon wrapped in tinfoil onto a table.

2. Ask a friend to shine the torch onto one side of the Moon.

3. Turn out the lights.

4. Move to the other side of the table and observe where the light is.

5. Slowly move yourself around the table watching the Moon and its light.

The Tides

AIM

To view the rise and fall of the tides.

MATERIALS

- bucket
- plastic ball or balloon
- water

STEPS

1. Half fill the bucket with water.
2. Place the ball in the bucket so it is floating.
3. Place both hands onto the ball and push down very slowly.
4. Let the ball come up again.

Did You Know?

Seventy per cent of Earth's surface is covered with oceans. Every twelve hours the tides rise and fall. This happens without the level of water changing. As Earth and the Moon spin, gravity pulls them together and the Moon pulls at the ocean water directly beneath it, causing it to rise and fall. When it is high tide on one side of Earth, it will be low tide on the other side.

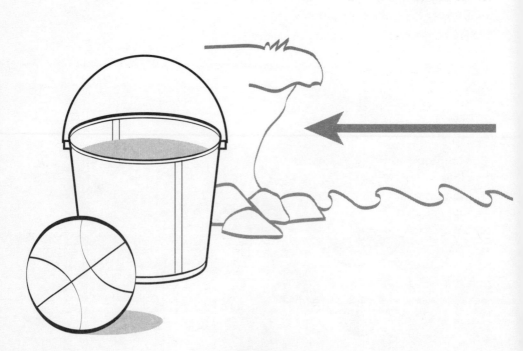

Star Gazing

 ✓

SUPERVISED

 ✓
 ✓

ACTIVITY

AIM

To view the movement of stars.

MATERIALS

- pencil
- paper
- clipboard

STEPS

1. Wait until it is dark. Find a place away from street and house lights that has a good view of the stars.

2. Record the exact spot that you are standing on so you can return to it later.

3. Observe the night sky.

4. Choose a star that is bright or easily located (near a tree top or roof).

5. Sketch the star, and if you can, any surrounding stars.

6. Use your finger, hand or arm to measure and describe distances between stars and objects.

7. You can record your findings in words and illustrations. Remember to also record the time.

8. Wait half an hour and repeat steps 5 to 7.

9. Wait another half an hour and repeat again.

10. You can continue this until bedtime!

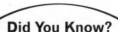

Did You Know?

Earth is like a grain of sand on the beach of the Universe! Our Sun is just one of billions in the Universe. There are about 100,000 million stars in the Milky Way. The nearest star to our Sun is so far away that its light takes about four years to reach Earth. To travel across our galaxy would take about 100,000 years. There is an estimated 100,000 million galaxies – and that is just what we can see with our largest telescopes!

EXPERIMENT

48

Gravity

AIM

To experience the pull of gravity.

MATERIALS

- elastic
- ball or balloon

STEPS

1. Whirl a ball or balloon on the end of a piece of elastic.

2. The stretch of the elastic is the gravitational pull of the Sun.

Did You Know?

The planets in our solar system are kept in place by gravity. The further the planet is from the Sun the longer it takes to orbit (travel) around. One trip around the Sun is equal to a year.

EXPERIMENT
49

Moon Gazing

 ✓
 ✓
 ✓

AIM

To view the phases of the Moon.

MATERIALS

- pencil
- paper
- clipboard
- clock

STEPS

1. Draw eight round moon-like shapes

   e.g. 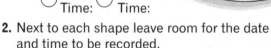 ◯ Date: ◯ Date:
        Time: Time:

2. Next to each shape leave room for the date and time to be recorded.

3. Choose a clear night and go outside and observe the shape of the Moon. Colour the first moon-like shape identical to the Moon in the sky.

4. Wait two nights and observe the shape of the Moon again and colour the second circle.

5. Continue this until each of the eight moon-like shapes are completed.

Did You Know?

The Moon does not shine any of its own light onto Earth. We can see the Moon from Earth because it is reflecting the light from the Sun. On Earth it looks like the Moon is changing shape but the Moon is spinning slowly on its axis as it orbits Earth – this changes the amount of light.

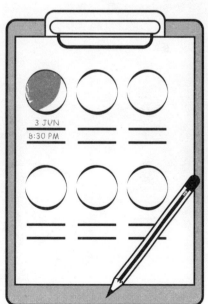

3 JUN
8:30 PM

EXPERIMENT
50

Splitting Light

SUPERVISED

ACTIVITY

AIM

To see how a spectroscope splits the light from stars and planets.

MATERIALS

- cardboard
- straight drinking glass
- water
- paper

STEPS

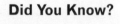

Did You Know?

Spectroscopes have allowed astronomers to study what the Universe is actually made of. Astronomers who study this are called astrophysicists.

1. Make a long narrow cut from the bottom of the cardboard to just above the height of the glass.

2. Sit the glass on the piece of paper in front of a window that lets in a lot of sun and place the cardboard between the glass and the window. (Remember to have the cut in the cardboard running the length of the glass.)

3. You should see the light split.

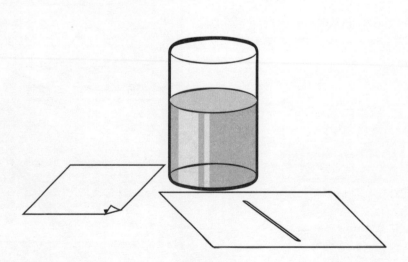

Your Weight on the Moon

AIM

To calculate your weight on the Moon.

MATERIALS

- bathroom scales
- calculator

STEPS

1. Weigh yourself on your bathroom scales.

2. Divide your weight by six because the strength of gravity on the Moon is about one-sixth of that on Earth.

Did You Know?

In 1969 Neil Armstrong and Edwin Aldrin were the first humans to ever walk on the Moon. This was eight years after Yuri Gagarin made the first human space flight.

Making a Spiral Galaxy

SUPERVISED ✓

ACTIVITY ✓ ✓

AIM

To make a spiral galaxy.

MATERIALS

- shallow dish
- coin
- water
- small circles of paper (confetti)

STEPS

1. Put the coin under the dish so that you can spin it easily.

2. Pour about 1 cm (½ in) of water into the dish.

3. Gently sprinkle your paper in the middle of the dish.

4. Slowly spin the dish and watch what happens to the paper in the middle.

Did You Know?

Galaxies live together in clusters just like cows live in a herd. Sometimes they bump into each other and disturb each other's shape. When this happens it can cause new stars to be born and this can create an amazing display of fireworks.

Images of the Sun

AIM

To safely view images of the Sun.

MATERIALS

- binoculars
- books
- mirror
- window and wall opposite to one another

Did You Know?

Scientists and astronomers call the super, super hot gas in the Sun plasma and its wispy atmosphere the corona. Sunstorms can occur when plasma explodes and escapes through the corona. We are safe on Earth, but satellites have been destroyed by sunstorms!

Warning: *Never stare directly at the Sun as it may cause damage to your eyes.*

STEPS

1. Place the binoculars on some books facing out of a window so they are catching shining light from the Sun.

2. Place a mirror at the eye piece of the binoculars.

3. Reflect the light from the Sun onto a wall opposite.

4. Adjust the image so it becomes more definite.

5. From time to time you will need to adjust the binoculars so they are in line with the Sun.

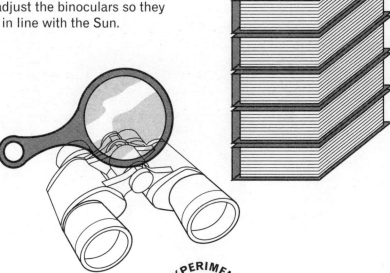

EXPERIMENT

The Sun and Us

 ✓

SUPERVISED

 ✓
 ✓
 ✓

ACTIVITY

AIM

To view the relationship between the Sun, Earth and the Moon.

MATERIALS

- one large balloon
- plasticine
- wire
- string
- sticky tape
- soft drink bottle
- straw

Did You Know?

Without the Sun humans would be unable to live. The Sun provides light, warmth and energy. The Sun is much bigger than any other planet in our solar system. In fact, compared to Earth, the Sun is 100 times bigger in diameter. 330,000 times heavier and a million times bigger in volume.

STEPS

1. Make a U-turn bend in the middle of a long piece of wire so that it can rest in the top of the soft drink bottle and still have either end lying horizontal.

2. Blow up a large balloon as big as possible and attach it to one end of the wire.

3. Make two round balls with the plasticine. One about the size of a ping pong ball (Earth) and the other a little smaller in size than a small marble (Moon).

4. Slide the straw through the middle of the larger ball and attach the straw to the end of the wire opposite to the balloon by sliding it over some of the wire. The straw should be tilted on approximately a 45 degree angle.

5. Attach another piece of wire approximately 6 cm (2½ in) in length to the end of the straw. If necessary secure with sticky tape.

6. Slide the smaller ball onto the end of this wire and bend the wire so the smaller ball is about 3 cm (1¼ in) from Earth.

7. Very gently give the wire resting in the soft drink container a push.

8. As this is happening, very gently give the smaller ball a push.

EXPERIMENT

Orbiting the Sun

✓
SUPERVISED

✓
✓
ACTIVITY

AIM

To view the orbit of planets.

MATERIALS

- piece of paper
- two pins
- pencil
- string

STEPS

1. On opposite sides of a piece of paper insert two pins.

2. Loosely fit a piece of string around the two pins.

3. Tie the string.

4. Pretend your pencil is a planet and place it on the inside of the string and move it in a circle around the pins so it tightens the string.

Did You Know?

At the centre of the solar system is a star, our Sun. Nine planets move around the Sun in circular paths or orbits. Pluto is known as the furthest planet from the Sun. However, at certain times Pluto's orbit actually moves in front of Neptune, making Neptune the furthest planet at that time.

Each time a planet orbits the Sun once, it has travelled one year. Each time you celebrate a birthday Earth is in the same place it was the day you were born!

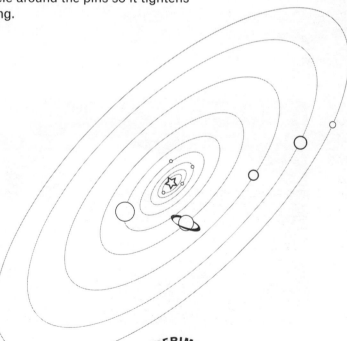

Speeding Stars

AIM

To experience the different speeds of outer and inner stars of spiral galaxies.

MATERIALS

- drinking glass
- paper strip about 20 cm (8 in) long × 5 cm (2 in) high
- cooking oil
- methylated spirits
- teaspoon
- water

Did You Know?

If you can find a clear night away from city lights you may be able to view the galaxies of the two clouds of Magellan and the Andromeda.

STEPS

1. Half fill a glass with water.
2. Place the paper strip inside the top section of the glass so it is lying over the water.
3. Gently add the methylated spirits.
4. Very carefully remove the paper.
5. Slowly add the oil and examine what happens.
6. Turn the glass sharply.
7. Leave for about 30 seconds and examine what has happened.

Gravity Pulls

 ✓

SUPERVISED

 ✓
 ✓

ACTIVITY

AIM

To explore the force of gravity.

MATERIALS

- ball
- jug
- lead sinker
- books

Did You Know?

Gravity makes all things on Earth stay on Earth. If gravity did not exist you and I, tables, chairs, food and everything would be floating around! Gravity also keeps the planets and the stars of the Milky Way in their place! Gravity acts in the same way on objects of differing size and weight.

STEPS

1. Prop a table up by placing some books under one end of it – about 5 cm (2 in).

2. Observe the speed of the ball as it rolls down the table.

3. Throw a ball into the air and observe its path.

4. Pour water from the jug and again observe its path.

5. The paths of these objects are called parabolic.

6. Now drop the lead sinker and the ball. Observe the difference.

EXPERIMENT
58

Space Clouds

SUPERVISED

ACTIVITY

AIM

To experience how a dust cloud would block an astronomer's view of space.

MATERIAL

- white balloon
- light or lamp
- tissue paper

Did You Know?

Dust and gas are a part of our galaxy. Coalsack is a cloud that is situated between the Southern Cross and the nearer Pointer. It blocks the light of stars behind it and prevents astronomers from seeing beyond it.

STEPS

1. Turn on a light or lamp.
2. Think about the colour of the light.
3. Blow up a balloon, hold it up to your face and look at the light.
4. Slowly let some of the air out of the balloon and look at the light again.
5. Look at the light through one sheet of tissue paper.
6. Try two pieces, then three.

Your Very Own Quadrant

AIM

To make your very own quadrant that can help you map the night sky.

MATERIALS

- cardboard
- scissors
- protractor
- ruler
- pen or pencil
- string
- plasticine

Did You Know?

Before astronomers had telescopes, they would use quadrants. Quadrants tell an astronomer the stars' elevation from the horizon. One of the very first astronomers was an Italian by the name of Galileo who, in 1609, turned a telescope upward into the night sky and saw, among many things, the details of the Moon.

STEPS

1. Cut the cardboard into a quarter of a circle shape.

2. Mark out the degrees onto the curved edge of the cardboard with a protractor and ruler.

3. Cut a piece of string a little longer than the cardboard.

4. Attach a ball of plasticine to the end of the string and tie the other end to the right angle of the quarter circle.

5. Cut two identical squares about 3 cm (1¼ in) apart to be your viewfinder.

6. Attach them to the upper side of your quadrant.

7. Point your quadrant to the sky and line up a star by the viewfinder. The string will dangle on the degrees of the star to the horizon.

Air Rockets

✓

SUPERVISED

✓

✓

✓

ACTIVITY

AIM

To make a roaring rocket.

MATERIALS

- balloon
- string
- a straw
- sticky tape
- scissors

Did You Know?

Two kinds of rockets take people, animals and objects into space. They are solid fuel and liquid fuel rockets. Both these rockets burn fuel to create enough gas to push the rocket forward. The first liquid rocket was launched by Dr Goddard in 1926. The rocket travelled only 12.5 m (13½ yds).

STEPS

1. Cut a 1 m (1 yd) length of string.
2. Thread the string through the straw.
3. Attach the string ends to opposite sides of the room.
4. Blow up a balloon and hold the end. Do not tie it.
5. With the other hand, sticky tape the balloon to the straw.
6. Pull the straw and the balloon to one end of the string.
7. Let the end of the balloon go!

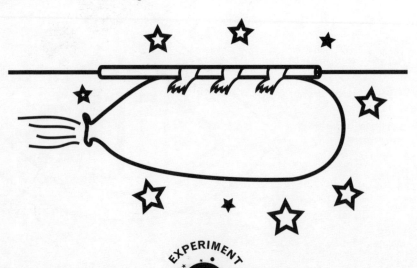

Making Gravity

AIM

To make your own gravity.

MATERIALS

- small can
- string
- water

STEPS

1. Attach a piece of string to a small can.

2. Half fill the can with water.

3. Do not put the lid back on.

4. Swing the can around your head very quickly.

Did You Know?

The surface gravity on the planets varies. If Earth has a surface gravity of one, the surface gravity on the planets would be as follows:

Mercury: 0.38   Venus: 0.91
Mars: 0.38   Jupiter: 2.36
Saturn: 0.92   Uranus: 0.89
Neptune: 1.12   Pluto: 0.07

Sunspots

AIM

To view images of the Sun.

MATERIALS

- 2 pieces of card
- sharp pencil

STEPS

1. Make a small hole with the sharp pencil in a piece of cardboard.

2. Go outside and stand with your back to the Sun.

3. Hold the card with the hole in it up to the Sun.

4. Hold the other piece of card about 20 cm (8 in) below it.

5. Observe what is happening.

6. Move the card pieces further apart.

7. Observe what is happening.

Did You Know?

Dark spots come and go all the time on the Sun's surface. These sunspots are dark because they are a few thousand degrees cooler than the gas around them. Astronomers have observed the Sun and now know that the Sun's equator spins around much faster than its probes!

Warning: *Never stare directly at the Sun as it may damage your eyes.*

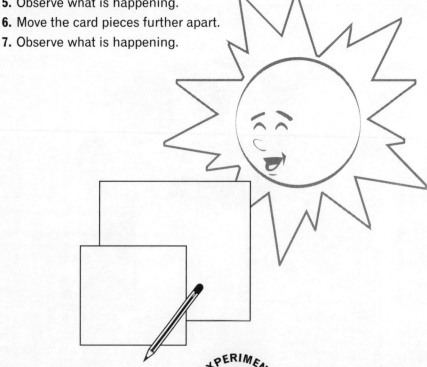

Pictures in the Sky

 ✓

 ✓
 ✓

AIM

To experience that close stars are not necessarily close.

MATERIALS

- yourself!

STEPS

1. Hold out your pointer finger on each hand.
2. Straighten your arms.
3. Close one eye, move one hand closer to the eyes, and move the two hands together laterally.
4. Stand very still and tilt your head sideways.

Did You Know?

For thousands of years people have been looking at groups of stars in the night sky and making pictures. These pictures are called constellations. One very famous constellation in Australia is the Southern Cross. It can only be viewed from the Southern Hemisphere. Stars that appear close together in a constellation may not necessarily be. It is the perspective of the viewer.

EXPERIMENT
64

Different Moons

 ✓

SUPERVISED

 ✓
 ✓

ACTIVITY

AIM

To view the different phases of the Moon.

MATERIALS

- shoe box
- black paint
- scissors or stanley knife
- plasticine
- ping pong ball
- torch

Did You Know?

The Moon spins exactly once during each orbit of Earth, which means we always see the same side. The other side remained a mystery until the Russian space probe *Luna 3* explored it in 1956. The probe sent back pictures that showed the other side had more craters!

STEPS

1. Paint the inside of a shoe box black.

2. Cut three holes, spread evenly along on each side of the shoe box. Make the holes about 7 mm (¼ in) in diameter.

3. Cut another hole of the same size at one end of the shoe box.

4. At the other end of the shoe box cut a big enough hole for a torch to shine through.

5. Hold the torch in place and turn it on.

6. Look into each hole.

Down with Gravity

AIM

To experiment with weight and the force of gravity.

MATERIALS

- grape
- 2 oranges
- newspaper
- chair

STEPS

1. Place newspaper on the floor.
2. Place a chair on top of the newspaper.
3. Very carefully stand on top of the chair.
4. Holding the two oranges in each hand, extend your arms. Each orange must be at the same height.
5. Let the oranges go at the same time and observe which one lands first.
6. Repeat from step 3 but this time hold an orange in one hand and a grape in the other.
7. Observe which one lands first.

Did You Know?

There is a force on Earth that pulls everything down. This force is called gravity. No matter how much an object weighs, gravity pulls it downward at the same speed.

Under the Night Sky

AIM

To make your very own night sky and constellations.

MATERIALS

- black umbrella
- chalk
- paper
- book of constellations (optional)

STEPS

1. Practise sketching the night sky or copy some of the constellations from a book onto a piece of paper.

2. When you are happy with your draft, copy the images using your chalk onto the inside of a black umbrella.

3. Stand under the umbrella and slowly turn.

Did You Know?

It would take about 500 years to reach, not our star, the Sun, but the next nearest star. From this star our own Sun would look like any other star. Just a tiny twinkle in the sky!

SUPERVISED ✓

ACTIVITY ✓ ✓

EXPERIMENT

67

Reflective Telescopes

AIM

To view how a reflective telescope works.

MATERIALS

- desk lamp
- dark piece of cardboard
- marker
- scissors
- sticky tape
- small mirror
- magnifying glass
- plasticine

Did You Know?

In a reflective telescope the light reflects off the primary mirror onto a secondary mirror, which is then focused and magnified by an eyepiece in the lens.

STEPS

1. Trace the area of your lamp onto the dark piece of cardboard.
2. Cut it out and then cut an arrow in the middle of the cardboard.
3. Stick the cardboard cut-out to the lamp with sticky tape so it is blocking the light.
4. Plug the lamp into a power source and set the mirror up so that it reflects the light onto a nearby wall.
5. Hold or sit the magnifying glass (you may need to use plasticine to keep it in place) so that the light reflecting from the mirror travels through it before hitting the wall.

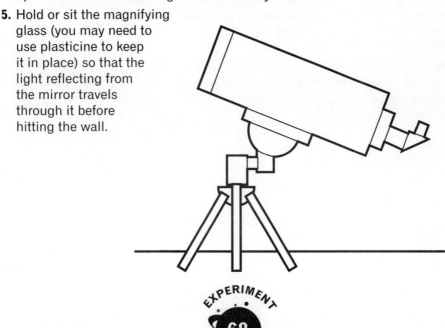

Refracting Telescopes

SUPERVISED

ACTIVITY

AIM

To view how a refracting telescope works.

MATERIALS

- desk lamp
- red cardboard
- marker
- scissors
- sticky tape
- 2 magnifying glasses
- plasticine

Did You Know?

Our brains work out how big an object is by using the angle of the light as it enters our eyes. A telescope makes distant objects appear larger by bending this light. The light rays from a distant object change direction as they move through the lens and again as they leave. The eyepiece or the lens brings the image into focus.

STEPS

1. Trace the area of your lamp onto the red piece of cardboard.

2. Cut it out, and cut a star shape out from the middle of the cardboard.

3. Stick the cardboard cut-out to the lamp with sticky tape so it is blocking the light.

4. Plug the lamp into a power source and position the lamp so it is shining onto a nearby wall.

5. Place a magnifying glass between the lamp and the wall so that the light passes through it. You may need plasticine to keep the magnifying glass in its place. Observe the image on the wall.

6. Place the second magnifying glass behind the first, again you may need plasticine. Gently move the second magnifying glass until the star image appears on the wall.

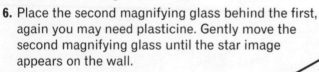

Signals and Satellites

 ✓

SUPERVISED

 ✓
✓

ACTIVITY

AIM

To view how satellites in space redirect signals and information.

MATERIALS

- dark cardboard
- scissors
- tin can
- sticky tape
- metre (yard) ruler
- mirror
- torch
- plasticine

Did You Know?

Communication satellites enable radio transmissions to be sent anywhere on Earth! They are transmitted from one side of the planet and are aimed at an orbiting satellite. The satellite then redirects this information to a receiver on the opposite side of the world!

STEPS

1. Cut out a piece of cardboard that is big enough to cover the tin can.

2. Stick the cardboard onto the can and stand the can upright.

3. Cut a 10 cm (4 in) square out of the piece of cardboard and stick it to the can so that it appears to one side (this will act as the antenna of the satellite).

4. Place the tin can onto the floor and measure approximately 1 m (3 ft).

5. Position the mirror at the end of the ruler.

6. Place the torch so it is level with the tin can but sitting about 20 cm (8 in) away.

7. Turn the lights off in the room and close the curtains.

8. Turn on the torch. Adjust the mirror so that it reflects the light from the torch onto the dark card on the side of the tin can (the antenna).

Orbiting Satellites

AIM

To experience how a satellite orbits (travels) around Earth and relays information.

MATERIALS

- friend
- string or wool
  (two different colours)
- coloured tape
  (two different colours)

Did You Know?

The movement or the orbit of a satellite around Earth is fixed. The satellite follows this orbit until it is no longer needed in space. There are about 500 satellites that humans have sent into space orbiting around Earth.

STEPS

1. Use one of the coloured tapes to make a circle about 50 cm (20 in) in diameter (Earth).

2. Stand inside the circle and take three very big steps.

3. Use the other coloured tape to make a circle at this spot (the orbit of the satellite).

4. Cut a piece of wool from both colours about 10 cm (4 in) bigger than the distance from the two circles.

5. Stand on the smaller circle and hold a piece of wool in each hand (to represent the transmitter and receiver).

6. Ask your friend to stand on the outer circle and hold both pieces of wool in one hand.

7. Both you and your friend slowly turn around by walking along the taped circle.

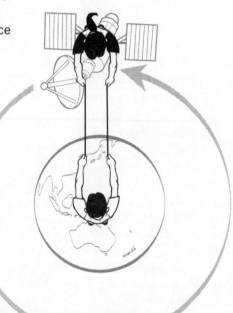

EXPERIMENT
71

Finding Your Bearings

SUPERVISED

ACTIVITY

AIM

To experience finding your bearings in space.

MATERIALS

- map (of where you are)
- compass
- protractor
- ruler
- pencil

STEPS

1. Look at an object that you can see on your map.

2. Point your compass north and read off the angle that points towards your object.

3. This is the object bearing from where you are standing.

4. Now on the map draw a line that runs through the object at the same angle to north as the bearing you took (the top of the map is usually north).

5. Repeat this for a different object.

6. Where the two lines cross on the map is your location.

Did You Know?

Global Positioning System (GPS) satellites orbit around Earth every 12 hours.

Rusty Mars

 ✓

SUPERVISED

 ✓

 ✓

ACTIVITY

AIM

To create the colour of Mars (rust).

MATERIALS

- a key (not stainless steel or galvanised)

STEPS

1. Take a new key and leave it outside.
2. Make sure the area is damp.
3. Collect the key in a couple of weeks.

Did You Know?

Mars is smaller than Earth and it gets less warmth from the Sun. Its average temperature is just minus 55°C (131°F).

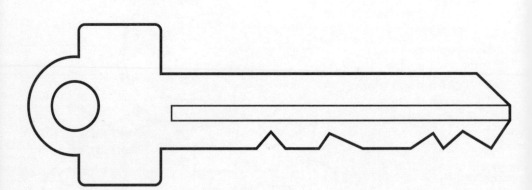

Jupiter's Rings

 ✓

 ✓

 ✓

AIM

To create swirling clouds to represent the bands on Jupiter.

MATERIALS

- shallow tray
- water
- liquid oil paints
- pointer
- paper

Did You Know?

Pictures taken of Jupiter show that its surface is made up of bands of clouds. These clouds are made of different chemicals including ammonia and water crystals.

STEPS

1. Fill the shallow tray with some water.

2. Pour some of the liquid oil paint onto the water.

3. Move the pointer across the floating paints in parallel lines to form bands.

4. Place a sheet of paper on top of the water so that it picks up the paints.

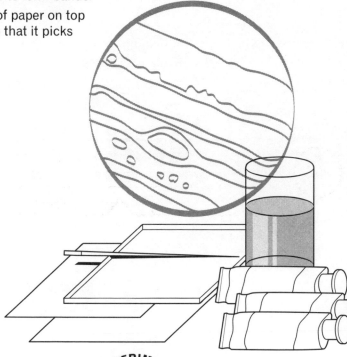

Dust Clouds

SUPERVISED

ACTIVITY

AIM

To create dust cloud patterns.

MATERIALS

- black cardboard
- glue
- sequins
- silver and white paint
- toothbrush
- pastels

Did You Know?

Stars die! When they die, they get rid of their outer layers. These form to become clouds of dust and gas. These clouds glow and are called planetary nebulae.

STEPS

1. Use your toothbrush to make spots on the black paper with your paint.
2. Use pastels to smudge the colours so they mix together.
3. Use glue to stick on sequins.

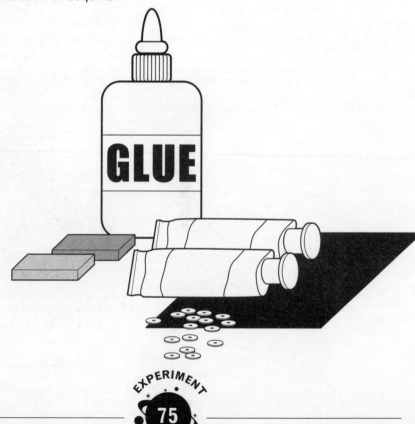

Revolving Space Station

SUPERVISED ✓

ACTIVITY ✓✓✓

AIM

To view how satellites in space redirect signals and information.

MATERIALS

- small boxes and pots
- tubes of paint
- plastic bottles
- gold thread wire
- newspaper
- glue
- sequins
- gold paper

Did You Know?

When astronauts are in space they have to drink using a straw because the liquid does not stay in the cup. They also need to have their food covered with a special jelly or the pieces will float away.

STEPS

1. Glue your pots, boxes, tubes and bottles together to create a space station shape (you may use books to help you).

2. Paste on strips of newspaper. Repeat this process until you can no longer see the boxes.

3. Paint the space station when the newspaper is dry.

4. Create an astronaut, probe, and a satellite and attach them with wires to the space station.

5. Hang the station by a thread and watch how the attachments move.

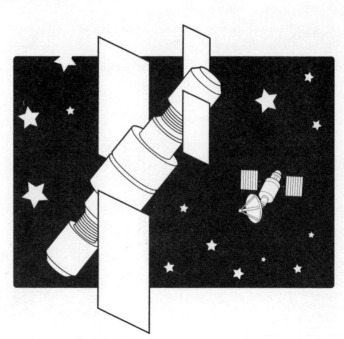

Star Gazers

AIM

To view the stages of a star's life.

MATERIALS

- cardboard
- black and white paper
- scissors
- glue
- paper fasteners
- glitter
- sequins
- silver paint
- pastels
- ruler
- pencil

Did You Know?

When a star dies it self-destructs and causes an explosion brighter than a million suns!

STEPS

1. Cut out a giant star from your cardboard and paint it silver. You can decorate it with sequins and glitter.

2. Draw two circles, one on the black paper and one on the white. Cut them out.

3. Divide the black circle into six equal parts. In each part use your pastels to draw the life cycle of a star (you may use a book to help).

4. Glue the black circle to the star.

5. Paint the other white circle to match your star, but cut out a part of it big enough to show one of the parts of your black circle.

6. Attach the new circle to the black one with a paper fastener.

7. Turn the disk around.

Our Solar System

AIM

To create a mobile that represents the planets of the solar system.

MATERIALS

- newspaper
- bucket
- glue
- paints
- bamboo sticks
- thread
- wire
- needle
- torch

Did You Know?

There are nine planets in our solar system. Our solar system was formed more than four billion years ago.

STEPS

1. Tear off the pieces of the newspaper and leave them overnight to soak in a bucket of water.
2. Squeeze the water out of the newspaper.
3. Make the round shapes of the planets by dipping the paper into the paste and moulding them into different sized balls.
4. Leave the shapes out to dry.
5. Paint the balls so that they are the different colours of the planets.
6. Make stars with your wire to hang next to your planets.
7. Push the needle through each ball, and thread the wire through the hole.
8. Attach your wire to the two bamboo sticks which have been made into a cross shape.
9. Turn the lights off and shine a torch onto the mobile.

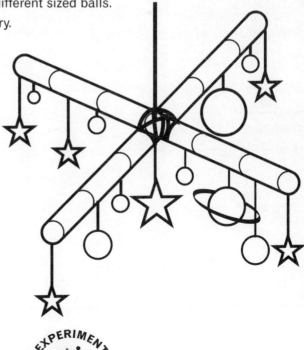

Bedroom Nights

 ✓
SUPERVISED

 ✓

 ✓

 ✓

 ✓

ACTIVITY

AIM

To make your very own night sky in your bedroom.

MATERIALS

- large black cardboard or paper
- glitter
- glue
- metallic paints
- silver thread
- shiny metallic paper
- torch
- scissors

Did You Know?

On a nice clear night you should be able to see thousands of stars twinkling in the night sky.

STEPS

1. Take the large piece of black cardboard or paper.

2. Use your glue to create night sky patterns.

3. Sprinkle your glitter over the glue.

4. Cut out stars from the metallic paper to stick on your paper.

5. Use the silver thread to outline your stars.

6. Stick the cardboard or paper on your bedroom ceiling. (Ask your mum or dad first.)

7. Before you go to bed shine your torch on your ceiling to see the sky.

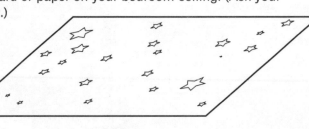

Aiming Probes

AIM

To experience how scientists aim a probe.

MATERIALS

- tree
- cardboard
- paper
- wind
- string
- scissors

Did You Know?

A probe makes observations of the solar system. Scientists do not use humans to probe space. Instead they use robots because it is safer and cheaper and they can go into places that people can't.

STEPS

1. Get your cardboard and cut it into a circle. Make a hole in the middle that measures 25 cm (25 in).

2. Use your string to hang the circle from a tree branch. (Make sure the branch is not too high.)

3. Scrunch your paper into a ball.

4. Take five steps backwards and try to throw your ball through the circle.

5. If it is a windy day you will see what a difficult job it is to launch a spaceship at a planet.

Uranus and the Sun

AIM
To see what Uranus looks like when it is orbiting the Sun.

MATERIALS
- stick
- glue
- paints
- cardboard
- pencils
- scissors
- glitter

Did You Know?
Uranus looks like it is lying on its side when it goes around the Sun. This means that one side of the planet is in darkness and away from light, while the other side is in the line of the Sun and is warmer.

STEPS
1. Draw two circles and cut them out.
2. Make a cut from the outside of the circle to the middle and make a cone shape. Leave a small hole at the top.
3. Poke a stick through the cones to join them together so that they look like a spinning top.
4. Paint and decorate the top half of the top with warm colours like reds and gold.
5. Paint and decorate the bottom half of the top with cold colours like blues and greens.
6. Spin the top as fast as you can and watch it spin.

The Moving Sun

SUPERVISED

ACTIVITY

AIM

To observe how the Sun moves through the day.

MATERIALS

- chalk
- 2 friends
- pen
- paper
- watch

Did You Know?

When it is summer in Australia it is winter on the other side of the world.

Warning: *Never look directly at the Sun as it can harm your eyes.*

STEPS

1. Choose three times of the day to go outside and measure the Sun. The best times are mid morning, noon and mid afternoon.

2. Before you go outside record the three times you will be outside in a table.

3. With your partners go outside with your chalk and your recording table.

4. Take turns to draw each other's shadows on the concrete.

5. Draw what your shadow looks like in your recording table. Draw a line through the middle of your shadow.

6. Go out for your second observation and stand in the exact same place as you did earlier. Trace around your shadow and draw a line down the middle of it. Record this on your table.

7. Do this for your third observation.

8. Compare the lines down the middle of each shadow. What do you notice?

Sunset in a Box

AIM

To create a sunset in a box.

MATERIALS

- clear box
- water
- milk
- torch

Did You Know?

Earth is surrounded by an atmosphere that is full of dust particles (similar to the ones you find under your bed). The particles scatter light and the red and yellow light of the Sun is harder to scatter, so that is why we see those colours during a sunset.

STEPS

1. Fill your box with the water.
2. Add a teaspoon of milk to the water.
3. Shine a torch straight down to see what the Sun looks like at midday.
4. Shine the torch sideways to see what the Sun looks like as it sets.

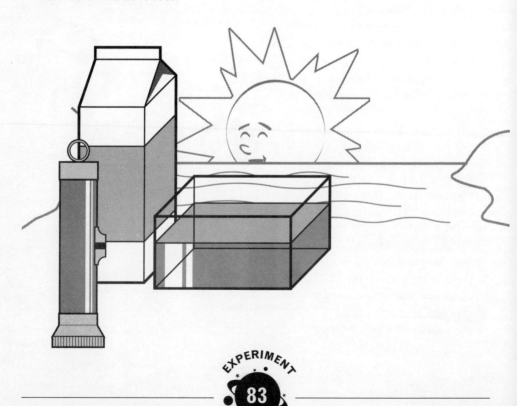

Observing Night and Day

5–12
AGES

SUPERVISED ✓

✓

✓

ACTIVITY

AIM

To experience the differences between night time and day time.

MATERIALS

- pencil
- clipboard
- paper

STEPS

Did You Know?

There are many animals that are nocturnal. This means that they sleep during the day and come out during the night. Some examples of nocturnal animals are possums and owls. Many people also sleep during the day and work at night. These people are called shift workers. Some examples of shift workers are doctors and police officers.

1. Find a spot that you are able to get to during different times of the day and night (sunrise, sunset, midday and just before bed are the best times).

2. At the above times go to the chosen spot and observe.

3. Look for things such as differences or similarities in what you see and feel. Look out for animals and birds, people, the temperature etc.

EXPERIMENT
84

Chemistry

Acid or Base?

AIM

To find out which chemicals are acids and which are bases.

MATERIALS

- few red cabbage leaves
- boiling water
- vinegar
- lemon juice or lemonade
- bicarbonate of soda
  (baking soda)
- laundry detergent

Did You Know?

Chemicals can be acids or bases. The 'cabbage juice' is called an indicator. It can show you whether a chemical is an acid or a base by changing its colour. Test some other chemicals around the house to see if they are acids or bases – try toothpaste and orange juice!

STEPS

1. Chop up the cabbage leaves into small pieces. Ask an adult to help boil some water and cover the pieces then let them soak for half an hour. Separate the cooled 'cabbage juice' from the leaves.

2. Pour some of each chemical (vinegar, lemon juice, bicarbonate of soda and laundry detergent) into a separate jar.

3. Add a dash of your cabbage juice to each chemical.

4. If the mixture turns pink, the chemical you tested is an acid. If the mixture turns blue/green, the chemical is a base.

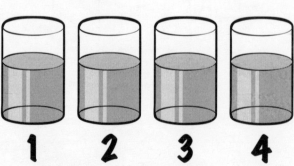

1 2 3 4

EXPERIMENT

85

Baked Ice-cream

SUPERVISED

ACTIVITY

AIM

Bake ice-cream in your oven without it melting.

MATERIALS

- 3 egg whites
- ½ cup sugar
- a big, thick biscuit or cookie
- 1 cup ice-cream
- tray
- foil
- oven

Did You Know?

When you beat the egg whites, a lot of tiny air bubbles were made and trapped in the foam. These air bubbles protected the ice-cream in the oven, slowing the hot air getting to the ice-cream, so that it did not melt! Yum! This works just like foam in an Esky keeping your drinks cold.

STEPS

1. Ask an adult to heat the oven to 260°C (500°F).
2. Place the foil on top of the baking tray.
3. Beat the egg whites with the sugar until you have glossy peaks.
4. Place the cookie on the foil, and top with the ice-cream. Spread the egg white all over the ice-cream, to cover it all.
5. Place the tray in the oven, near the bottom, for about five minutes. When the egg white has browned slightly, remove and eat!

"Ice-cream... straight from the OVEN?!?!?"

Blow It Up

SUPERVISED ✓

ACTIVITY ✓ ✓

AIM

To find out how temperature affects how much space gases take up.

MATERIALS

- 2 balloons
- fridge

STEPS

1. Blow up two balloons so that they are the same size.

2. Place one balloon into the fridge, and leave the other at room temperature.

3. After a few hours, compare the size of the balloons. What has happened to the gas inside each balloon?

Did You Know?

Gas molecules slow down and come closer together when they are cold. This means that the gas in the fridge takes up less space than the same amount of gas at room temperature. Try putting a balloon in the freezer!

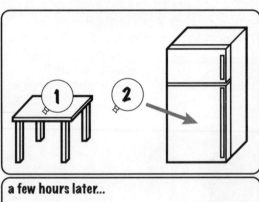

a few hours later...

EXPERIMENT
87

Blowing Bubbles

AIM

To find out which detergent is best for blowing bubbles.

MATERIALS

- different household detergents (shampoo, dishwashing liquid, bubble bath etc.)
- jars of water
- straws
- wire loops (florist wire works well)

Did You Know?

A bubble is actually a thin 'skin' of detergent, filled with air. The bubble pops if: the skin is stretched too thin; it hits something so the skin breaks; or the air inside expands too much.

STEPS

1. Add a few tablespoons of each detergent to a different jar of water. Mix well. Leave for a day if possible.

2. Dip one end of the straw into each jar, and try blowing bubbles. Which detergent works best?

3. Dip the wire loop into each jar, and try blowing bubbles. Does it work better than the straw?

4. How long do your bubbles last before they pop? Describe and draw the bubbles you blow!

Brown Apples

AIM

To stop a cut apple turning brown.

MATERIALS

- apple
- lemon juice
- knife

STEPS

1. Cut an apple in half.

2. Spread lemon juice over one cut half, and leave the other half untouched.

3. Leave both halves out in the air. Check every 15 minutes to notice any changes.

Did You Know?

Air contains a gas called oxygen. Oxygen reacts with some foods, like apples, to cause a brown colour. The foods 'oxidise'. Some chemicals, such as lemon juice, slow down this reaction. This can be used in fruit salads to keep the fruit looking nice! Try this experiment with other fruits.

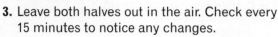

Bubbly Drink

 ✓
SUPERVISED

 ✓

 ✓
ACTIVITY

AIM

To make your own bubbly fruit drink.

MATERIALS

- orange
- water
- bicarbonate of soda (baking soda)
- glass
- sugar (optional)

Did You Know?

The bubbles are made from the reaction between the acid in the orange and the bicarbonate of soda. These bubbles are actually a gas, just like in a soft drink!

STEPS

1. Squeeze the orange juice into the glass.

2. Add the same amount of water to the glass.

3. Stir in a teaspoon of bicarbonate of soda.

4. Take a sip to taste the bubbles! Add a little sugar to make it sweeter, if you like.

EXPERIMENT

90

Carbon, Carbon Everywhere

SUPERVISED

 ✓

 ✓

ACTIVITY

AIM

To show that all living things contain carbon.

MATERIALS

- 1 lit candle
- paper
- pencil
- leaves
- sugar
- tin lid
- tongs
- bowl of water

Did You Know?

You were burning some materials that were once alive. When the burning is completed only carbon is left. Carbon is an element represented by the symbol C. The paper, leaves and sugar turned black – carbon. If carbon is heated to a very high temperature, it can form the gas carbon dioxide. Topsoil is darker than subsoil, because it contains rotten plants and animals, which have become carbon.

STEPS

1. Ask an adult to light the candle. Hold a tin lid in the candle flame with the tongs. Cool the lid, then wipe off the black stuff called soot. This is actually carbon.

2. Make a pencil mark on paper then rub your finger on it. The black mark on your finger is carbon.

3. Burn paper and leaves. What happens to them?

4. Heat up some sugar on a tin lid. What happens to the sugar?

EXPERIMENT

91

Chalky Gift-wrap

SUPERVISED

ACTIVITY

AIM

To make your own coloured swirly paper.

MATERIALS

- coloured chalk
- plastic bags
- rolling pin
- tray of water
- vinegar
- cups
- cooking oil
- white paper

Did You Know?

The chalk, vinegar and paper stick to each other. This gives the swirls and streaky patterns on your paper. Use it for gift-wrapping presents!

STEPS

1. Add five tablespoons of vinegar to the tray of water.
2. Place the chalk inside the plastic bags, and crush the chalk into fine powders with the rolling pin.
3. In cups, add a tablespoon of oil to each coloured powder.
4. Carefully pour each colour into the tray of water. The coloured oils will float on top of the water.
5. Dip each piece of paper onto the surface of the tray. Leave the paper to dry overnight.

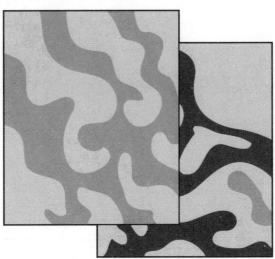

Changing Shape

AIM

To find out which materials can easily change shape.

MATERIALS

- pieces of different household and garden materials (newspaper, clingwrap, wood, baking paper, foil, metal, fabrics, twigs, sand, rocks, bone, clay, sheep's wool, glass, plastic, paper, cardboard, leaves, feathers etc.)

Did You Know?

Some materials are easily changed. For example, an elastic band needs to easily stretch and change back to its original form to do its job. Other materials, such as brick, are very hard to change, so give strength to a wall.

STEPS

1. Test each material to see if it can squash, bend, twist or stretch.
2. Sort the materials into two groups – those that can easily change shape, and those that can't. Can you change them back to their original shape?

Clean Cleaner

SUPERVISED

ACTIVITY

AIM

To compare the cleaning action of vinegar and a supermarket cleaner.

MATERIALS

- vinegar
- cleaning product for mirrors (supermarket)
- newspaper
- a cleaning cloth (supermarket)

Did You Know?

Many cleaning products contain toxic chemicals that pollute our waterways. Vinegar is a good cleaner, and is non-toxic. A lot of energy goes into making cleaning cloths. Recycling newspaper means you don't need to buy cleaning cloths!

STEPS

1. Find a dirty mirror!

2. Scrunch up a sheet of newspaper and pour some vinegar on it. Scrub half of the mirror.

3. Spray some cleaning product onto the mirror. Using the cleaning cloth, scrub the other half of the mirror.

4. Which half of the mirror is cleaner? Is there much of a difference? Which way is more environmentally friendly?

Clean Money

AIM

To clean some coins using acids.

MATERIALS

- glass of cola drink
- dirty coins

STEPS

1. Drop the dirty coins into the glass of cola drink.
2. Check the coins after a day or two. What happened?

Did You Know?

Cola drinks contain food acids. The acids react with the dirt on the coins, and so 'clean' them. Try cola to clean a dirty toilet!

Climbing Colours

SUPERVISED

ACTIVITY

AIM

To discover all the hidden colours inside ink.

MATERIALS

- different coloured textas (water-based, not permanent)
- coffee filter paper or paper towel
- drinking glass
- water
- scissors

Did You Know?

Many inks are actually mixtures of different colours. As the water carries the ink up through the paper, these colours separate because some move further and faster than others. This way, you can discover which colours are used to make up the ink.

STEPS

1. Cut some strips of dry filter paper. Each one should be 2–3 cm (1–2 in) wide and long enough to reach the bottom of the glass.

2. Draw a dot with a texta, 2–3 cm ($\frac{1}{2}$–$1\frac{1}{2}$ in) from the bottom of one strip.

3. Place the strip into 1 cm ($\frac{1}{2}$ in) of water in the glass, leaning the strip against the edge of the glass. Make sure the water level is below the dot!

4. The water should rise up the paper, past the dot, and carry the ink upwards. The ink will separate into its different colours.

5. Repeat with the other strips, with different coloured dots on each strip.

Colourful Sugar

AIM

To create colourful sugar crystals.

MATERIALS

- 4 spoonfuls of sugar
- 20 spoonfuls of water
- food colouring
- bowl
- sunny spot

Did You Know?

With the Sun's heat, the water will evaporate from the bowl, leaving the sugar and colour behind for you to enjoy!

STEPS

1. Stir the sugar into the water until it dissolves (disappears).
2. Add a few drops of food colouring.
3. Leave the bowl in a sunny spot for a few days. What happens?

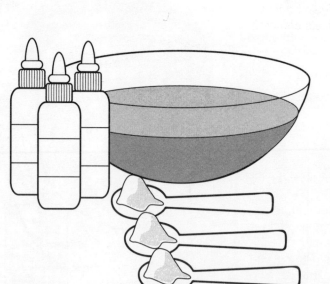

Conduction

AIM

To find out which material is a better conductor of heat.

MATERIALS

- hot water
- drinking glass
- ceramic mug
- polystyrene cup

STEPS

1. Ask an adult to fill the glass, the mug and the cup with the hot water.

2. Gently place your hand around the outside of each container, one at a time.

3. Which feels hottest? Which feels coolest?

Did You Know?

Some materials let heat through more easily than others. These are called good 'conductors' of heat. The heat travels or 'conducts' through the material. The glass should have felt the hottest, since it is the best conductor of heat. The polystyrene should have felt the coolest, since it is a poor conductor of heat. This is why hot drinks are often served in polystyrene, to keep the heat in the drink for longer.

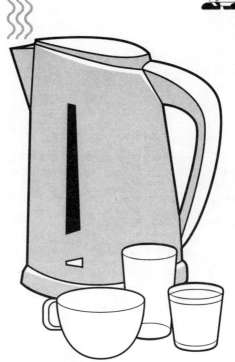

Cooling Down

 ✓

 ✓
 ✓

AIM

To find out what happens to different materials when they are cooled.

MATERIALS

- different household materials (water, vinegar, tomato sauce, bread, rice, butter etc.)
- containers
- freezer

Did You Know?

Cooling materials can change them. For example, some liquids will have changed into a solid, such as water into ice. Some materials may not have changed much at all, such as the rice. We can cool foods to keep them fresh for longer.

STEPS

1. Place each material into a container. Draw a picture, and describe its feel.

2. Place the containers in the freezer overnight.

3. Check the materials the next day – what are they like now? Draw a second picture and describe their feel.

Corny Goo

AIM

To make a goo with strange behaviour.

MATERIALS

- water
- 2 tablespoons of cornflour
- bowl
- spoon

Did You Know?

When you roll the goo, it feels dry and hard, like a solid. When you stop rolling, it slowly spreads over your fingers, like a liquid. Cornflour particles float in water. When you roll the flour and water, the particles are forced together. When you stop rolling, the cornflour and water separate again. Corny goo behaves much like quicksand!

STEPS

1. Put two tablespoons of cornflour into the bowl.

2. Add a tablespoon of water to the flour, one at a time, stirring well with the spoon. Keep adding water until the goo is thick and creamy.

3. Pick up the goo and roll it between your fingers. Stop rolling – what happens?

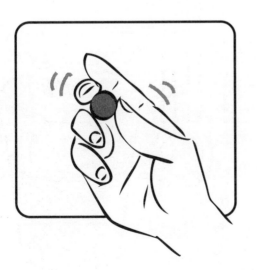

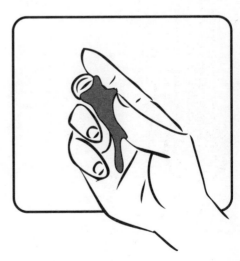

Crystal Star

AIM

To make your own crystal star.

MATERIALS

- borax (laundry section in supermarket)
- hot water
- jar
- popstick
- cotton string
- pipe cleaner
- food colour
- scissors

Did You Know?

The borax powder dissolves in the water. When the water evaporates, the borax is left behind, and attaches to the pipe cleaner 'star' as tiny crystals.

STEPS

1. Cut a pipe cleaner into four pieces, and twist the lengths together to form a star shape.

2. Tie a length of string to one 'arm' of the star. Tie the other end around the popstick.

3. Ask an adult to dissolve the borax in boiling water, about three tablespoons per cup of water. Half fill the jar. Add a few drops of food colour if you like. Borax powder is poisonous – wash your hands after touching it.

4. Place the popstick across the top of the jar, so your star hangs into the borax water. Wait a few days for your star to grow!

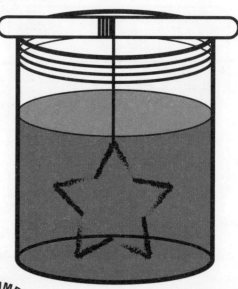

Crystal Stars Everywhere

SUPERVISED

ACTIVITY

AIM

To watch stars appear when tiny crystals grow.

MATERIALS

- card
- large sheet of black poster paper
- scissors
- ½ cup of hot water
- Epsom salts (from laundry section in supermarket)
- small sponge

Did You Know?

The Epsom salts dissolve in the hot water. When you use it to paint on the black paper, the water evaporates, and the Epsom salts are left behind, forming small crystals on the paper.

STEPS

1. Cut a star shape out of the card, so you are left with a stencil. Throw out the star.

2. Dissolve the Epsom salts in half a cup of hot water. Keep adding salt until no more will dissolve.

3. Dip the sponge into the salt water. Placing the stencil over the black paper, rub the sponge over the star shape, onto the black poster paper.

4. Carefully lift the stencil to another area on the paper. 'Paint' more star shapes with your salt water until you run out of room on the black paper.

5. Let your paper dry until the crystal stars appear!

Disappearing Act

SUPERVISED ✓

ACTIVITY ✓ ✓ ✓

AIM

To find out which materials can dissolve in water.

MATERIALS

- warm water
- 3 glasses
- salt
- sugar
- spoons

Did You Know?

Some materials, such as sugar and salt, easily dissolve in water. They break down until we can't see them anymore, but if we tasted the water, we would notice they were still there! Some materials, such as sand, do not dissolve in water, and so will never 'disappear'. Imagine how much salt is dissolved in sea water!

STEPS

1. Fill the glasses three quarters full with warm water.

2. Place two teaspoons of salt into one glass. Stir quickly, and count until the salt has disappeared.

3. Place two teaspoons of sugar into another glass. Stir quickly, and count until the sugar has disappeared.

4. Repeat with two teaspoons of sand in the third glass. What happens?

Dissolving

AIM

To test how to dissolve a solid in water faster.

MATERIALS

- salt
- 3 glasses
- water
- spoon

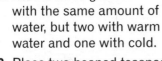

Did You Know?

Stirring and warm water both help to dissolve a solid into water faster. Doing both at the same time should have been the fastest way to dissolve the salt!

STEPS

1. Fill the three glasses with the same amount of water, but two with warm water and one with cold.

2. Place two heaped teaspoons of salt into the first glass of cold water. Stir it, and count how long it takes to dissolve.

3. Place two heaped teaspoons of salt into the second glass of warm water – don't stir! Count how long it takes to dissolve.

4. Place two heaped teaspoons of salt into the third glass of warm water. Stir it, and count how long it takes to dissolve. What did you notice?

EXPERIMENT
104

Diving Currants

AIM

To make currants dive up and down without touching them.

MATERIALS

- 10 currants
- 1 tall glass
- 2 tablespoons of bicarbonate of soda (baking soda)
- white vinegar

STEPS

1. Place the bicarbonate of soda into the glass.

2. Slowly pour the vinegar into the glass, taking care it does not overflow!

3. Drop the currants into the glass, and watch them bounce up and down!

Did You Know?

The bicarbonate of soda and vinegar mix together to make a gas, called carbon dioxide. The bubbles of gas attach to the currants, and carry them up to the surface. At the surface, the bubbles pop, which sends the currant diving down to the bottom again! Does this experiment work in a glass of fizzy lemonade? The bubbles in soft drink are also carbon dioxide gas.

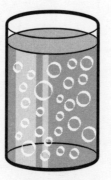

Dry Washing

5–12
AGES

SUPERVISED ✓

ACTIVITY ✓

AIM

To discover where washing will dry fastest.

MATERIALS

- 4 handkerchiefs
- water
- clock
- pegs
- paper and pencil

Did You Know?

The handkerchief in the sunny and windy spot should have dried first. Evaporation happens faster in warmer places, and the wind would also pick up water droplets from the cloth.

STEPS

1. Soak the handkerchiefs thoroughly with water, so that they are dripping wet.
2. Hang one in a sunny, windy spot (it might need a peg).
3. Hang another in a sunny, but still, spot.
4. Hang another in a shady, windy spot.
5. Hang another in a shady, but still, spot.
6. Record the time it takes for each handkerchief to dry.

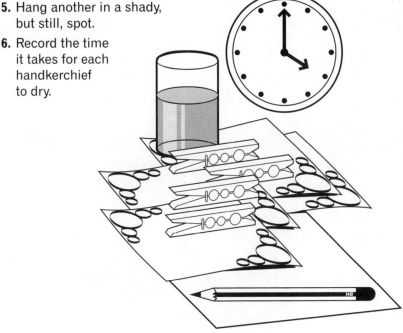

EXPERIMENT

Fast Rust

AIM

To quickly rust steel.

MATERIALS

- steel wool (not the soapy kind)
- jar
- water
- vinegar
- bleach

Did You Know?

Rust forms when iron is combined with oxygen and water. The vinegar strips any protective coating off the steel, and oxygen in the bleach combines with the iron in the steel. This made the wet steel go rusty very quickly. If you wrapped the steel around the bulb of a thermometer, you should be able to see the temperature rise! This is because this chemical reaction gives off heat energy.

STEPS

1. Place the steel wool into the jar then cover it with water.

2. Pour in a dash of vinegar and a dash of bleach.

3. Wait for a few hours, and watch the steel go rusty!

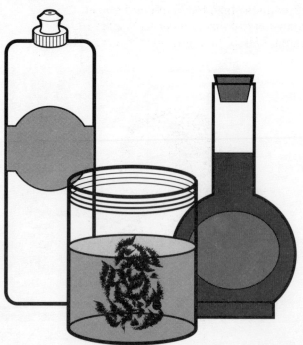

Fire Extinguisher

SUPERVISED

ACTIVITY

AIM

To put out a candle flame (not using your breath).

MATERIALS

- a lit candle
- empty film canister
- bicarbonate of soda (baking soda)
- vinegar

Did You Know?

The bicarbonate of soda and vinegar mix together and make a gas called carbon dioxide. This gas poured out of the canister and down over the flame, stopping air from fuelling the fire.

STEPS

1. Ask an adult to light the candle.
2. Place a teaspoon of bicarbonate of soda into the film canister.
3. Pour a little vinegar into the canister, and quickly put the lid on.
4. Shake the canister, take the lid off and quickly point the opening of the canister just above the candle flame. Watch the flame suddenly go out!

Fizzy Sherbet

SUPERVISED

ACTIVITY

AIM

To make your own delicious fizzy sherbet.

MATERIALS

- 20 teaspoons icing sugar
- 1 teaspoon citric or tartaric acid
- 1 teaspoon bicarbonate of soda (baking soda)
- 1 teaspoon jelly crystals

Did You Know?

The acid makes the icing sugar taste tangy. When the baking soda is added, it reacts with the acid to make bubbles of carbon dioxide gas, which makes the sherbet fizzy on your tongue! Be careful – if you eat too much, you will burp a lot from all that gas!

STEPS

1. In a bowl, mix the icing sugar, acid and baking soda together. Add the jelly crystals.
2. Eat!

Floating Drops

 ✓

 ✓
 ✓
 ✓

AIM

To make drops of oil sink and rise again.

MATERIALS

- water
- cooking oil
- red food colouring
- tall glass
- salt

Did You Know?

The oil forms a separate layer above the water, since it is lighter, or less dense. Oil and water do not mix. The salt sinks down into the water since it is denser than both oil and water, and carries an oil droplet with it. When the salt dissolves into the water, the oil droplet floats up again. This effect should continue as long as you keep adding salt!

STEPS

1. Pour water into the glass so it is one-third full. Add a few drops of red food colouring.

2. Add the same amount of oil to the glass, so it is two-thirds full. What happens?

3. Slowly sprinkle salt onto the oil. What happens?

Gas to Liquid

SUPERVISED

ACTIVITY

AIM

To see the water that exists in air.

MATERIALS

- glass jar with lid
- ice cubes
- salt
- tissue

STEPS

1. Fill the jar with ice cubes and add two tablespoons of salt. Screw on the lid then shake!

2. Slowly watch water droplets appear on the outside of the jar. Wrap the tissue around the jar, then take it off to see how wet it is!

Did You Know?

The salted ice quickly makes the glass sides of the jar very cold. The water that exists in the air as a gas cools down and changes into a liquid when it hits the cold sides of the jar. This process is called condensation (which is the opposite to evaporation). This allows you to see the water that is usually invisible in the air! You can collect the water using the tissue.

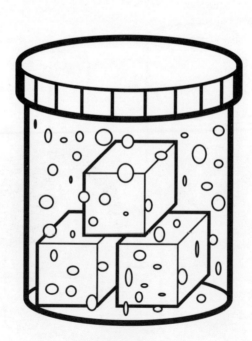

Green Slime

AIM

To make a jelly-like green slime.

MATERIALS

- white PVA glue
- borax powder (laundry section in supermarket)
- green food colouring
- water

Did You Know?

The glue and borax mix together to make a new chemical – the slime! The borax stops the glue flowing like a liquid. The slime is very elastic, so it can even bounce if you roll it into a ball!

STEPS

1. In a container, mix together one tablespoon of glue, one tablespoon of water, and one drop of green food colouring.

2. In a separate container, dissolve one teaspoon of borax powder in one tablespoon of water. Borax powder is poisonous – wash your hands after touching it or your slime!

3. Pour the borax solution into your glue mixture. Mix with your fingers – a 'slime' should form instantly!

4. Store in an airtight container.

Green to Red

✓

SUPERVISED

✓

✓

ACTIVITY

AIM

To watch a tomato ripen.

MATERIALS

- 2 green tomatoes
- 1 banana
- 2 paper bags

STEPS

1. Place one tomato in each paper bag.

2. Add the banana to one of the bags, and close the openings of the bags.

3. Place the bags in a cool place.

4. Every day, check the tomatoes. After a few days, the tomato with the banana should turn red first.

Did You Know?

Ethylene is a natural gas that ripens fruit. Without ethylene, some fruits, such as bananas, would never ripen. The banana's ethylene gas helps to ripen the tomato in the bag. The tomato without the banana will also make its own ethylene, it just won't ripen as quickly. Ethylene also wilts flowers, so keep your bananas away from your fresh-cut flowers!

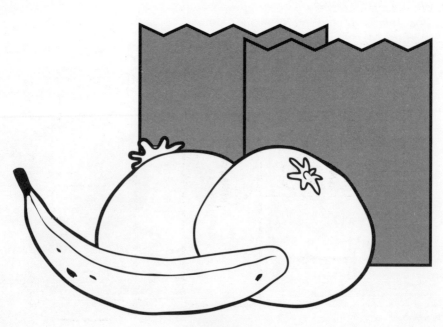

Hard and Soft Water

AIM

To see the difference between a 'hard' and a 'soft' water.

MATERIALS

- 2 clean empty soft drink bottles with lids
- Epsom salts (laundry section in supermarket)
- dishwashing liquid

Did You Know?

The bottle with the Epsom salts should have many less bubbles than the plain water. This is because you have made the water 'hard'. Water in some areas is hard because it has minerals dissolved in it. These minerals interfere with the action of detergents. Chemicals can be added to hard water to make it 'soft' again, so that detergents can do their work.

STEPS

1. Place two cups of water into each bottle. Add two teaspoons of Epsom salts to one of the bottles. Screw the lids on and shake.

2. Add a few drops of dishwashing liquid to both bottles. Replace the lids and shake.

3. What do you notice?

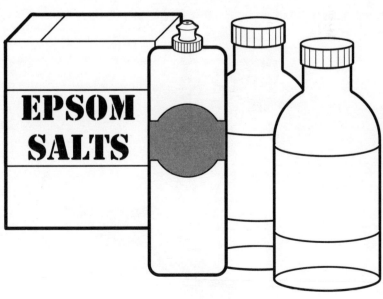

Heated Up

AIM

To find out how materials change when they are heated up.

MATERIALS

- aluminium foil, cut into 4 squares
- knob of butter
- sugar
- salt
- piece of bread
- oven

Did You Know?

Some materials, such as sugar, bread and butter, are quickly changed by heat. Sugar changes into a brown 'caramel', bread changes into brown toast, and butter melts into a liquid. The salt does not change, because its melting temperature is 850°C (1562°F)! The bread and sugar can never be changed back to how they were, but the butter could be cooled back into a solid again.

STEPS

1. Fold up the edges of aluminium foil squares, to make 4 small 'plates'.

2. Place the knob of butter, a tablespoon of sugar, a tablespoon of salt and a small piece of bread into separate foil plates.

3. Put the plates onto a baking tray, and ask an adult to bake them in an oven at 200°C (400°F).

4. Take them out after half an hour. Which materials have changed?

Heating Up

AIM

To see how heat can change materials.

MATERIALS

- popping corn
- cooking oil
- saucepan
- bread
- toaster
- candle
- match

Did You Know?

Heating materials often changes them for good, that is, you can't change them back to what they were like before. A new material is made, such as the brown colour of the toast, the popped corn or the melted wax and smoke. We can use heat to change foods to become easier to eat, or to just make them yummier!

STEPS

1. Draw the bread, popping corn and candle, writing three words about each to describe how they look, feel and smell.

2. Ask an adult to cook the popcorn, toast the bread and light the candle.

3. Now repeat your pictures and three describing words for each material. How has heat changed them?

EXPERIMENT

Home-made Glue

✓

SUPERVISED

✓

✓

ACTIVITY

AIM

To make a non-toxic, environmentally friendly glue.

MATERIALS

- flour
- water
- jar with lid
- spoon
- brush

STEPS

1. Mix one cup flour with half a cup of water together in the jar, stirring well. This becomes the glue!

2. Use your brush to glue newspaper pages together into shapes. Let them dry. What happens?

Did You Know?

This is a chemical reaction, and the paste sets hard when it dries. After your newspaper shapes have dried, you can even paint them different colours!

Hot and Cold

AIM

To find out how temperature affects how quickly liquids mix.

MATERIALS

- 1 glass of cold water
- 1 glass of hot water
- food colouring
- eye dropper

STEPS

1. Gently add four drops of food colouring to the glass of cold water. Count how many seconds the colour takes to mix into the water completely.

2. Gently add four drops of food colouring to the glass of hot water (watch out for burns!). Count how many seconds the colour takes to mix in completely.

Did You Know?

Water and other liquids are made up of tiny molecules that you can't see. The molecules in hot water have more energy than those in cold water, and so move around faster. The faster they move around the food colouring molecules, the faster the food colouring is spread through the whole glass! Try dissolving a teaspoon of salt in cold and hot water to see the same effect.

How Sweet

SUPERVISED

ACTIVITY

AIM

To test how water temperature affects dissolving.

MATERIALS

- sugar
- 4 glasses
- cold water, tap water, warm water, hot water
- spoon

Did You Know?

The warmer the water, the faster the particles are moving around. This means the faster the water and sugar particles will mix together, so the boiling water should have dissolved the sugar fastest. The cooled water should have dissolved the sugar the slowest, since the particles will be moving around much more slowly.

STEPS

1. Fill one glass with water and place in the fridge for an hour.

2. Add two heaped teaspoons of sugar to the glass, and stir. Count how long it takes for the sugar to dissolve.

3. Repeat with cold water from the tap. Make sure the amount of water is about the same!

4. Repeat with warm water from the tap.

5. Ask an adult to boil some water. Repeat the dissolving. What did you find out?

Ice Pick-up

AIM

To pick up an ice cube without touching it.

MATERIALS

- ice cube
- glass of water
- piece of string
- salt

Did You Know?

The salt melts the ice around the string, making a little puddle. After a few minutes, the coldness of the ice cube freezes the little puddle of water into ice again, around the string. This lets you pick up the ice cube. In countries where snow stops people using roads, salt is used to melt the ice away faster.

STEPS

1. Place the ice cube on top of the full glass of water.
2. Carefully place the string across the ice cube.
3. Sprinkle some salt onto the ice cube, where the string lies.
4. After a few minutes, try to lift the ice cube out of the glass by holding the ends of the string.

EXPERIMENT
120

Invisible Ink

AIM

To write an invisible message and watch it re-appear.

MATERIALS

- lemon juice (bottled is fine)
- a cotton bud
- a piece of white writing paper
- clothes iron

Did You Know?

The heat changes the lemon juice into a new chemical. This has a brown colour, and so your message can be seen on the white paper. Eventually, the paper would also turn brown and burn, but the lemon juice changes more quickly. Try using other acids such as vinegar as your ink!

STEPS

1. Dip the cotton bud into the lemon juice, and use this 'pen' to write an invisible message or picture on the paper.

2. Wait for your 'ink' to air-dry and completely disappear.

3. Ask an adult to iron over the dry paper. Watch your message reveal itself!

Light It Up

AIM

To observe the changes in a burning candle.

MATERIALS

- candle
- match
- container to catch the dripping wax

Did You Know?

When you light a candle the wick burns to produce heat. This heat melts solid wax to become a liquid, then a gas. This gas burns to form the candle flame and makes heat. Fire can be very useful, for example when cooking food. It can also be dangerous. Its heat can burn property, or even you. Always keep flammable things, such as paper or dry grass, away from the flame.

STEPS

1. Stand a candle in the container.

2. Ask an adult to light the candle. Watch the flame carefully. What shape is the flame? Is the shape always the same? What colours can you see in the flame? Is the candlewick straight or bent? Draw a picture.

3. What happens to the candle? Does the candle get smaller? What happens to the wax just below the flame? Where does the melted wax go?

4. Measure the length of the candle every two hours. Draw a graph to show how the length of the candle changes over the day.

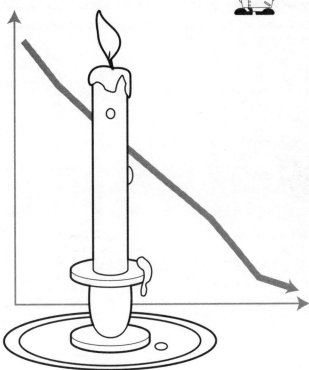

Lights Out

SUPERVISED

ACTIVITY

AIM

To make a candle go out without blowing it.

MATERIALS

- 1 lit candle
- a glass
- a metal lid

STEPS

1. Ask an adult to gently place a candle into a glass and light it. The candle needs to be shorter than the glass!

2. Carefully place a metal lid on top of the glass that completely covers the opening.

3. Watch the candle go out after a minute!

Did You Know?

Fire needs fuel and oxygen to burn. The wax of the candle is the fuel, and the oxygen comes from the air. When you place the lid on top of the glass, you block the oxygen getting to the flame, and the fire will go out. This is the reason heaping sand over a campfire will make it go out by suffocating the fire!

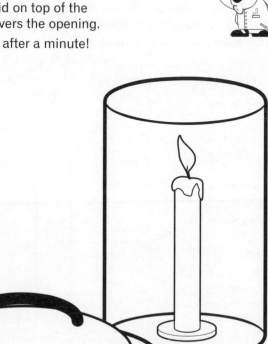

EXPERIMENT

123

Liquids on the Windowsill

 ✓

SUPERVISED

 ✓

 ✓

ACTIVITY

AIM

To observe the changes when you leave liquids in the sunshine.

MATERIALS

- different household liquids (water, salty water, methylated spirits etc.)
- same-sized bowls
- windowsill or sunny spot
- plastic ruler

Did You Know?

Liquids can evaporate, or change into a gas, when they are heated up. The salt dissolved in the water cannot evaporate, so it is left behind in the bowl. Alcohol, such as spirits, evaporates more quickly than water. Evaporation helps to cool us down when we sweat.

STEPS

1. Pour the same amount of each liquid into separate bowls.

2. Leave the bowls in a sunny spot for an hour. Measure how deep each is.

3. Measure the depth every two hours now. Which liquid goes down fastest?

4. After a few days, what is left in the bowls?

Lolly Molecules

AIM

To make lolly models of molecules.

MATERIALS

- different coloured gum-drop lollies
- toothpicks
- bowl

Did You Know?

Water (H_2O) is the most important liquid on Earth. Carbon dioxide (CO_2) is a gas that we breathe out. There are more than 100 different atoms, so you would need 100 different coloured lollies to make every possible molecule!

STEPS

1. Give each different atom a colour, for example, hydrogen = red, oxygen = yellow, and carbon = green.

2. Make a water molecule (H_2O) – this means that two hydrogen atoms are joined to one oxygen atom inside water. So, join two red lollies to one yellow lolly with toothpicks. Put your water molecule in a bowl. Make more!

3. Make a carbon dioxide molecule (CO_2) – this means that two oxygen atoms are joined to one carbon atom. So, join two yellow lollies to one green lolly with toothpicks. Put your carbon dioxide molecule in the bowl. Make more!

4. Eat! Which molecule are you eating?

Making Starch

SUPERVISED

ACTIVITY

AIM

To separate a powder called starch from potatoes.

MATERIALS

- 5 large potatoes
- grater
- bowl
- water

STEPS

1. Peel the potatoes.
   Grate them into a bowl.

2. Fill the bowl with water to cover the potatoes. Squeeze the potato with your fingers for several minutes. Leave for half an hour. Repeat the squeezing.

3. Take the potato out of the bowl, leaving behind the cloudy water.

4. Try to pour off the clear layer of water, leaving the cloudy stuff in the bowl. Let all the water dry up in a sunny place. What happens?

Did You Know?

You should be left with a white powder in the bowl called starch. Starch is present in many plants, because it is a way they store energy. When you eat potatoes, your body changes this starch back into sugar for energy. This process starts in your mouth, with chemicals in your saliva (spit) breaking down the starch.

Making Water

SUPERVISED

ACTIVITY

AIM

To find out what happens when steam cools down.

MATERIALS

- kettle
- water
- freezer
- metal tray

Did You Know?

When the water boils, the liquid changes into a gas. This is called evaporation. When the steam hits the cold tray, it changes into a liquid again, and is seen as water droplets. This is called condensation, and is the same process as rain forming in clouds when they get colder.

STEPS

1. Place the metal tray in the freezer for an hour.

2. Ask an adult to fill the kettle and boil the water.

3. Look at the steam escaping from the kettle. Hold the cold tray above the steam. What happens?

Materials and Their Uses

AIM

To find out the different uses of materials.

MATERIALS

- house
- garden
- paper
- pencil

 ✓
SUPERVISED

Did You Know?

Choosing the right materials for different uses is very important. For example, a glass chair or a plastic saucepan would not be very easy to use! New materials are being invented all the time to suit different uses, for example, polar fleece for light, yet warm, clothing.

 ✓
 ✓
 ✓
ACTIVITY

STEPS

1. Walk around the house and garden looking for all the things made of wood. Record the uses of that wood, for example, wood is used for fences, spoons, chairs etc.

2. Repeat the survey for plastic, metal and glass.

3. Which do you think is the most useful material to humans? Why?

Melt or Burn?

5–12
AGES

SUPERVISED

ACTIVITY

AIM

To observe the changes when you heat different solids.

MATERIALS

- different household solids (ice, plastic, glass, metal, wool, leaf, paper, cardboard, rock)
- lit candle
- container of water
- tongs

Did You Know?

Different substances change in different ways when you heat them. Some you can change back to their original form (ice into water), and these are called reversible changes. Irreversible changes are when you can't reverse the change, like when paper burns into ash and smoke.

STEPS

1. Ask an adult to light the candle.

2. Hold a solid with tongs and heat it over the flame for about a minute.

3. Observe carefully what happens to each solid. Does it change? Does it melt or burn? If it burns is anything left when it stops burning?

4. Drop the solid into the cold water. Draw a picture of what happened to the solid.

5. Repeat for all the solids. Do all substances change the same way when they are heated? Which substances change when they are hot but go back to their original form when they cool again? Which substances change permanently?

Melting Ice

 ✓
 ✓
 ✓
 ✓
 ✓

AIM

To find out which spot in the house or garden is warmest.

MATERIALS

- 5 containers
- 10 ice cubes

Did You Know?

Placing the container in a sunny place, or close to a light bulb or a heater, would have melted the ice quickly. Dark and cool places, such as inside a cupboard, would probably keep the ice cold longer.

STEPS

1. Place two ice cubes in each container.
2. Place the five containers in different spots around the house and garden. Guess which will melt first, and which last.
3. Check to see which ice melts first, second, third, fourth and fifth. Why do you think this happened?

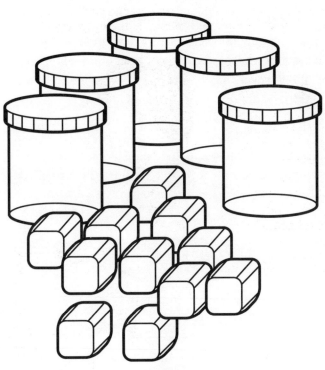

Metal, Metal Everywhere

SUPERVISED

ACTIVITY

AIM

To discover different metals around the house and garden.

MATERIALS

- different household metal objects
- paper and pencil

Did You Know?

Some of the metals you find are mixtures. Coins are made of a mixture of copper and nickel. Old bits of metal may show corrosion – they are no longer shiny. Lead can become covered with a dark grey substance. Iron gets covered with a brown-orange rust. Corrosion can destroy metals.

STEPS

1. Walk around the house and garden, drawing as many objects made of metal as you can.

2. Look closely at each object. Try and find out which metal it is made of.

Iron:	shiny, can go rusty (nails, knives, tools, cans)
Lead:	soft, usually grey, looks like silver when scratched (old water pipes)
Aluminium:	shiny (kitchen foil, drink cans)
Copper:	red-brown, quite soft (electrical wire)
Zinc:	grey (covers things made of iron, iron roofing and fencing)
Chromium:	shiny (covers steel parts of a car with a thin layer)
Tin:	shiny, white (covers cans made of iron)
Brass:	hard, yellow, mixture of copper and zinc (taps, keys)
Steel:	very springy, strong, mainly iron with some carbon (razor blades, screw, pin, paper clip, food cans)
Silver:	shiny, can go black (jewellery, cutlery, ornaments)
Gold:	shiny, yellow or white (jewellery)

EXPERIMENT

Milky Plastic

AIM

To make a milky plastic.

MATERIALS

- glass of full-fat milk
- vinegar
- eye dropper

STEPS

1. Ask an adult to warm up the milk by microwaving it for a minute or placing it in a bowl of hot water.

2. Slowly squirt the vinegar into the warm milk and stir.

3. Slowly pour the milk out onto your hand (over the sink!), 'catching' the plastic in your fingers!

Did You Know?

Milk contains a chemical called casein. Casein can be separated from the rest of the milk using the vinegar. This is a type of plastic, which is a chemical made of long chains of many small parts joined together.

EXPERIMENT

132

Mini Packages

SUPERVISED

ACTIVITY

AIM

To change chip and nut packets into mini packets.

MATERIALS

- empty chip or nut packets
- oven
- baking tray

Did You Know?

The packets shrink because during the baking, the plastic changes to new chemicals. You could make them into keyrings or brooches!

STEPS

1. Eat the chips or nuts!
2. Ask an adult to heat the oven to a moderate temperature.
3. Place the empty packets on a baking tray, and bake them for two to five minutes. Watch them shrink!

Mix and Separate

AIM

To separate a mixture of salt, sand and water.

MATERIALS

- jar of water
- 5 tablespoons of salt
- 5 tablespoons of sand
- coffee filter paper or paper towel

Did You Know?

The sand does not dissolve into the water, so you can filter the water to separate it from the sand. The salt stays dissolved in the water, so it can pass through the paper. When the water is warmed up by the sun and turns into steam (evaporates), the salt is left behind in the bowl. Try this experiment with sugar instead of salt!

STEPS

1. Dissolve the salt into the jar of water by mixing well. The salt should disappear.

2. Add the sand to the salty water and mix well. The sand will not disappear.

3. Slowly pour the water through the filter paper, letting the water drip into a bowl.

4. Leave the bowl in a sunny place. Wait several days, and see the salt re-appear!

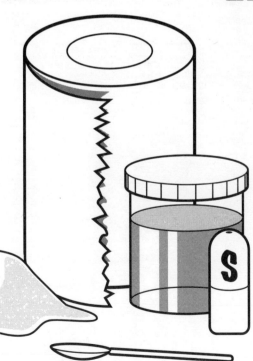

Modelling Dough

SUPERVISED

ACTIVITY

AIM

To make you own modelling dough to sculpt with.

MATERIALS

- flour
- salt
- cornflour
- vegetable oil
- food colouring
- water
- 2 cups

Did You Know?

The solids and liquids in this recipe combine to make a new product that is unlike the original ingredients. It is smooth and stretchy, so it allows you to make it into different shapes.

STEPS

1. Place two tablespoons of water in a cup, and add two drops of food colouring. Add one tablespoon of salt, stirring until it dissolves.

2. Place four tablespoons of flour, one tablespoon of cornflour and one tablespoon of vegetable oil to the second cup and mix well.

3. Add the salty water to the second cup, and knead well with your fingers.

4. Use your modelling dough to make any shapes you like! Store your dough in a plastic bag.

Natural or Processed?

 ✓

 ✓
 ✓

AIM

To sort materials into natural and processed groups.

MATERIALS

- pieces of different materials (newspaper, clingwrap, wood, baking paper, foil, metal, fabrics, twigs, sand, rocks, bone, clay, sheep's wool, glass, plastic, paper, cardboard, leaves, feathers etc.)
- 2 sheets of poster paper
- PVA glue

Did You Know?

Some materials are natural, but then are changed by people to become new things. For example, a tree can be changed into a tissue, or a wooden ruler. Even many plastics come from natural sources such as gas and oil found under the ground.

STEPS

1. Sort the materials into two groups – natural and processed (man-made) materials.

2. On one sheet of poster paper, glue all the natural materials into a collage. Add some pictures.

3. On the second sheet of paper, glue all the processed materials into a collage. Add some pictures.

Ocean in a Bottle

SUPERVISED

ACTIVITY

AIM

To make your own ocean in a bottle.

MATERIALS

- one long jar with a lid
- water
- blue food colouring
- cooking oil

Did You Know?

Oil and water do not mix. This means that your heavier 'waves' of water make a separate layer under the lighter 'sky' of oil. If you shake the jar really hard, you will see droplets of oil in the water. When you stop shaking, the two layers re-form. Adding detergent to the oil would let it mix with the water.

STEPS

1. Half fill the jar with water.

2. Add a few drops of blue food colouring to the water and mix.

3. Fill up the rest of the jar to the rim with cooking oil.

4. Screw on the lid.

5. Tip the jar onto its side, and watch the blue 'waves' rock when you gently shake the jar!

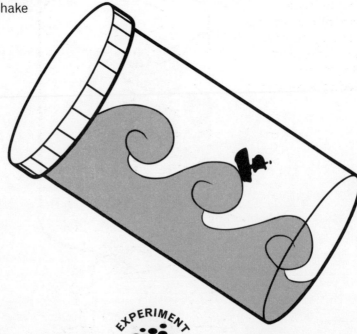

Paper Strength

AIM

To compare different types of paper.

MATERIALS

- different types of paper (tissue, toilet, writing, gift-wrap, cards, baking paper, newspaper)
- scissors

Did You Know?

Toilet paper is quite weak as it needs to break down easily in sewage treatment processes. Newspaper needs to be quite strong, as it needs to withstand printing processes and people reading it.

STEPS

1. Guess how strong each paper type is, writing down the order you think, from weakest to strongest.

2. Cut each paper into a square, with 10 cm (4 in) sides.

3. One at a time, tear each piece of paper, writing down how easy it was.

4. Now write down the paper types, in order of weakest to strongest. Was your guess close? Why do some need to be stronger?

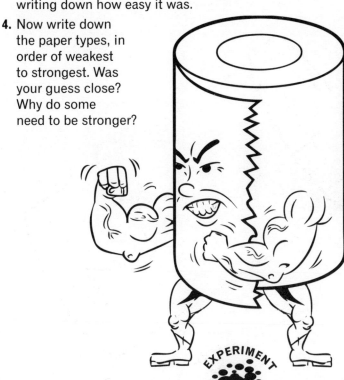

EXPERIMENT

Peppery Skin

AIM

To prove that water has an invisible 'skin'.

MATERIALS

- large flat bowl
- water
- pepper
- dishwashing liquid

Did You Know?

You should have seen the surface of pepper split, or fracture, when you dropped the detergent in. This is because detergent breaks up the invisible 'skin' of water, and the pepper allows you to see this happening.

STEPS

1. Fill the bowl with water.

2. Sprinkle pepper all over the surface of the water.

3. Gently add a drop of detergent to the middle of the bowl. What happens?

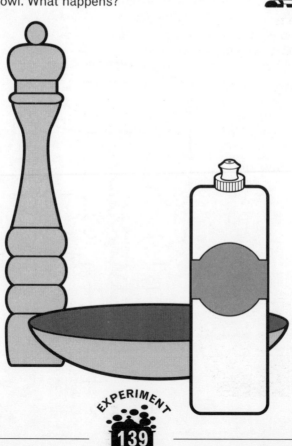

EXPERIMENT
139

Preserving Food

AIM

To compare different ways of stopping bread going mouldy.

MATERIALS

- 4 pieces of bread
- 4 jars with lids
- vinegar
- water
- salt

Did You Know?

Foods contain yeasts and bacteria, which after some time, can grow and make the food go mouldy and unhealthy to eat. Vinegar and salt kill most of these organisms, so pieces of bread soaked in these jars should go mouldy last, or not at all! Before fridges were invented, salt was an important way to preserve foods.

STEPS

1. Place a piece of bread into each jar.
2. Add water to one jar so it just covers the bread.
3. Add vinegar to the next jar, so it just covers the bread.
4. Dissolve a few teaspoons of salt in some water. Add this to a jar, just covering the bread.
5. Leave the fourth piece of bread untouched.
6. Leave the jars for several days. Each day, check if any mould has grown.

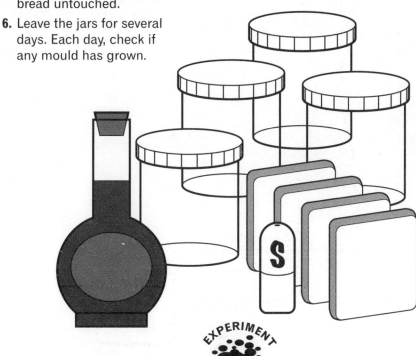

EXPERIMENT

Rise Up

AIM

To change materials into a loaf of bread.

MATERIALS

- 1 tablespoon sugar
- 1 tablespoon olive oil
- 1 tablespoon yeast
- 1¼ cup warm water
- 3½ cups flour
- 1 tablespoon salt
- 2 bowls
- 1 baking tin
- pastry brush
- oven

Did You Know?

The warm water activates the yeast, which begins feeding on the sugar. The yeast organisms make carbon dioxide, which is a gas. These bubbles of gas get trapped in the baking dough, so make the dough 'rise up'.

STEPS

1. Mix the sugar, oil, yeast and water in a bowl. It should start to froth.

2. In another bowl, mix the flour and salt.

3. Add the liquids to the solids. Mix and then knead with your hands until smooth and elastic. Brush the ball of dough with oil, and cover with clingfilm. Leave in a warm place for an hour.

4. Ask an adult to preheat the oven to 220°C (425°F).

5. Roll the dough into a round roll. Brush with butter if you like. Place in a baking tin and bake for 40–60 minutes or until the top is brown. Cool and eat!

Rubbery Egg

SUPERVISED ✓

ACTIVITY ✓ ✓ ✓

AIM

To make an eggshell go soft.

MATERIALS

- 1 egg
- drinking glass
- vinegar

Did You Know?

The vinegar reacts with the calcium in the eggshell, dissolving it. This makes the shell feel rubbery. This shows the importance of calcium to make the shell strong, just like the calcium in our bones. Keep drinking that milk!

STEPS

1. Gently place the egg into the glass.

2. Pour vinegar over the egg to completely cover it.

3. Wait several days. Take the egg out of the glass, and feel the shell.

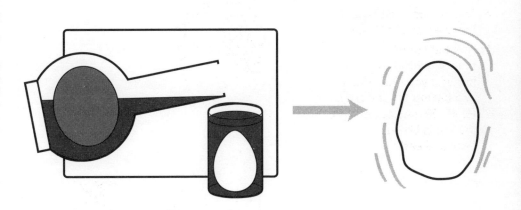

Salty Drops

5–12
AGES

SUPERVISED

ACTIVITY

AIM

To catch and taste some steam.

MATERIALS

- salty water
- metal spoon
- freezer

STEPS

1. Place the metal spoon in the freezer for an hour.
2. Ask an adult to boil some salty water in a saucepan.
3. When the water is steaming, hold the metal spoon above the saucepan until water droplets form on it. Guess whether you think the droplets will taste salty. Check!

Did You Know?

The water droplets would not taste salty, because when the water evaporates from the saucepan, the salt is left behind.

Salty Ice

AIM

To melt an ice cube quickly.

MATERIALS

- 2 ice cubes
- salt
- 2 bowls

STEPS

1. Place each ice cube into a separate bowl.

2. Sprinkle a teaspoon of salt onto one of the ice cubes.

3. Watch the ice cubes melt. Which one wins the melting race?

Did You Know?

The salt makes the ice cube melt faster. Plain water freezes at 0°C (32°F). Salt lowers the freezing temperature of water, so the ice cube in salt would have to be made much colder than 0°C (32°F) to stay frozen. At room temperature this is not possible, so the ice has to melt.

Save our Chemicals!

 ✓
 ✓
 ✓

AIM

To look after our environment and recycle chemicals.

MATERIALS

- house
- garden
- park
- streets
- plastic bags
- gardening gloves

Did You Know?

A lot of energy goes into making new chemicals, or getting them out of our Earth. We can recycle many chemicals, such as glass, paper and aluminium, and make them into new objects. This means that we can save energy and limit the damage done to our environment.

STEPS

1. Search the house and garden, and a local park or street (with the permission of an adult) for chemicals you can recycle. For example, collect empty drink cans and old newspapers.

2. Collect all the paper in one plastic bag, drink cans in another bag, glass bottles in another. Leave them for the recycling company to pick up!

EXPERIMENT

145

Shiny Silver

ACTIVITY

AIM

To clean silver without using toxic chemicals or polishing.

MATERIALS

- bicarbonate of soda (baking soda)
- water
- large saucepan
- sink
- aluminium foil
- a dirty (tarnished) piece of silver
- stove

Did You Know?

Air reacts with silver to make a chemical with a black colour on the surface of the silver. Here, the bicarbonate of soda brings that black chemical and aluminium foil together, and they react to make a new chemical on the foil, so that the silver is clean again!

STEPS

1. Lay the aluminium foil across the bottom of the sink.

2. Place the piece of dirty silver on top of the foil.

3. Ask an adult to help you boil water in the saucepan and add one cup of bicarbonate of soda for every four cups of water.

4. Carefully pour the water into the sink over the silver.

5. Watch as the piece of silver cleans itself!

EXPERIMENT
146

Smell That Gas

AIM

To time the travel of a gas.

MATERIALS

- perfume or air freshener
- large room

STEPS

1. Spray the perfume or air freshener in one corner of the room.
2. Run over to the other corner of the room, and count how long before you can smell the perfume.

Did You Know?

The perfume is a liquid, but when we spray it, it evaporates into a gas. This gas spreads out and travels through the gases of the air. When we breathe in air, the smell is noticed in our nose. Because many gases are invisible and poisonous, they can be dangerous. This is why natural gas has a smell added to it, so we know when it is in the air around us.

1-ONE-THOUSAND... 2-ONE-THOUSAND... 3-ONE-THOUSAND...

EXPERIMENT
147

Soak It Up

AIM

To find out which paper would be best for mopping up a spill.

MATERIALS

- squares of different paper types (newspaper, tissue, toilet paper, writing paper, cardboard, paper towel, baking paper, giftcard etc.)
- water
- dropper

Did You Know?

To make your test fair, you need to use the same size squares of each paper, and add the same number of drops of water onto each. You were testing how absorbent the paper was, or how well it soaks up water. Try this experiment with a cup of water and different brands of nappies!

STEPS

1. On each square of paper, place five drops of water in the middle.

2. How much water soaks into the paper? How much water stays on top of the square?

3. Which do you think is the most suitable paper type to mop up a spill? Why?

Soap Boats

 ✓
 ✓
 ✓

AIM

To make a boat move across water using soap.

MATERIALS

- one plastic bread-bag tie, or a piece of card cut into a boat shape, with a 'V' shape cut into one edge (see picture to the right)
- large bowl or tub of water
- dishwashing liquid or small piece of soap

STEPS

1. Place the plastic tie or card boat onto the water.

2. Carefully place a few drops of dishwashing liquid into the 'V' shape of the boat.

3. Watch your boat move forward across the water!

Did You Know?

The dishwashing liquid mixes into the water, and weakens the attraction between the water and the back of the boat. The pull of the water on the front of the boat is now stronger, so moves the boat forwards. Try this experiment by wedging a small piece of hand soap into the 'V'.

Sorting Materials

AIM

To describe and sort materials.

MATERIALS

- a collection of different materials (spoons, keys, wooden objects, papers, fabrics)
- paper
- pencils

Did You Know?

In science we often sort things into groups, depending on their characteristics. For example, animals can be divided into mammals, reptiles, birds and insects.

STEPS

1. Look at each material closely. Draw a picture of it.

2. Around the picture, write different words to describe the material. Use words such as hard, soft, shiny, dull, bendy etc.

3. Are there any groups you could sort the materials into, for example, heavy and light? How many different ways can you sort your objects?

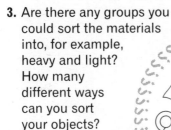

EXPERIMENT
150

Squishy Ice-cream

AIM

To create your own ice-cream.

MATERIALS

- ½ cup full-fat milk
- 1 tablespoon sugar
- 1 teaspoon vanilla essence
- 1 large zip-lock bag
- 1 small zip-lock bag
- 2 cups crushed ice
- 6 tablespoons of salt

Did You Know?

The salt makes the ice even colder, and so freezes the milk mixture. Because you keep squishing, the mixture becomes creamy!

STEPS

1. Mix the milk, sugar and essence in the small bag, seal and shake!

2. Mix the ice and salt in the bigger bag.

3. Put the small bag inside the big bag. Squish them together for 10 minutes or so, with your fingers. The longer you knead, the creamier the ice-cream!

4. Eat!

Stretchy Stockings

 ✓

 ✓

✓

AIM

To discover which pair of tights is the most stretchy.

MATERIALS

- different pairs of tights
- a weight, such as a rock
- ruler

STEPS

1. Hang a pair of tights up high on the washing line.

2. Place the weight into one 'foot'. With the ruler, measure how much the tights stretched down.

3. Repeat your test for the other pairs of tights. Draw a bar graph of the different lengths the tights stretched.

Did You Know?

Before the invention of nylon, stockings were made from wool, silk and cotton. The first nylon stockings went on sale in 1940. At first, they were made to the exact shape of the leg, since they could not stretch. In 1959, lycra was invented, which could stretch up to seven times its original length without breaking!

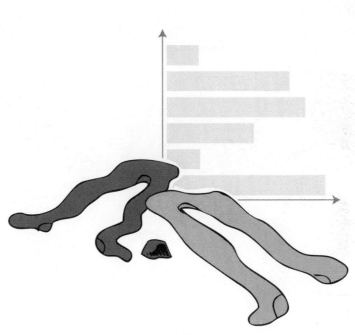

Sweaty Eggplants

AIM

To watch an eggplant 'sweat'.

MATERIALS

- 2 slices of eggplant (aubergine)
- 2 teaspoons of salt

STEPS

1. Ask an adult to cut two slices off an eggplant.

2. Sprinkle two teaspoons of salt over one of the slices, and leave the other untouched.

3. After half an hour, look closely at both slices. The salted slice will appear 'sweaty', with drops of water coming out of it!

Did You Know?

An eggplant is a plant, so water can flow in or out of its tiny cells. When you sprinkle salt onto the eggplant slice, there is more salt in the surroundings than inside the plant, so water leaves the cells. This makes the eggplant appear to 'sweat'. This process is used in cooking to take the bitterness out of the eggplant.

EXPERIMENT

153

Sweet Dissolving

5–12
AGES

✓
SUPERVISED

✓
✓
ACTIVITY

AIM

To test dissolving under different conditions.

MATERIALS

- 3 hard lollies (such as Minties), about the same size
- timer or clock

STEPS

1. Place one lolly into your mouth. Time how long it takes to dissolve, without using your tongue or your teeth to help!

2. Place the second lolly into your mouth. Time how long it takes to dissolve, using only your tongue.

3. Place the third lolly into your mouth. Time how long it takes to dissolve, using both your tongue and your teeth.

4. Compare the three times taken. What do you notice?

Did You Know?

Dissolving is easier if the pieces are smaller, and if you can 'stir'. So the lolly should have dissolved fastest when you could use your tongue and teeth to help!

Swirly Colours

 ✓

SUPERVISED

 ✓
 ✓

ACTIVITY

AIM

To make swirly coloured patterns in milk.

MATERIALS

- flat bowl or deep plate
- dishwashing liquid
- different food colourings
- milk

Did You Know?

The detergent changes the surface of the milk, making the water in the milk flow more easily. This causes a swirling motion, easily seen by the movement of the food colouring. Try this activity with low-fat milk to see whether this makes any difference!

STEPS

1. Fill the bowl or plate with milk, 2–3 cm (½–2 in) deep.

2. Add a few drops of different food colourings on top of the milk, around the edges of the plate or bowl, keeping the colours separate. Do not mix them into the milk!

3. Add a few drops of dishwashing liquid in the centre of the bowl.

4. Watch the swirly coloured patterns form!

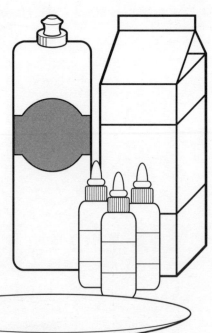

EXPERIMENT

155

Tall or Short?

SUPERVISED

ACTIVITY

AIM

To observe how fast evaporation happens in different containers.

MATERIALS

- narrow tall container
- wide shallow container
- water
- plastic ruler
- sunny spot

Did You Know?

Liquids can evaporate, or change into a gas, when they are heated up. The water in the wide, shallow container should evaporate first, because there is more surface area where it can change into a gas.

STEPS

1. Pour the same amount of water into both containers. Measure the depth of each.

2. Leave the bowls in a sunny spot. Measure how deep each is every hour.

3. Which liquid goes down fastest? After a few days, which container is dry first?

EXPERIMENT

156

The Big Freeze

AIM

To find out how quickly water freezes.

MATERIALS

- 2 ice cube trays
- freezer
- warm water
- cold water

Did You Know?

The warm water will take longer to freeze, since it takes more energy to turn warm water into a solid than cold water. This is because in warm water the particles are moving faster around each other than in cold water, and so it takes more energy to slow them down into a solid.

STEPS

1. Fill one ice cube tray with cold water, and the other with warm water.
2. Place them both in a freezer. Which will freeze first?
3. Every 15 minutes, check the ice cubes. What happens?

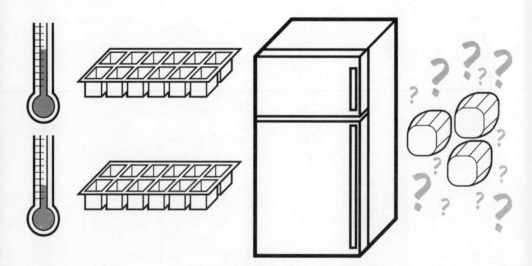

The Big Ice

SUPERVISED

ACTIVITY

AIM

To measure how much space ice takes up.

MATERIALS

- glass of water
- ice cube

STEPS

1. Fill the glass with water, almost up to the rim.

2. Carefully place the ice cube on top of the water.

3. Watch as the ice cube melts. Have a guess whether the water will overflow out of the glass!

Did You Know?

Ice takes up more space than liquid water. This is why, when the ice cube melts, the water should not overflow. The ice cube will melt into liquid water which will take up less space than the original ice cube took up.

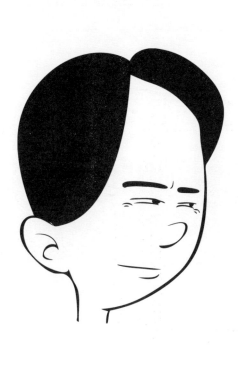

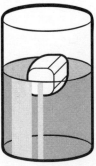

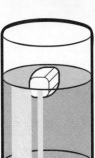

The Floating Egg

AIM

To find out which liquids an egg will float in.

MATERIALS

- 4 glasses of water
- salt
- sugar
- flour
- egg

Did You Know?

Density is how tightly the matter of a mixture is packed together. For example, an egg is more dense than plain water, so the egg sinks. Salt water, however, is more dense than an egg, and so the egg floats! Are you more or less dense than sea water?

STEPS

1. Fill each glass three-quarters full with water.

2. Stir a few tablespoons of salt into one glass of water, until it dissolves.

3. Stir the same amount of sugar into the second glass of water.

4. Stir the same amount of flour into the third glass of water. Leave the fourth glass of water plain.

5. Guess which glass of liquid the egg will float in. Now try them all!

EXPERIMENT

159

Tilted Bottle

AIM

To discover what happens to the water level in a tilted bottle.

MATERIALS

- a plastic see-through bottle with lid
- water
- paper
- pencil

Did You Know?

The water level always stays flat, or horizontal. It stays parallel with the ground, because gravity pulls it down equally on all sides.

STEPS

1. Half fill the bottle with water and screw the lid on. Draw the bottle and the water level.
2. Tilt the bottle a little on its side. Draw it again, noting the water level.
3. Tilt the bottle further towards the table and draw it and the water level again.
4. Lie the bottle flat on the table. Draw it and the water level again. What did you notice?

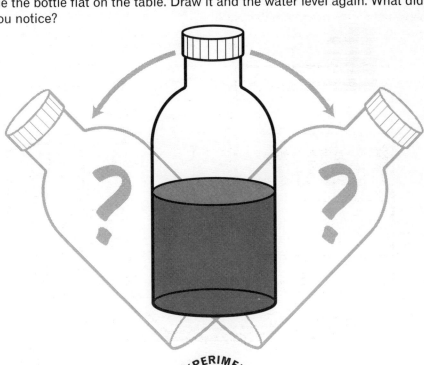

Underwater Volcano

SUPERVISED

ACTIVITY

AIM

To create an underwater volcano eruption.

MATERIALS

- small glass bottle
- warm water
- red food colouring
- string
- large jar of cold water

Did You Know?

The red food colouring lets you see where the warm water molecules travel. Warm water always rises up to the surface, and cooler water molecules sink. This also happens to warm and cool air.

STEPS

1. Tie the string around the neck of the small bottle.

2. Fill the small bottle with warm water and a few drops of red food colouring.

3. Slowly lower the bottle into the large jar of cold water. Try to place the bottle at the bottom of the jar.

4. Watch the red water rise from the bottle, just like lava and smoke from a volcano!

EXPERIMENT

Volume

SUPERVISED

ACTIVITY

AIM

To find out how much water is moved by different weights.

MATERIALS

- 2 same-sized glasses
- 2 same-sized jars with lids (smaller than the glasses)
- sand
- water

Did You Know?

When something sinks, it moves some water aside. In a glass, the water must move up. Because the full jar of sand is heavier, it needs to move aside more water. This is why the water will move up higher in the glass.

STEPS

1. Half fill each of the glasses with water, to the same level.
2. Fill one jar with sand and fill the other jar only half full. Screw on the lids.
3. Sink the half-full jar into one glass of water. How much does the water rise?
4. Sink the full jar into the second glass. How much did the water rise this time?

Wash It Clean

SUPERVISED

ACTIVITY

AIM

To test which detergent is the best cleaner.

MATERIALS

- 4 handkerchiefs
- 3 household detergents (dishwashing liquid, laundry detergent, shampoo, bubble bath etc.)
- 4 cups, half filled with water
- container with dirt
- eye dropper
- newspaper

Did You Know?

Detergents clean by making it easier for the water to spread out and wet the surface. Some detergents are stronger cleaners than others.

STEPS

1. Add a little water to the dirt. Scrub each handkerchief in the mixture, so they are all about as dirty as each other. Leave them to dry, flat on a newspaper.

2. Dissolve two tablespoons of each detergent in half a cup of water. Leave one cup of water plain.

3. Place 20 drops of one mixture in the centre of one handkerchief. Repeat with the other mixtures on the other handkerchiefs. Which detergent did the best job of cleaning?

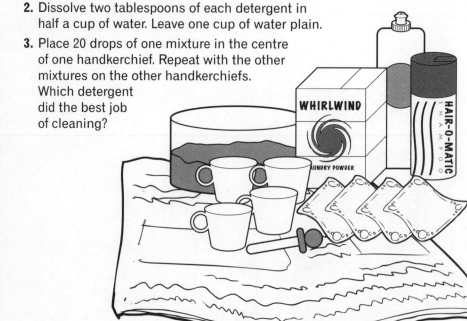

WHIRLWIND

LAUNDRY POWDER

HAIR-O-MATIC
SHAMPOO

EXPERIMENT

163

Waterproof?

AIM

To find out which materials are waterproof.

MATERIALS

- pieces of different materials (newspaper, cling wrap, wood, baking paper, foil, metal, fabrics etc.)
- water
- dropper

Did You Know?

Some materials are more waterproof than others. For example, while wood and metal may both hold back 10 drops of water, a bucket of water would soak through wood, but not metal!

STEPS

1. Guess which materials will be waterproof.

2. Testing one material at a time, place 10 drops of water onto each piece of material.

3. Check to see whether the table is wet underneath. Which would you choose to make an umbrella?

TISSUES ARE NOT WATERPROOF...

What Is It?

SUPERVISED

ACTIVITY

AIM

To identify materials using your senses (except sight and taste).

MATERIALS

- a collection of different objects (spoons, keys, wooden objects, papers, fabrics)
- large bag

Did You Know?

We often use our senses to work out what is in the world around us. For some people, who are blind or deaf, this process becomes much more difficult. In this activity, the sense of touch was probably the most useful.

STEPS

1. Ask an adult or a friend to place different objects into the bag for you – don't look!

2. Using your sense of touch, hearing and smell, pick up each object in the bag and try to guess what it is.

3. Give yourself a point for each one you guess correctly. Swap – this time you place objects in the bag for a friend to guess! Which sense was the most useful in this activity?

Will It Mix?

AIM

To find out which liquids will mix with water.

MATERIALS

- different household liquids (methylated spirits, fruit juice, cooking oil, sunscreen, ink, detergent, cordial, milk, vinegar, engine oil etc.)
- jar of water
- stirrers
- soapy water

Did You Know?

Not all liquids can mix with water. For example, oil and water do not mix, unless you add a detergent to them.

STEPS

1. Add a few tablespoons of one of the liquids to the jar of water. Mix well.

2. Look closely at the mixture. Has the liquid mixed in with the water, or does it float on top or settle on the bottom?

3. Rinse the jar in soapy water, and test all the liquids. Do they all mix with water?

MUMBLE...
GRUMBLE...

GRRRR...
RASSUM FRASSUM...

OIL AND WATER DON'T MIX...

Wrinkly Apple

AIM

To create your own mummified apple face.

MATERIALS

- 1 apple
- 1 popstick
- 1 plastic bag
- ¼ cup salt
- ½ cup sodium carbonate (powder bleach)
- ½ cup bicarbonate of soda (baking soda)

Did You Know?

The powders take all the moisture out of the apple, and make it difficult for bacteria to grow. Without the water and bacteria, the apple cannot decay, so it just shrivels and dries up. Do not eat this apple!

STEPS

1. Mix the salt, sodium carbonate and bicarbonate of soda together in the bag.

2. Cut a face into the apple using the popstick. Push the popstick into the top of your apple so it makes a handle.

3. Put the apple into the mixture in the bag, so it is covered.

4. Leave the bag open, in a warm place. Watch what happens to the apple!

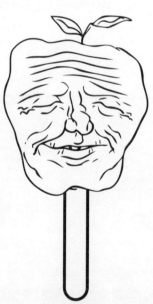

Geology and Geography

Making Sandstone

AIM

To make your very own piece of sandstone.

MATERIALS

- dry sand
- cementing solution
  (2 parts water to 1 part
  Epsom salts)
- paper cups
- paper towel

Did You Know?

Sandstone is classified as a sedimentary rock. Sedimentary rocks can take thousands of years to form. You made your very own in two days!

STEPS

1. Half fill a small paper cup with sand.

2. Slowly add the cementing solution until it completely covers the sand.

3. Now you have to let your mixture set. Make sure you place the cup in a warm place (i.e. cupboard). Keep it there overnight.

4. In the morning remove the dry mixture from the cup. It may still be a little wet, but should still be dry enough to hold its shape. Place the mixture on a paper towel for a further two days, or until it is completely dry.

5. Congratulations! You now have your very own piece of sandstone.

EPSOM SALTS

The Thirsty Brick

SUPERVISED

ACTIVITY

AIM

To investigate whether rocks can absorb water.

MATERIALS

- large plastic container
- measuring cup (must have level markings)
- brick

Did You Know?

Most rocks in the environment absorb water. However, the amount of water they can absorb depends on a number of factors. One factor is how absorbent the rock is.

STEPS

1. Pour a measured amount of water into the container. Make sure you pour enough water so that it completely covers the brick.

2. Put the brick in the middle of the water-filled container. Can you see anything happening to the water level?

3. Leave the brick in the container for 45 minutes.

4. Remove the brick from the container. Make sure you allow the excess water to drain off before completely removing the brick.

5. Calculate how much water was soaked up by the brick. This can be done by pouring the excess water back into the measuring container.

Making Limestone

 ✓

 ✓
✓

AIM

To make a piece of limestone.

MATERIALS

- shoe box
- plastic garbage bag
- paper cups
- dry plaster
- water
- pieces of shells

Did You Know?

Limestone is a type of sedimentary rock made up mostly of calcium carbonate. When microscopic marine animals die, they fall to the sea floor where their hard parts (shells) collect and eventually form limestone.

STEPS

1. Line the shoe box with plastic.

2. Add the plaster and water, taking care to mix it thoroughly.

3. Add the shell pieces and thoroughly mix them in with the plaster.

4. Pour the mixture into the cups.

5. Place the cups in a warm area (cupboard), where they will not be disturbed for three to four days.

6. Remove limestone from cups. Describe what the limestone looks and feels like.

Making Conglomerate Rock

SUPERVISED

ACTIVITY

AIM

To make a piece of conglomerate rock.

MATERIALS

- shoe box
- plastic garbage bag
- paper cups
- sandwich bags
- dry cement
- dry sand
- water
- rocks

Did You Know?

Conglomerate rock is a rock made up of particles of different sizes. Rocks are made up of minerals and scientists classify different types of rock according to their grain size and what each rock is made up of.

STEPS

1. Line the shoe box with plastic.

2. Add one cup of dry cement, one cup of dry sand, and one cup of cold water. Mix thoroughly.

3. Add rocks to the mixture and mix again.

4. Line the small cups with the sandwich bags and pour the mixture.

5. Place the cups in a warm area (cupboard) until the mixture is dry. Describe the texture of the rock.

At-home Palaeontologist

AIM

To make your very own fossilised footprint.

MATERIALS

- 1 two-litre milk or juice carton
- bucket of sand
- small cup
- large cup
- water
- plaster
- scissors

Did You Know?

Fossilised evidence is one method scientists use to discover what types of plants and animals lived many thousands of years ago. Without fossils we may have never known what type of dinosaurs once roamed our planet.

STEPS

1. Carefully cut a milk carton lengthwise.

2. Fill the cut milk carton with a layer of sand about 6 cm (2¼ in) deep.

3. Place one leg on top of the sand, and carefully press on the sand so that your footprint remains on the sand.

4. Fill the small cup with plaster and pour it into the larger cup. Now add another small cup of plaster. Add one small cup of water and let the large cup sit until all of the water has been absorbed. The plaster will be our pretend mud that is needed in the fossilisation process.

5. After the plaster has been mixed carefully pour it into the milk carton. Make sure to completely cover the footprint with plaster.

6. After the plaster has set, carefully lift your fossilised footprint out of the sand and give it a quick clean. Now you can compare your plaster fossil to the original footprint.

EXPERIMENT

172

Searching for Missing Footprints

AIM

To search for and fossilise footprints.

MATERIALS

- small cup
- large cup
- water and plaster
- brush
- footprint

Did You Know?

Some fossils, such as bone, may consist of the actual remains of the organism. However, most fossils consist only of the impression left in the rock by the organism after the remains have decomposed or dissolved.

STEPS

1. Go outside to your garden bed or to a nearby park, and look for a footprint impression within the soil.

2. Although to us it is only a footprint made only a few hours or a couple of days ago, palaeontologists spend years looking for similar things.

3. Fill the small cup with plaster and pour it into the larger cup (this will be our pretend mud that is needed to fossilise the footprint). Now add another small cup of plaster. Add one small cup of water and let the large cup sit until all of the water has been absorbed.

4. After the plaster has been mixed, carefully pour it into and over your footprint. Make sure you completely cover the footprint with the plaster mixture.

5. After the plaster has set, carefully lift your fossilised footprint out of the garden bed. Now you can compare your plaster footprint to the original footprint you found in the garden.

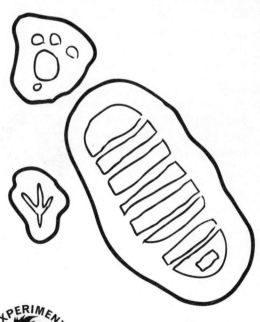

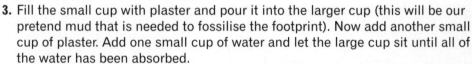

EXPERIMENT
173

Soil Search

 ✓

 ✓
 ✓
 ✓

AIM

To investigate what lives in soil.

MATERIALS

- small bucket of soil
- large bucket
- kitchen sieve or strainer
- magnifying glass
- pen and paper
- newspaper

Did You Know?

Although its chief component is weathered rock, a true soil also contains water, air, bacteria, and decayed plant and animal materials. Did you find any of these?

STEPS

1. Go out to the garden and collect yourself half a bucket of soil. Remember the bucket may be heavy so ask an adult to help you carry the bucket inside.

2. Empty the contents of the small bucket, so the dirt falls through the kitchen strainer and into the big bucket.

3. Spread some newspaper on the table and empty the contents of the strainer.

4. Using the pen and paper write down all the living things that you find in the soil.

5. Now write down all the non-living things that you find.

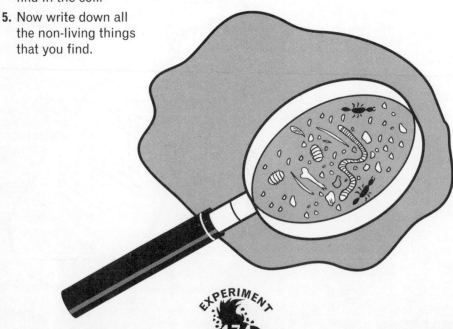

Studying Rocks

AIM

To study and classify different types of rocks.

MATERIALS

- small collection of rocks
- pen and paper

STEPS

1. Collect some rocks in your garden or on a trip to the park.

2. Classify the rocks according to size and weight.

Did You Know?

Rocks are all made up of minerals. If you have a rock that is predominately red in colour, then it most likely has a high iron content. Calcium is the mineral found mostly in white coloured rocks. Did you have any red or white rocks?

3. Classify the rocks according to their grain size and hardness.

4. Which rocks are layered? Which rocks are not?

5. Classify your rocks according to their shine, i.e. separate the shiny rocks from the dull rocks.

6. See which rocks you can draw with on the asphalt or pavement (hard or soft).

What's in Dirt?

 ✓

SUPERVISED

 ✓
 ✓
 ✓

ACTIVITY

AIM

To analyse different soil samples.

MATERIALS

- 3 medium-sized cups
- 3 kitchen sieves
- paper and pen

Did You Know?

Soil or dirt is really made from the erosion of rocks. This process can take thousands of years. Just think, the dirt you collected today was once a big rock!

STEPS

1. Collect three different soil samples.

2. Each soil sample should be collected in a large cup.

3. The soil samples should be taken from three different locations. Areas may include: a sandpit, near a pond or stream, from a garden bed.

4. Each soil sample should then be put through a kitchen sieve.

5. Make sure you hold on to what is left in the sieve. The soil that passes through the sieve can then be put back.

6. Record what was found in each sieve. Were there many differences between the contents of the three sieves?

Just Rockin' Around

SUPERVISED ✓

ACTIVITY ✓ ✓

AIM

To identify and group rocks.

MATERIALS

- 12 different types of rocks
- pen
- paper
- drop sheet

Did You Know?

Scientists have identified over 2000 different minerals in Earth's crust, and there are only three different ways that rocks are made.

STEPS

1. Cover your work area with the drop sheet. Spread your assorted rock collection over your work area.

2. See if you can divide your rock collection into two different groups. Describe why you grouped your rocks as you did to a friend. Listen and share ideas.

3. Now see if you can divide your rock collection into three different groups. Describe why you grouped your rocks as you did to your friend. Listen and share ideas.

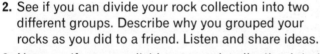

Rock Search

AIM

To find and group rocks according to texture, grain size and colour.

MATERIALS

- rock collection (6–10 rocks should be sufficient)
- paper
- pen
- drop sheet
- magnifying glass

Did You Know?

The rocks that make up the world's continents are all made of minerals, and about 3,000 different minerals have been identified in Earth's crust.

STEPS

1. Place the drop sheet over your workspace. Spread out your rocks and look them over.

2. Group your rocks according to colour. One group should contain lightly coloured rocks, the other group should contain dark coloured rocks.

3. Group your rocks according to texture. One group should contain rocks that have a fine or smooth texture. The other group should contain rocks with a coarse or rough texture.

4. Now using your magnifying glass, group your rocks according to their grain size. One group should contain the rocks with the small or fine grains. The other group should contain the rocks with the larger grains.

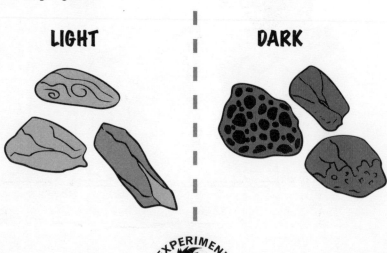

LIGHT   DARK

At-home Volcano

 ✓

 ✓

 ✓

AIM

To make your very own working volcano.

MATERIALS

- play dough
- empty film canister
- tablespoon of bicarbonate of soda (baking soda)
- tablespoon of vinegar

Did You Know?

Volcanoes erupt every day someplace on Earth. The Stromboli volcano near southern Italy is erupting this very minute, as are less famous continually active volcanoes in Ethiopia, Indonesia and elsewhere. The next big eruption will be ... we don't know where!

STEPS

1. Sculpt the play dough so that it forms the shape of a volcano.

2. Leave a hole on top of the volcano. The hole should be big enough so that the empty film canister can fit into it.

3. Insert the empty film canister into the hole.

4. Now it is time to add the ingredients that form the flowing molten lava.

5. Ask an adult to help. First add a tablespoon of baking soda to the empty canister. Now add the vinegar. Step back and watch your volcano come to life.

EXPERIMENT

179

Volcano in the Sandpit!

SUPERVISED

ACTIVITY

AIM

To make a volcano in the sandpit.

MATERIALS

- sandpit
- empty film canister
- bicarbonate of soda (baking soda)
- vinegar
- food colouring

Did You Know?

The biggest volcano on Earth is Mauna Loa on the island of Hawaii in the middle of the Pacific Ocean.

STEPS

1. Sculpt a volcano out of sand in the sandpit.

2. Dig a hole in the top of the volcano. The hole should be big enough so that an empty film canister can fit into it.

3. Insert the empty film canister into the hole.

4. Now it is time to make the volcano explode.

5. Ask an adult to help. First add a tablespoon of baking soda into the empty canister and the food colouring. Now add the vinegar.

6. Step back and watch your volcano come to life.

EXPERIMENT
180

Rock or Not!

 ✓

 ✓
 ✓

AIM

To identify buildings made from rocks.

MATERIALS

- pen
- paper
- map of your neighbourhood

Did You Know?

The rocks that make up the world's continents are all made of minerals. Manufactured materials such as brick, plastic, plaster and cement are not minerals because they are not natural in origin. Therefore, they are not considered rocks.

STEPS

1. With an adult and some friends, walk around your neighbourhood and try to identify which of the buildings are made from rock.

2. Write down which buildings you think are made from rock and which are not.

3. Get together with your friends and discuss your answers.

4. Remember! Buildings made from sandstone, bluestone and granite are made from rock. Whereas buildings made with brick and cement are not made from rock.

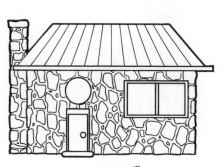

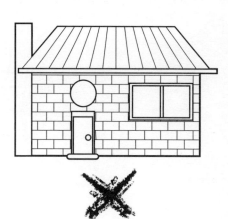

Rock Hunt

SUPERVISED ✓

 ✓

✓

ACTIVITY

AIM

To identify and group rocks.

MATERIALS

- rock collection
- pen
- paper

Did You Know?

Meteorites, which are rocks from space, help scientists learn about the solar system and are very valuable too!

STEPS

1. Go outside or to a nearby park.

2. Collect six rocks, making sure they are all collected from different areas (a garden bed, next to a lake or from the school oval).

3. Write down all the differences that you can spot between all of the rocks.

4. Do you think that the location of where the rocks were found accounts for any of the differences identified?

EXPERIMENT
182

The Amazing Floating Rock

SUPERVISED

ACTIVITY

AIM

To see whether a rock can actually float on water.

MATERIALS

- pumice stone (the bathroom should have one)
- plastic see-through container
- enough water to just fill the plastic container

Did You Know?

The pumice stone is used to get rid of all those yucky bits found on your feet. It is actually made from rock which is found only in volcanoes!

STEPS

1. Fill the plastic see-through container with water.
2. Drop the pumice stone into the container.
3. Does it sink to the bottom or float to the top?

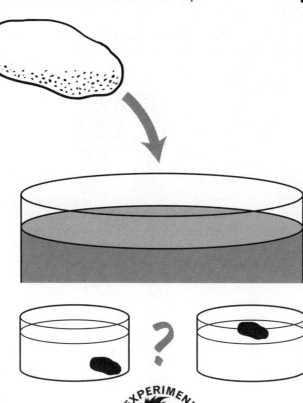

EXPERIMENT
183

Float or Sink?

✓

SUPERVISED

✓

✓

ACTIVITY

AIM

To predict which rock will float or sink.

MATERIALS

- pumice stone (the bathroom should have one)
- small piece of sandstone
- small piece of granite
- small brick or small piece of cement
- plastic see-through container
- enough water to just fill the plastic container
- pen
- paper

Did You Know?

Diamonds are the hardest rock and granite is the second hardest.

STEPS

1. Take your pen and paper and predict which rocks will float and which rocks will sink. Write your prediction down.

2. Fill the plastic see-through container with water.

3. Drop all your rocks into the container.

4. How many did you get right? How many did your friends get right?

EXPERIMENT
184

Styrofoam Earth

AIM

To make a model of Earth's interior using a styrofoam ball.

MATERIALS

- styrofoam ball
- set of coloured markers or paints
- knife
- fishing line (optional)

Did You Know?

The distance from the surface of Earth to the centre is about 6,378 kilometres (3,963 miles). Much of Earth's interior is made up of fluid and the mostly solid skin of the planet is only 66 kilometres (41 miles) thick.

STEPS

1. On the outside of the styrofoam ball, draw and colour in Earth's continents and oceans. Don't forget to also include the north and south poles. Other features you may also want to draw include: Mount Everest, the Nile River and your capital city.

2. Cut the styrofoam ball in half – have an adult to do this for you.

3. Earth's core is the hot spot that is located in the middle of the planet. Using a red marker or paint, draw and colour Earth's core on the styrofoam ball.

4. Earth's mantle is the area between Earth's core and Earth's crust. Using a brown marker or paint, colour in Earth's mantle.

5. Now you have your very own model of Earth. If you have some fishing line, why not hang it up? If you really want to get into it, why not make a model of the Moon and add that to your Earth model?

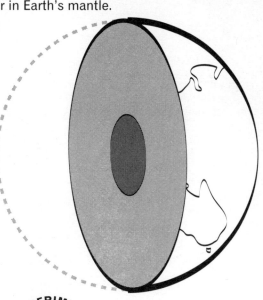

Journey to the Centre of the Earth

 ✓

AIM

To identify the sections of Earth's interior using an apple model.

MATERIALS

- apple
- knife
- ink pad
- large sheet of paper
- pen
- ruler

Did You Know?

The Earth's outermost surface is called the crust. The crust is typically about 40 km (25 miles) thick beneath the continents, and about 10.5 km (6.5 miles) thick beneath the oceans. On your ink model the crust was represented by just the apple skin!

STEPS

1. Take the knife (ask an adult to do this) and cut the apple in half from the stem, through the core, to the base.

2. Dip one half of the apple onto the ink pad and carefully place it onto the large piece of paper.

3. Leave the apple on the paper for a few seconds while applying a little pressure.

4. Carefully remove the apple from the paper. You should now have an ink imprint of the apple.

5. Notice any similarities between your stamp of the apple and that of Earth's interior?

6. Finish off by labelling your stamp. Write in where you think Earth's crust would be on your stamp. (Hint! Where the apple skin is.) Also, fill in where you think Earth's core and mantle would be.

EXPERIMENT 186

Which Rock is the Thirstiest?

 ✓

 ✓
 ✓

SUPERVISED

ACTIVITY

AIM

To identify what type of rock is most porous.

MATERIALS

- 3 large plastic containers
- measuring cup
- piece of granite
- piece of sandstone
- piece of limestone

Did You Know?

The colour of granite ranges from pink to light grey.

STEPS

1. Measure and pour the same amount of water into the three containers.

2. Make note of how much water was poured into each container.

3. Put each rock in the middle of each water-filled container.

4. Make sure there is enough water to cover each rock completely.

5. Ensure you leave each rock in the water for at least 30 minutes. Can you see anything happening to the water level?

6. Carefully remove the rocks from their containers. Make sure you allow all of the excess water to drain.

7. Calculate how much water was soaked up by each rock. This can be done by pouring the excess water back into the measuring container.

Living in Soil

✓

SUPERVISED

✓

✓

✓

ACTIVITY

AIM

To try and identify some of the organic (living) and inorganic (non-living) organisms that live in soil.

MATERIALS

- 3 collection containers
- soil from a sandpit (high sand content)
- soil from a football oval (high clay content)
- soil from a garden bed (high organic content)
- drop sheet
- magnifying glass
- pen
- paper

Did You Know?

Some earthworms are known to have lived for as long as six years. However, the average life span for an earthworm is only 20 months. Imagine having to live underground for that long! Yuk!

STEPS

1. Collect three soil samples using your collection containers.

2. Spread your drop sheet over your working area. Spread your soil samples out. Try to avoid mixing the three samples.

3. Lightly coloured soils usually indicate a high sand content, while dark coloured soils indicate a high organic content. Can you identify any differences in colour between your three samples?

4. Using your magnifying glass, try to identify the differences in particle size between your three samples. Which sample has the big particles?

5. See if you can find any living things in any of the soil samples. Which sample has the most? Which sample has the biggest living thing? Which soil sample has the smallest living thing?

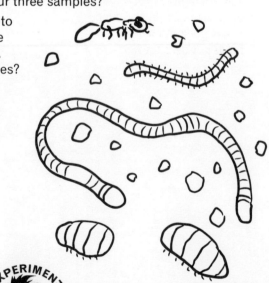

Melting Polar Ice Caps

✓

SUPERVISED

✓

✓

ACTIVITY

AIM

To predict whether rising sea levels will result from the melting polar ice caps.

MATERIALS

- tray of ice blocks
- large cup (milkshake cup is perfect)
- enough water to fill the cup

Did You Know?

It is not the melting polar ice caps that will contribute to the rising of the sea level. The major contributor will be the snow melting from the mountain areas, such as the Himalayas.

STEPS

1. The ice in this experiment represents the polar ice cups. Empty the tray of ice cubes into the cup. Filling the cup halfway should be sufficient for this experiment to work.

2. Carefully fill the cup with water. Try to get the water level as close to the rim of the cup as possible without overfilling it. The water in this experiment represents the oceans of the world.

3. Now, just kick back and wait for the polar ice caps (really the ice) to melt. Predict what you think will happen. Do you think the water will rise and overflow, stay the same or decrease?

EXPERIMENT
189

Biodegradable Bags

5–12
AGES

✓

✓

✓

SUPERVISED

ACTIVITY

AIM

To investigate the biodegradability of a plastic and a paper bag.

MATERIALS

- plastic shopping bag
- paper bag (preferably the same size as the plastic bag)
- shovel
- garden

Did You Know?

The biggest problem with plastic bags is that they do not readily break down. It has been estimated that it takes them from between 20 to 1000 years to decompose. I wonder how long your bag will take?

STEPS

1. Use the shovel to dig two small holes in your yard. (Ask an adult for permission first.) Make sure that the holes are no further than 1 m (3 ft) apart and approximately 20 cm (8 in) deep (you may need help from an adult to do this bit).
2. Place the plastic bag in one hole and the paper bag in the other hole.
3. Fill both holes with soil, ensuring that they are fully covered.
4. Now all you have to do is leave the bags covered for a month.
5. Come back after a month and dig both bags up. Which bag has biodegraded the most?

999 years in the future...

I'm still going!

EXPERIMENT
190

The Slow-moving Glacier

AIM

To demonstrate the movement of a glacier using a block of ice as a model.

MATERIALS

- medium sized zip-lock bags
- handful of pebbles
- handful of twigs
- water
- freezer

Did You Know?

Every continent on Earth has glaciers except Australia. Australia did have glaciers thousands of years ago. But with the onset of global warming they all melted away in much the same way as your miniaturised glaciers!

STEPS

1. The first step is to make our miniaturised glaciers.

2. Fill the zip-lock bags with water. Do not fill them right to the top, otherwise they will burst while freezing.

3. Before zip locking the bag add some twigs and pebbles.

4. Zip lock the bag, and put it into the freezer. Leave it there overnight or until the water is frozen.

5. Once it is frozen, remove the bag by simply ripping the plastic off. You have just made your very own, miniaturised glacier.

6. Go outside and find an asphalt area that has a slight decline.

7. Push down on the ice block and watch it move slowly forwards as it melts.

8. Make note of the debris left behind. Real life glaciers change our Earth's crust in much the same way, but on a much bigger scale.

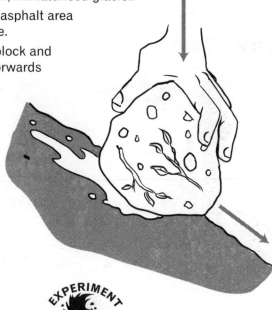

Soil Erosion

AIM

To investigate the influence that plants and water have on soil erosion.

MATERIALS

- 3 pans or plastic containers
- water
- 3 cups of sand
- styrofoam cup
- jug of water
- pen
- paper
- tissue

Did You Know?

Erosion is the wearing away of soil and rock, and the down slope movement of soil and rock. Some factors that influence erosion include: gravity, glaciers, wind and waves.

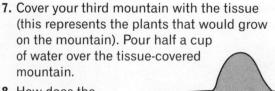

STEPS

1. Place one cup of sand into the middle of each pan.

2. Shape two piles of sand into small mountains. Smooth the third pile of sand so that it covers the whole pan.

3. Predict what you believe would happen if rain fell on one of your mountains and what would happen if it fell on the flattened sand.

4. Make a small hole in the bottom of the styrofoam cup. Place your finger over the hole and half fill it with water from the jug.

5. Hold the cup approximately 30 cm (12 in) away from the centre of your smooth pan. Move your finger so that the water trickles out. Record what happens.

6. Repeat the same procedure, this time on the pan with the mountain of sand. Record the results.

7. Cover your third mountain with the tissue (this represents the plants that would grow on the mountain). Pour half a cup of water over the tissue-covered mountain.

8. How does the shape of the land influence the amount of erosion? How does the tissue covering the mountain influence the erosion?

EXPERIMENT
192

Making Mountains Last

 ✓

 ✓

SUPERVISED

 ✓

ACTIVITY

AIM

To see how structures made of different materials are affected by water.

MATERIALS

- soil
- sand
- rocks
- drinking glass or cup
- water

Did You Know?

Different materials in the earth are affected in different ways by rain and water. This is one way that different land formations come about.

STEPS

1. In your garden build three mountains: one from rocks; one from sand; and one from soil. Make the mountains as secure as you can.

2. Now take the glass and fill it with water. Pour the water over the mountain made from rocks. What happens?

3. Repeat step 2 but this time pour the water over the mountain made of soil. What happens this time?

4. Finally pour some water over the mountain made of sand. What happens this time?

Digging for Dinosaurs

SUPERVISED

ACTIVITY

AIM

To see how dinosaur bones are found and put together.

MATERIALS

- dinosaur model
- 3–5 shoe boxes or similar
- friend

Did You Know?

The study of fossils and extinct animals and plants is called palaeontology.

STEPS

1. Take your shoe boxes and cut some holes in the lids just big enough to put your hand through.

2. Invite your friend to place the pieces of the dinosaur model in the shoe boxes. Ask your friend to mix them up so that they are not in any order. (To be clever your friend could leave some out.)

3. Have your friend arrange the shoe boxes on the floor.

4. Now place your hand in the various boxes and pull out the pieces of dinosaur model. Can you put together a dinosaur from the pieces you have found?

Help, I'm Caving In!

AIM

To see how caves and rivers are formed.

MATERIALS

- sugar cubes
- freshly made icing or frosting
- drinking glass
- water
- flat tray

Did You Know?

Caves and caverns once had water flowing through them. This is how they were formed.

STEPS

1. Take your tray and place it on a table.

2. Pour some of the icing onto the tray to make a small square a least 10 cm (4 in) wide and long.

3. Place your sugar cubes on the icing to make the base of your mountain.

4. Now pour more icing on the layer of sugar cubes and add another layer of sugar cubes. Keep repeating this process until you have made a mountain. (Your mountain can be any shape – a cube is fine.)

5. Now slowly pour water over your mountain. Can you see rivers forming?

6. To finish, break open your mountain. What can you see on the inside?

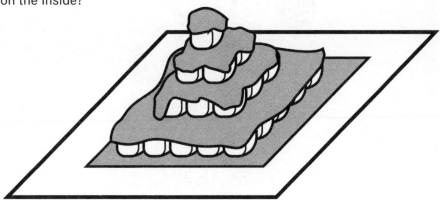

Metamorphic Pancakes

AIM

To see how metamorphic rock is formed.

MATERIALS

- pancake mix
- sultanas
- coconut
- nuts
- frying pan
- stove

Did You Know?

Metamorphic rock is sedimentary rock changed by heat caused by the pressure of the upper layers of the earth.

STEPS

1. Make up your pancake mix following the recipe. (You may need an adult to help you with this.)

2. Now add in some sultanas, some coconut and some nuts. What you have made is similar to sedimentary rock.

3. Now heat your pan and fry your pancake. What has happened? Has the pancake hardened and taken a specific shape?

EXPERIMENT
196

Magnetic Rocks!

SUPERVISED

ACTIVITY

AIM

To see how rocks are made of different minerals.

MATERIALS

- sheet of cardboard
- rocks
- magnet

STEPS

1. Collect some rocks from your garden. Get as many different types of rock as you can.

2. Place the rocks on your cardboard. Spread them out.

3. Now place your magnet close to each of the rocks. Are some attracted to the magnet and others not?

Did You Know?

There are many different types of minerals in rocks. The rocks that are attracted to your magnet have iron in them. This is why they move to the magnet.

EXPERIMENT

197

Hey, I'm Eroding Away!

SUPERVISED

ACTIVITY

AIM

To see how water causes erosion.

MATERIALS

- clear flat patch of earth
- drinking glass
- water

Did You Know?

The effect of water on land is to erode it away. When land is cleared of trees and bush the soil is eroded much more quickly because the trees and bush hold the earth together. Soil erosion is a big environmental problem.

STEPS

1. Clear a bit of ground in your backyard. Flatten out the ground so that it is even.

2. Fill your glass with water. Hold it at about a height of 15 cm (6 in) from the ground and pour the water. Note what happens.

3. Now fill your glass with water again. On another spot of cleared earth pour the water, this time from a height of about 30 cm (12 in) from the earth. Is the result the same? Did the water affect the earth differently?

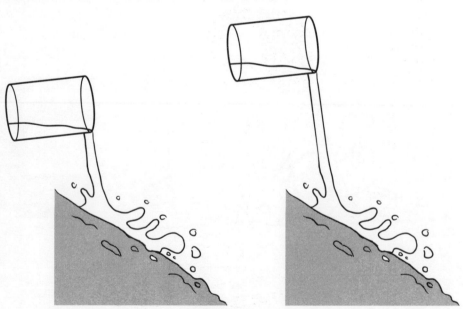

EXPERIMENT
198

Rubbing the Glacial Way

5–12
AGES

AIM

To see how glaciers affect the surface of Earth.

MATERIALS

- 1–2 ice cubes
- cup of sand
- modelling clay
- newspaper

SUPERVISED

Did You Know?

Ten per cent of Earth is covered by glaciers. But during the last ice age 32 per cent of Earth was covered by glaciers. That's a lot of ice!

STEPS

1. Spread some newspaper so that your work area stays clean.

2. Place the modelling clay on the ground and flatten it out.

3. Take an ice cube and rub it over the surface of the modelling clay. What do you notice happening?

4. Sprinkle some sand on the modelling clay and rub an ice cube over it as before. Is the effect the same or different to when you rubbed the ice on the clay without the sand?

ACTIVITY

EXPERIMENT
199

Pangaea: The Ancient Continent

AIM

To investigate the shape of the continents and the history of Earth.

MATERIALS

- map of the world
- large sheet of butcher's paper the same size as your map
- scissors
- glue

Did You Know?

Because the continents are shaped in the way they are, scientists think that they were once joined as one super continent. This means that fossils of animals that live in only one place today can be found in places all over the world.

STEPS

1. Cut the seven continents out from your map of the world. (If you don't know what a continent is ask an adult or your teacher.)

2. Spread the butcher's paper on a table.

3. Take the continents you have cut out and place them on the paper. Play around with the continents and see how you can get them to fit together. Do any of them fit together like the pieces of a jigsaw?

4. When you have found some pieces that match, glue them next to each other on your butcher's paper. Glue the other continents around the outside. Now you have Pangaea.

NOW...

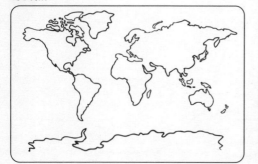

THEN...

Eggs Continental

AIM

To see how Earth's tectonic plates work.

MATERIALS

- boiled egg

STEPS

1. Take the boiled egg and crack it on its side. (What you want are two or three large pieces of egg, not a lot of little shards.) Note the way the outside of the egg looks.

2. Take your egg and try to move the pieces of the shell horizontally around the egg so that the pieces move against each other.

3. Do the pieces of shell move over each other? Do they buckle or move upwards?

Did You Know?

You have made something similar to the surface of Earth in this experiment with your shell being what is called tectonic plates. Earth's surface is actually made up of these plates which move at the rate of about 3–5 cm (1¼ in–2 in) a year. This movement is called continental drift.

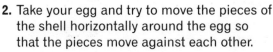

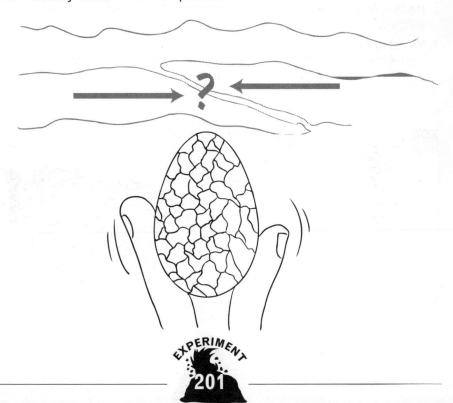

Dishing up the Crystals

5–12
AGES

SUPERVISED

ACTIVITY

AIM

To see how crystals are formed.

MATERIALS

- saucepan
- 500 g (1 lb) of Epsom salts
- bowl
- 2 pieces of charcoal
- spoon
- warm water

Did You Know?

Gems get their colour from the minerals that they are formed from. Out of all the minerals in the world there are only a few that produce the beautiful colours of gems.

STEPS

1. Warm two or three cups of water in the saucepan. (You may need an adult to help you with this.)

2. Stir the Epsom salts into the water until no more will dissolve.

3. Tip the water into the bowl and add the two pieces of charcoal.

4. Now leave your bowl in a safe place and check it over the next five days. Have crystals formed in your dish?

EPSOM SALTS

EXPERIMENT

202

Salty Painting

AIM

To see how salt reacts to water.

MATERIALS

- food colouring
- salt
- water
- paintbrush
- large sheet of paper

Did You Know?

One of the properties of salt is that it absorbs water. This is why the seas are salty. The salt is attracted to the water.

STEPS

1. With your ingredients make a solution of salt, water and food colouring. This will be your paint.

2. Take your paintbrush and paint whatever you like on the paper.

3. When you have finished leave the paper to dry. The water will dry leaving the salt behind. Have you made a nice picture?

EXPERIMENT
203

Make Your Own Sandpaper

AIM

To see how things from the earth are used in everyday life.

MATERIALS

- sheet of A4 paper
- glue
- sand
- strainer (optional)

Did You Know?

There are many things around your house that make use of things from the ground. Have you ever wondered what toothpaste is made of? See if you can find out.

STEPS

1. Spread your piece of paper out flat.

2. Lightly cover the paper with glue.

3. While the glue is still wet cover the paper with sand. (You could use a strainer to do this if you want to spread the sand evenly.)

4. Leave the glue to dry. When it is dry test your sandpaper by sanding a piece of wood.

EXPERIMENT
204

Like a Crystal on a String

AIM

To see how crystals grow on a string.

MATERIALS

- salt (you can also use alum or sugar)
- saucepan
- narrow glass
- string about 30 cm (12 in) long
- water
- stove

Did You Know?

The study of caves is called speleology.

STEPS

1. Warm the water in a saucepan on a low heat. (You may need an adult to help you with this.)
2. Add salt to the water until no more will dissolve.
3. Leave this to cool so the crystals will form.
4. Take out the largest crystal and add as much salt to the solution as the crystal displaced.
5. Heat the solution again until the salt dissolves.
6. Cool this solution and pour it into a narrow glass.
7. Tie the thread around the crystal and place it in the solution. Leave. What do you notice after a number of days?

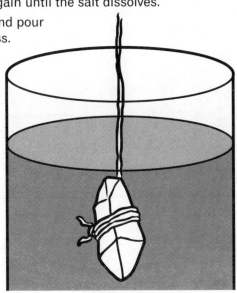

Stalagmite or Stalactite?

SUPERVISED

ACTIVITY

AIM

To see how stalagmites and stalactites are formed.

MATERIALS

- Epsom salts (you can also use alum or sugar)
- saucepan
- 2 glasses
- string about 40 cm (16 in) long
- water
- small plate

Did You Know?

A *stalagmite* is a pointed rock formation formed by rock dripping down from above. The force of gravity pulling molten rock downwards causes a *stalactite*.

STEPS

1. Warm the water in the saucepan and add in salt until no more will dissolve.

2. Place the glasses about 15 cm (6 in) apart and put the plate in between.

3. Now place one end of the string in one glass of water and the other end in the other one.

4. Pour the salty solution into the glasses in even amounts and leave it for at least three days. If the experiment has worked there should be crystals hanging from the string and underneath it.

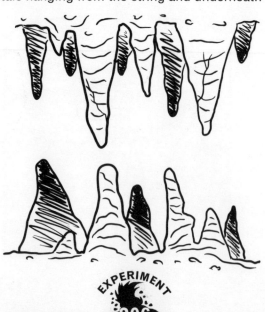

This is Very Hard!

SUPERVISED

ACTIVITY

AIM

To test the hardness of different minerals.

MATERIALS

- piece of quartz
- piece of soapstone
- coin
- nail
- your fingernail

Did You Know?

Rocks are different from minerals. Minerals are made up of one substance only, whereas rocks are made up of many minerals. The largest rock in the world is Uluru in the Northern Territory, Australia.

STEPS

1. Take your mineral specimens and lay them on a table.

2. With your fingernail try to scratch the surface of each of the rocks. (Be careful not to hurt yourself.)

3. With the coin try to scratch the surface of each of the rocks. Which ones were difficult scratch?

4. Finally try to scratch the surface of each of the rocks with the nail. (Be very careful this time.)

5. Now place the rocks in a line from softest to hardest.

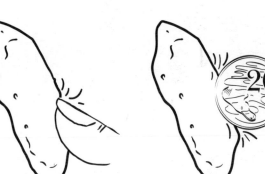

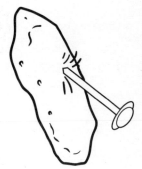

That's Volcanic!

AIM

To show how pressure can cause a volcanic eruption.

MATERIALS

- metal funnel
- modelling clay (you will only need a little)
- frying pan
- water

Did You Know?

One of earliest detailed reports of a volcanic eruption was by Pliny the Younger. He wrote about the eruption of Mount Vesuvius in 79 AD, which was the cause of the destruction of Pompeii. Pompeii is still being excavated today for information on how the Romans lived.

STEPS

1. Take the metal funnel and cover the narrow end with a very thin strip of modelling clay. (You may need an adult to help you with this.)
2. Take your frying pan, fill it a third full with water and place it on the stove.
3. Heat the water.
4. Place the funnel wide-end down in the water.
5. Turn up the heat and stand clear!

EXPERIMENT
208

Too Much Salt!

AIM

To see how salt can affect the ways plants grow.

MATERIALS

- 2 glasses
- 2 cotton buds
- 10 wheat seeds
- salt

Did You Know?

Salination occurs when water under the earth rises in level and the salt contained in the water comes to the surface. Salination is a big environmental problem in Australia.

STEPS

1. Place a cotton bud in each of the glasses.
2. Sprinkle one with salt.
3. Place five wheat seeds on each of the cotton buds.
4. Wet the cotton bud in each of the glasses. Keep them moist and over the next few days watch how the wheat grows. Which seeds sprouted more quickly?

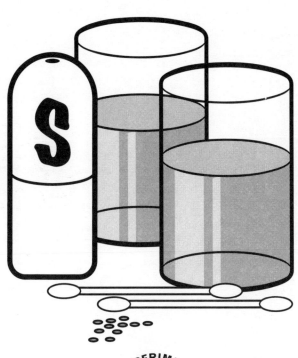

EXPERIMENT
209

Lava Icing

SUPERVISED

ACTIVITY

AIM

To see how lava at different temperatures flows and creates different types of rocks.

MATERIALS

- 500 g (1 lb) of icing or frosting
- 2 bowls
- 2 plates

Did You Know?

Magma can reach a temperature of about 1000 degrees centigrade (1832 Fahrenheit). Not only that, volcanoes can produce different kinds of rocks including basalt, granite and obsidian.

STEPS

1. Make up your icing.
2. Divide the icing evenly between the two bowls.
3. Leave one of the bowls on the bench and put the other in the fridge.
4. Take the bowl from the fridge when the icing has cooled but is still able to be poured.
5. On one of the plates pour the warm mixture, on the other pour the cool mixture. What do you notice about how the icing pours?

ICING MIX

Mapping the Ocean Floor

SUPERVISED

 ✓
 ✓
✓

ACTIVITY

AIM

To see how surfaces can be mapped.

MATERIALS

- largish lunch box
- chopstick
- ruler
- modelling clay
- 2 pieces of cardboard large enough to cover the lunch box
- friend

Did You Know?

The technical term for the instrument used to measure a landscape in this way is a probe. The ocean floor was once actually mapped in this way using long lines with lead weights on the bottom. Today oceanographers use radars or sonar.

STEPS

1. Ask your friend to construct a landscape with mountains and a valley inside the lunch box using the modelling clay. (If you need help to do this ask an adult.)

2. Now ask your friend to cover the lunch box with the two pieces of cardboard so that there is a small gap lengthways down the lunch box. This gap should be big enough to put the chopstick through, but not so wide that you can see into the lunch box.

3. Put your chopstick into the box at different points along the length of the box. Each time you do this (you probably only need to do it three or four times) measure with the ruler how much of the chopstick can be seen above the cardboard. Make sure that your chopstick is always straight up.

4. From your measurements can you get an idea of some of the physical aspects of the bottom of the lunch box? Did you find high places, did you find low places?

Where's the North Pole?

AIM

To see how Earth has a magnetic north pole.

MATERIALS

- magnet
- needle
- glass of water
- sliver of cork
- sticky tape

Did You Know?

Earth is like a great big magnet. This is the reason why we can make compasses that tell us where magnetic north is.

STEPS

1. Run the needle along the magnet in only one direction about 60 times.

2. Tape the needle to the sliver of cork and place it gently in the water.

3. Spin it gently. Is it starting to point in one direction? That is magnetic north.

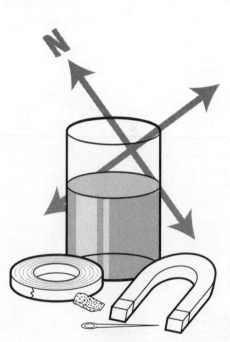

EXPERIMENT
212

Minerals, Minerals Everywhere

✓

SUPERVISED

✓

✓

ACTIVITY

AIM

To see how minerals are part of our lives.

MATERIALS

- pen
- paper
- your best eyesight

Did You Know?

Diamonds are the hardest things known to scientists. They affect light in a certain way so they are also used to make laser beams.

STEPS

1. Take your pen and paper.
2. Now wander around your home and write down anything that you think is made from minerals.
3. Make a list as long as you can and check it with an adult.
4. Hint – Do you have salt in your kitchen? What is your stove made of? What is in your pencil?

EXPERIMENT
213

Avalanche!

AIM

To see how different materials can be stable or unstable and cause an avalanche.

MATERIALS

- 1 kg (2 lb) of sugar
- 1 kg (2 lb) of flour
- 300 g (10 oz) of dried coconut
- piece of cardboard 60 cm x 60 cm (24 in x 24 in)
- newspaper

Did You Know?

Avalanches are caused by a weakening of the bond between layers of earth or snow. This weakening causes the earth or snow on the top to slide down making an avalanche. Avalanches can occur very suddenly and unexpectedly.

STEPS

1. Go outside and spread the newspaper on the ground so it covers a space wider than the size of the cardboard.

2. Take your piece of cardboard and lay it flat on the newspaper.

3. In layers place some sugar, coconut and flour in any order on the cardboard. Make a note of the order in which you layered them.

4. Raise the cardboard and note how your materials fall.

5. Repeat these steps two or three times but layer your materials in a different order each time. (Remember to note the order in which you layer them.)

6. Which combination made the best 'avalanche'?

EXPERIMENT
214

Slidin' Mudslides

SUPERVISED

ACTIVITY

AIM

To see how earth slides down a mountain.

MATERIALS

- newspaper
- piece of canvas
- half a bucket of sand and gravel
- water
- bucket
- 4 bricks

Did You Know?

Mudslides can often be caused by deforestation. This is when a mountain has had all of its trees removed. When the environment is changed in this way it can have disastrous results, for example, a mudslide.

STEPS

1. Twist up the newspaper so that you have enough to make a steady pile about 20 cm (8 in) high.

2. On some flat ground outside pile up your newspaper to make the shape of a mountain.

3. Cover the newspaper with some canvas and secure it with bricks. This is your mountain so make it a little uneven like a real mountain.

4. In the bucket, mix the soil and gravel with water to make mud.

5. Now pour the mud over your mountain. How does the mud flow down the mountain? Did it flow in the way you expected?

EXPERIMENT
215

Making Pet Rocks

AIM

To examine different kinds of rocks.

MATERIALS

- rocks
- paint
- marker pens
- things to decorate a rock with, i.e. string for hair, buttons for eyes etc.
- newspaper
- glue

Did You Know?

There are three different types of rocks – sedimentary, metamorphic and igneous.

STEPS

1. Spread the newspaper on the ground.
2. Put the rocks out on the newspaper.
3. Look at the rocks. Do you notice any differences between the rocks?
4. Take your paint and materials and go for it!

Wondrous Woodchips

SUPERVISED

AIM

To see how convection causes the surface of Earth to move.

MATERIALS

- plastic lunch box
- heat source
  (perhaps a stove)
- tray of ice
- woodchips
- 2 different colours
  of food colouring

Did You Know?

This process is called convection.
The ocean currents are created by
convection because some water is very
cold near the North and South poles
and some water is very warm near
the equator. This causes the
water to move around the
surface of Earth.

ACTIVITY

STEPS

1. Put the end of the lunch box
   near the heat source and put the ice at the other end.

2. Put one colour of food colouring at one end of the
   lunch box and the other colour at the other end of
   the lunch box. What happens?

3. Now drop the woodchips
   into the lunch box. What
   happens to them?

EXPERIMENT
217

My Crust is Bent!

AIM

To see how earthquakes affect Earth's surface.

MATERIALS

- 2 long blocks of wood
- modelling clay
- rolling pin
- marker pen

Did You Know?

Earthquakes happen when two plates moving against each other slip. This is why they occur frequently in places where two tectonic plates meet.

STEPS

1. Place the two blocks together.

2. Roll out the clay so it will cover both the blocks of wood.

3. Cover the blocks with the clay.

4. If you like you can draw a road on the clay.

5. Move one of the blocks in one direction against the other block. What happens to the clay?

EXPERIMENT
218

A Sedimentary Situation

AIM

To make and examine sedimentary rock.

MATERIALS

- large glass jar
- cement
- sand
- plaster
- water
- food colouring

Did You Know?

Sedimentary rock makes up the upper layers of the earth. It is not so hard as rock found deeper in the earth and has a high content of sand.

STEPS

1. Half fill the jar with water.
2. Pour in a layer of cement about 4 cm (1½ in).
3. Leave for a few days.
4. Pour in another layer, this time of sand mixed with cement. Allow to harden.
5. Pour in another layer, this time of plaster and sand. Allow to harden.
6. Pour in some water and food colouring.
7. Pour in another layer of plaster and sand. Allow to harden.
8. Remove the glass. (Ask an adult to do this.) You have made your own sedimentary rock.

EXPERIMENT
219

Is This Soil Thirsty?

AIM

To examine soil.

MATERIALS

- large funnel
- large glass
- soil
- jug
- water

Did You Know?

Soil with a high clay content will hold a lot of water, whereas soil with a high sand content will allow a lot of water to pass through it. Was your soil sandy or full of clay?

STEPS

1. Place the funnel in the glass.
2. Half fill the funnel with soil.
3. Now pour the water through the soil.
4. Measure how much water comes through into the glass. How thirsty was your water?

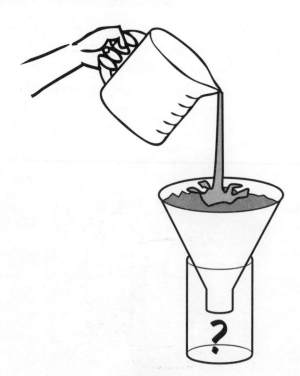

What's in This Soil?

AIM

To look at what is in soil.

MATERIALS

- bottle
- soil
- water

STEPS

1. Fill the bottle less than a third of the way with soil.
2. Put in twice as much water.
3. Now shake up the bottle.
4. Allow it to sit for a while. Now you can see what was in your soil.

Did You Know?

Soil is made up of sand, clay, dead plants and animals. Coal is formed over millions of years from the dead plants and animals in soil.

Savoury Volcanic Mud

AIM

To see what lava does when it is hot.

MATERIALS

- gravy mix
- water
- saucepan

Did You Know?

This is the way volcanic mud reacts when it is hot. The mud is so hot that it forces the air in it to the top. This is a very volatile substance.

STEPS

1. Mix your gravy mix with some water in a bowl. (Following the recipe on the side.)

2. Place the saucepan on the stove and tip the mixture into it. (Ask an adult to help you.)

3. Heat it up. Watch what happens. Do you see bubbles rising to the surface?

EXPERIMENT
222

We're Making Rivers

SUPERVISED

ACTIVITY

AIM

To see how rivers and lakes are formed.

MATERIALS

- sheet of A4 paper
- sheet of A4 cardboard
- spray bottles
- water
- food colouring

Did You Know?

Some famous rivers are the Amazon, the Nile and the Yangtze. These rivers took thousands of years to form.

STEPS

1. Crumple up the paper but not too tightly.

2. Stretch it out now and tape it about 3 cm (1 in) within the border of the cardboard. If the paper is standing up it should make a mountainous-looking region.

3. Put some water in your spray bottles and add the food colouring.

4. Now spray water over the paper. Can you see rivers forming on the paper? Try spraying a little harder. What happens now?

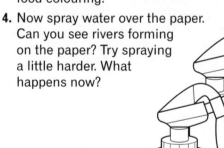
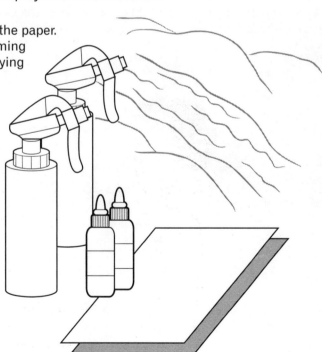

EXPERIMENT
223

What's in Sand?

 ✓

 ✓

 ✓

AIM

To see what is in sand.

MATERIALS

- different types of sand (coarse and fine sand)
- vinegar
- bowls (1 bowl for each type of sand)

Did You Know?

Sand is made up of rocks that have been worn down, but it can also contain shells washed up from the sea. Shells are the remains of dead sea animals.

STEPS

1. Put your sand samples in different bowls.

2. Now to each bowl add vinegar so that the sand is covered.

3. What happens to your sand samples after you add the vinegar?

4. If you noticed a reaction in one, it is because the vinegar has affected some shells in one of your samples.

EXPERIMENT
224

Chalk Talk

AIM

To see how acids can affect minerals.

MATERIALS

- chalk
- drinking glass
- vinegar

Did You Know?

Chalk is made from a type of mineral called calcium carbonate. This mineral dissolves when it comes into contact with an acid like vinegar. Chemical reactions like the one you have performed can also happen on Earth to produce geographical structures.

STEPS

1. Take the piece of chalk and place it in the glass with a little vinegar.
2. Leave for five to ten minutes.
3. Now check the chalk. What has happened to it?

EXPERIMENT
225

Play Dough Mountains

5–12
AGES

 ✓

SUPERVISED

 ✓

ACTIVITY

AIM

To see how the earth is affected by different forces which create mountains.

MATERIALS

- large amount of play dough
- newspaper
- your hands

Did You Know?

You have simulated what happens to the earth due to the movement of the tectonic plates. These plates move very slowly and force the earth in different directions to form mountains and valleys.

STEPS

1. Take your play dough and on the newspaper roll it into a long shape like a cylinder.

2. Now from both ends push the play dough together. Does it rise in the middle?

3. Roll your play dough out again but this time pull it apart from the ends. What happens now?

4. Finally, make your play dough into a rectangular shape. Now push the play dough along the length in opposite directions. What shape is made in the play dough now?

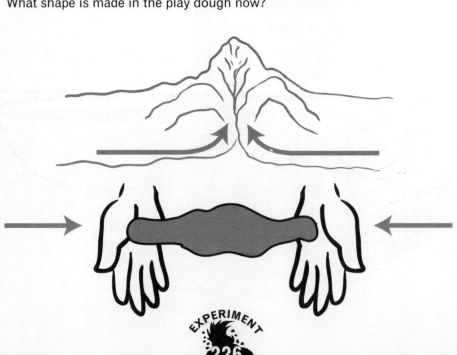

EXPERIMENT
226

Shell We Give It a Go?

 ✓

SUPERVISED

 ✓
 ✓

ACTIVITY

AIM
To see what makes up a shell.

MATERIALS
- shells
- vinegar
- bowl

STEPS
1. Put a little vinegar in a bowl.
2. Now put a shell or two into the bowl.
3. Leave this for two to three days. Keep the other shells handy.
4. Now remove the shells from the bowl. First try to break some of the shells you put aside. Now try to break the shells that you placed in the vinegar. Are they easier to break?

Did You Know?
Shells are made up of a mineral called calcium carbonate. The vinegar's effect on this mineral is to soften it. Can you find out about anything else that is made from this mineral?

Filtering Water

AIM

To see how rocks and earth can be used to filter water.

MATERIALS

- small plastic plant pot
- piece of paper towel
- gravel
- water
- bottle
- tray
- soil

Did You Know?

A similar process to the one you have just performed is used in water treatment plants. It is not the whole process but it is a very important part.

STEPS

1. Take your pot and place the paper towel into the bottom of it.

2. Put in a layer of gravel about the length of your finger.

3. Now pour in about twice as much soil. Leave some room at the top of the pot for water to pool. This is your filter.

4. Now mix soil and water in the bottle. Pour this through the filter.

5. When all the water has drained through repeat step 4 and keep repeating it until the water starts to become clearer. You have just filtered water!

Can Soil Breathe?

AIM

To see if there is air in soil.

MATERIALS

- soil
- water that has been boiled and cooled (Ask an adult to help.)
- large bowl

Did You Know?

This experiment shows that there is air in soil but it's not enough for you to be able to breathe under there!

STEPS

1. Put the soil into the bowl.
2. Now cover the soil with the water you have prepared.
3. What happens? Do you notice bubbles in the water?

CAN WE BREATHE UNDER THE SOIL?

EXPERIMENT
229

Rockin' Bubbles

5–12
AGES

 ✓

SUPERVISED

 ✓

ACTIVITY ✓

AIM

To learn about porous rocks.

MATERIALS

- pieces of brick
- tray
- water

STEPS

1. Fill the tray with water.

2. Put your pieces of brick into the water and make sure they are covered.

3. Observe what happens. You may have to look closely. Can you see bubbles?

Did You Know?

I bet you thought rocks were completely solid but they are not. Some rocks are full of holes where air can get caught. They are called porous rocks. When these rocks are put under water the air in them rises to the surface of the water.

A Home-made Seismograph

AIM

To make a device for measuring tremors.

MATERIALS

- shoe box with a lid
- pencil
- pen
- weights
- tape
- can of fruit or vegetables etc.
- string

Did You Know?

This is the way that earthquakes are measured. There is also a scale to make a distinction between earthquakes of different intensity. This scale is called the Richter scale.

STEPS

1. Stand the shoe box up on its end and place the can on the bottom in the box so it sits firmly.

2. Now tape the lid of the shoe box to the end raised in the air so that it makes an L shape.

3. To the pointed end of your pencil tape the weights. Make sure they are secure.

4. To the other end of the pencil tie the string securely.

5. On the shoe box lid at the end sticking out make a little hole big enough for a piece of string to fit through.

6. Take the other end of the string that you attached to the pencil and feed it through the hole you have made.

7. Tie this end of string to the middle of the pen. You must make sure that the pencil will hang down so that its tip is level with the bottom of the shoe box. Now rest the pen flat on the topside of the shoe box lid.

8. Place your seismograph on a table and place a piece of paper under the pencil.

9. Shake the table gently. Are you getting a reading on your home-made seismograph?

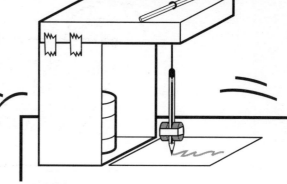

Too Hot to Handle

AIM

To see how things heat up under pressure.

MATERIALS

- wire coat hanger
- candle

STEPS

Did You Know?

The pressure of rocks on top of rocks causes heat like the heat you produced with the coat hanger. This heat causes rocks to change and become harder.

1. Unwind the coat hanger so that you have one long piece.

2. Now take the coat hanger in both your hands about 20 cm (8 in) apart and make a bend in it.

3. Now twist the coat hanger as quickly as you can about 40 times.

4. Now put the middle of the length you have been twisting onto the candle.
   What do you notice?
   Does it melt?

Hey, You're Blocking My Funnel!

AIM

To see how clay absorbs water.

MATERIALS

- clay from the back garden
- funnel
- drinking glass
- water

STEPS

1. Put the funnel in the glass.
2. Now put some clay into the funnel. (Make sure all the edges are covered.)
3. Tip some water into the funnel. What happens?
4. Leave the clay for a while and check it again in half and hour. Can you see any water coming through?

Did You Know?

Clay has very small particles that are very tightly held together. Ground that becomes waterlogged may have a lot of clay in it. Clay is a very common material found in the soil.

Water, Water Everywhere

AIM

To see how the shape of landscapes can affect erosion.

MATERIALS

- 3 milk cartons
- wet soil
- water
- drinking glass
- scissors

Did You Know?

You can see by this experiment that landscapes with different shapes can hold different amounts of water. The shape of land can change and more or less erosion may occur.

STEPS

1. Take your milk cartons and cut off the side behind the mouth.

2. Place your three milk cartons (you may want to do this outside) with the mouth on the ground.

3. In one carton put some soil so that it makes a straight incline in the milk carton. In the second carton make the soil into the shape of a set of stairs. In the third carton make a hill with ridges and valleys. Leave to dry.

4. Now pour water into the three milk cartons. Which one holds the most water?

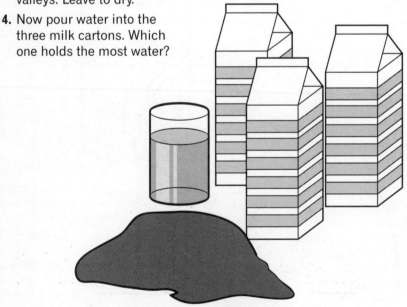

EXPERIMENT
234

Pretend Panning

AIM

To see how panning for gold works.

MATERIALS

- birdseed
- sieve or colander
- flat tray
- water
- gold paint

Did You Know?

Gold fossickers pan for gold in this way because gold can be found in riverbeds. The gold travels through the water and ends up in the stones and rocks of the river. Fair sized pieces of gold can be found using the process of panning.

STEPS

1. Fill the tray with water to a shallow level.

2. Pour the birdseed in the water.

3. Take your colander and scoop some of the birdseed out of the water.

4. Shake your colander so that the small particles fall through the holes while the larger ones remain. Pick out a particular type of seed. This is your pretend gold.

5. Repeat this process until you have a pile of seed.

6. When you have finished take the pile of seed and paint it gold. When the paint has dried pan for your 'real' gold this time.

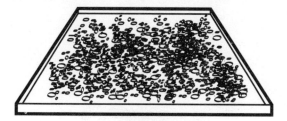

EXPERIMENT
235

It's a Watery Old Earth

AIM

To see how much of Earth is covered by ocean.

MATERIALS

- world globe
- friend

STEPS

1. You are going to throw the globe to your friend but first, ask your friend to make a guess. Does your friend think his or her hands will touch water more times than they will touch land? Does your friend think he or she will touch land more times?

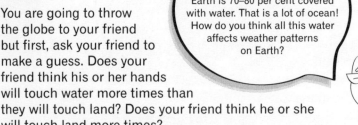

Did You Know?

Earth is 70–80 per cent covered with water. That is a lot of ocean! How do you think all this water affects weather patterns on Earth?

2. After your friend has guessed take the globe and have your friend stand about 1½ m (5 ft) away.

3. Now throw the globe to your friend.

4. Your friend has to catch the globe and count how many times his or her hands touch water and how many times they touch land. If you need help remembering make a note of it on a sheet of paper.

5. Now check your results with your friend's guess. Was the guess correct or not? Do you think the surface of Earth has more water on it or more land?

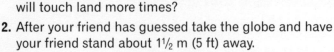

Making Soil

AIM

To see what soil is made of and how well plants grow in different soils.

MATERIALS

- sand
- silt
- clay
- old plants (you will find old leaves and things in the garden)
- 3 or 4 plant pots
- seasonal seeds

Did You Know?

What is in the soil greatly affects the ability of things to grow. Soil that is very sandy will not hold much water. Do you think that you would have to water plants more that are planted in sandy soil?

STEPS

1. In your plant pots put various mixtures of sand, soil, clay and plants. Make a note of which ones have more or less of each material.

2. When you have made your mixtures water them through.

3. Now plant your seeds. You will have to wait for your seeds to sprout. Be patient. Which one of the pots had seeds that sprouted first? Do you think that some of the materials helped the seeds to sprout while others didn't?

Making Mountains

5–12
AGES

SUPERVISED

ACTIVITY

AIM

To use a contour map to make a mountain.

MATERIALS

- contour map of a mountain in your area
- tracing paper
- Stanley knife
- pencil
- large piece of 3 mm (1/8 in) cardboard
- scissors
- an adult

Did You Know?

Maps are used all the time to help people get from place to place. The making of maps is called cartography.

STEPS

1. Take your map and with the tracing paper trace out the different contours of the mountain.

2. Now cut out the various contours.

3. Carefully draw the contours onto the cardboard.

4. Using the help of an adult cut out the contours from the cardboard with the Stanley knife.

5. Now glue your contours together from largest to smallest following the picture on the contour map. You have made your mountain.

6. If you want you could cover your mountain with foil or with paper and paint it.

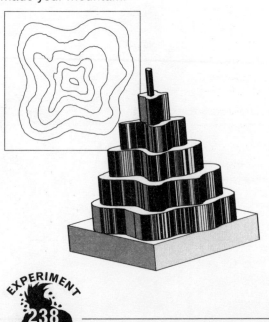

Mapping It Out

 ✓

 ✓
 ✓

AIM

To see how maps are made and make your own.

MATERIALS

- ruler
- bedroom
- pencil
- sheet of paper
- large piece of butcher's paper
- piece of note paper

Did You Know?

All maps have a legend and a scale so that they can be read accurately. Have you ever seen a map of your city?

STEPS

1. The first thing you need to do is make a legend. A legend is an explanation of the symbols placed on a map. On your sheet of paper draw a picture of all the things in your room. Next to each object draw a symbol, i.e. next to the picture of a desk draw a square, next to the chairs draw an 'x' and so on.

2. Now you need to measure the distances between various objects in the room. Use your ruler for this and take note of your measurements.

3. Now you need to draw the objects in the room onto your sheet of butcher's paper. Use your legend to represent the objects in the room. Because the sheet of paper is smaller than the room you need to 'scale' the distances down. To scale your measurements down divide them by ten. If the measurements are still too large divide them by a larger number.

4. Draw the objects in the room onto your map.

5. How accurate is your map? Could you navigate around the room using the map?

To Compost or Not to Compost?

AIM

To see how the earth can recycle materials.

MATERIALS

- old milk carton
- soil
- fruit and vegetable scraps

Did You Know?

A large part of soil is made up of things that have decomposed in it. Decomposition is the ability of soil to reduce things to simple chemical elements.

STEPS

1. Open up the top of your milk carton.

2. Put some soil in the bottom of the milk carton.

3. Place some food scraps into the milk carton and close the lid.

4. Put your compost bin outside in the garden. You can keep adding scraps to your bin but don't overfill it. Keep it closed.

5. After a few weeks cut open your compost bin and see what is inside. Have your food scraps changed?

EXPERIMENT
240

Fizzin' Minerals!

 ✓

 ✓

AIM

To see how various minerals react to vinegar.

MATERIALS

- piece each of granite, sandstone and limestone
- vinegar
- bowl

Did You Know?

Some minerals react to acids such as vinegar whereas other minerals don't react at all. The limestone in your experiment actually gives off a gas when it comes into contact with vinegar.

STEPS

1. Fill your bowl with vinegar.
2. Place the granite in the vinegar. What happens?
3. Next place the sandstone in the vinegar. What happens?
4. Finally place the limestone in the vinegar. What happens? Does it fizz?

EXPERIMENT
241

Watch Out for the Quicksand!

AIM

To see how quicksand works and its interesting qualities.

MATERIALS

- cornflour
- water
- bowl

Did You Know?

Quicksand is a mixture of water and sand. In real life quicksand can be dangerous because the surface of it looks hard and solid but when it is walked on it can cause objects to sink in to it.

STEPS

1. Fill the bowl about half way with cornflour.

2. Now add water to it and stir thoroughly until it makes a thick paste. This is your 'quicksand'.

3. Now with two fingers pretend to 'walk' across the quicksand. Do it quickly first. Did you make it across the quicksand?

4. Now try to walk across the quicksand slowly. Can you make it across this time?

EVER HAVE THAT SINKING FEELING?

EXPERIMENT
242

Tough Plates

AIM

To see how Earth's tectonic plates work.

MATERIALS

- 2 blocks of wood
- 2 sheets of sandpaper
- thumb tacks
- hammer

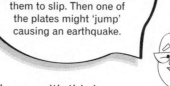

Did You Know?

When two tectonic plates are moving against each other, sometimes the friction causes them to slip. Then one of the plates might 'jump' causing an earthquake.

STEPS

1. Attach the sandpaper to the long ends of the blocks of wood with the tacks and the hammer. (You may need an adult to help you with this.)

2. Now rub the blocks of wood together on the side that is sandpapered.

3. Is this difficult to do? Do they slip sometimes?

4. An even simpler way to try the experiment is with your hands. Rub them together. Do your hands jump when you try to do this?

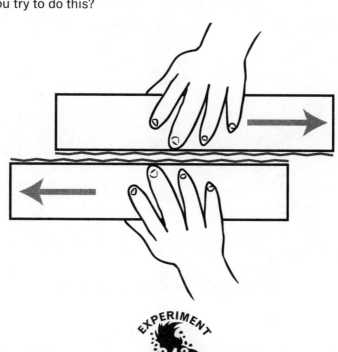

Litter! Yuk!

 ✓

 ✓

 ✓

AIM

To see how litter affects the environment.

MATERIALS

- rubber gloves
- 2 glass jars
- water and soil
- 2 old cigarette butts

STEPS

1. Put your rubber gloves on and go outside and pick up two old cigarette butts. (You should ask your parents if they are happy for you to do this.)

2. Fill one of the glass jars with some soil and water.

3. Place one of the butts in the empty glass jar and one in the glass jar of water and soil.

4. Leave the butts for a number of days. What happens to the water in the jar?

Did You Know?

Cigarette butts contain toxins (bad stuff) that seep into the soil and contaminate it.

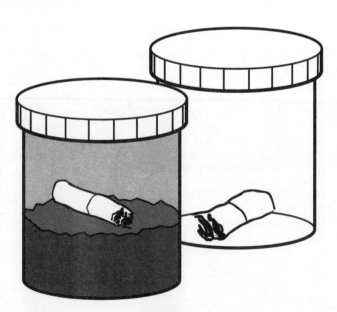

Is That Gas?

SUPERVISED

ACTIVITY

AIM

To see how volcanoes give off gas.

MATERIALS

- glass jar
- bicarbonate of soda (baking powder)
- vinegar
- funnel
- balloon

Did You Know?

Volcanoes not only spew out lava but they also release a deadly gas called carbon dioxide. This gas can kill people. So in a volcanic eruption there is not only the danger from lava but also the danger from poisonous gas.

STEPS

1. Place some baking soda on the bottom of the jar.
2. Place the funnel in the top of the jar and pour in the vinegar.
3. Now remove the funnel.
4. Place the balloon over the lid of the jar. What happens? (Be careful not to inflate the balloon too much – it might explode!) What do you think has happened?

Glacial Matters

SUPERVISED

ACTIVITY

AIM

To make a glacier.

MATERIALS

- blender
- tray of ice
- tray
- rubber gloves

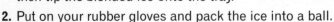

Did You Know?

This is what happens to snow when it is changed into glaciers. Snow is like the crushed ice you made. When the snow is compressed together and melts and freezes it is made into huge rocks of ice. Anyone like some ice in their drink?

STEPS

1. Blend the ice
   (you may need to
   ask an adult to do this)
   then tip the blended ice onto the tray.
2. Put on your rubber gloves and pack the ice into a ball.
3. Let it melt for a minute and place the ice ball in the freezer.
4. Take out your ice ball. Is it a big clump of ice?

EXPERIMENT
246

Happening Hair Dryers

SUPERVISED

ACTIVITY

AIM

To see how wind can affect topsoil.

MATERIALS

- hair dryer
- tray
- loose soil
- extension cord

Did You Know?

Soil can be affected by the weather. When soil is exposed it can be shifted by wind as well as rain. Wind is one major factor in soil erosion.

STEPS

1. Lay the soil loosely in the tray. (You may want to do this outside as you could make a mess.)

2. Now from the side have the hair dryer blow air over the soil. What happens? Is some of the soil being blown away?

Home-made Geodes

 ✓

 ✓
 ✓

AIM

To find out about the rocks called geodes by making some.

MATERIALS

- Epsom salts
- 500 ml (2 cups) of warm water
- eggshell halves
- food colouring (different colours if you like)

Did You Know?

Geodes are sphere-like stones with crystals in the middle. Sometimes the crystals inside can be of different colours because of the different minerals that are inside the rock. If you can, get a whole geode and break it open. You may be surprised at what you find inside.

STEPS

1. Spoon Epsom salts into the warm water until no more will dissolve. (Ask an adult to help.)

2. Add food colouring to the solution.

3. Pour this solution into the eggshell halves and leave the water to evaporate. (This may take a few days so be patient.)

4. Check your eggshells. Now you have made your very own geodes!

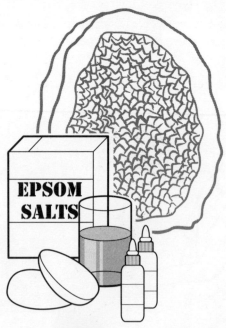

EPSOM SALTS

EXPERIMENT
248

Settle Down, Pencil!

5–12
AGES

SUPERVISED

ACTIVITY

AIM

To see how seismographs work.

MATERIALS

- pencil
- sheet of paper
- something firm to rest your paper on
- trip in the car

Did You Know?

Seismographs work in a similar way to your experiment but they react to the movement of the earth and measure earthquakes.

STEPS

1. When you go for your next trip in the car take your materials.

2. Get seated (don't forget to put your seat belt on!) and place the firm flat object on your lap with the paper on top.

3. Hold the pencil in your hand so it is just touching the paper. Don't hold it too firmly but so that it can react readily to the movement of the car.

4. Do this as the car moves. What kind of picture have you made?

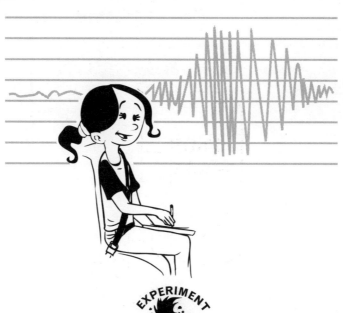

EXPERIMENT
249

Catching Colourful Rain Drops

5–12
AGES

 ✓
SUPERVISED

 ✓
✓
ACTIVITY

AIM
To observe the difference in the size of rain drops.

MATERIALS
- coloured tissue paper (one colour is fine, but lots of colours make it more colourful)
- paper clips
- white cardboard
- eye dropper
- water

Did You Know?
Every rain drop is made up of over a million tiny droplets of water!

STEPS
1. Secure the tissue paper with the paperclips on top of the cardboard.
2. Carefully drip some rain drops onto the tissue paper and let the water seep through to the cardboard.
3. Let the cardboard and tissue paper dry.
4. Take the paperclips off and take off the tissue paper.
5. The cardboard will now be covered with different sized colourful rain drops.

EXPERIMENT
250

Freezing Cold – Part A

SUPERVISED ✓

ACTIVITY ✓ ✓

AIM

To measure how long it takes water to freeze.

MATERIALS

- clock
- small plastic toy (optional)
- clear plastic cup

Did You Know?

Ice is a solid! When you heat ice its molecules move really fast and that is how the ice melts to become a liquid.

STEPS

1. Fill the plastic cup with water and put the plastic toy in the cup.
2. Place the plastic cup in the freezer.
3. Start timing! Check the cup at half-hour intervals until the water has frozen. (This may take a few hours.)
4. Record what you see each half hour.

Freezing Cold – Part B

SUPERVISED

ACTIVITY

AIM

To measure how long it takes ice to melt.

MATERIALS

- clock
- plastic toy in ice (see Experiment 251)
- tray

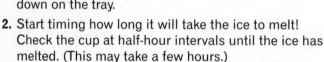

Did You Know?

The warmer the air, the faster the molecules in the air will move. The faster the molecules in the air move, the faster ice will melt!

STEPS

1. Using the frozen plastic toy from Part A of this experiment, place it upside down on the tray.

2. Start timing how long it will take the ice to melt! Check the cup at half-hour intervals until the ice has melted. (This may take a few hours.)

3. Record what you see each half hour. Which one took longer – the ice to melt or the water to freeze?

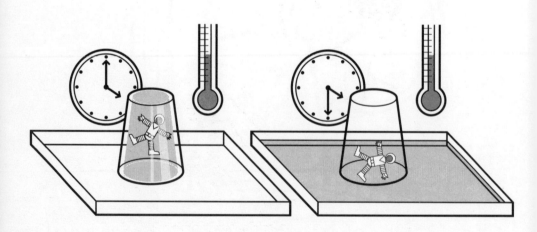

Living in Ice

ACTIVITY

AIM

To observe the effects salt has on ice.

MATERIALS

- lots of ice cubes
- salt shaker with salt

STEPS

Did You Know?

Salt helps ice stick together!

1. Use the ice cubes to build an igloo (or a square shaped house). You will notice the difference between building with blocks and building with ice.

2. Sprinkle the ice with salt. Has this made a difference to your building?

Melting Salty Ice

AIM

To observe the difference between melting salty water and non-salty water.

MATERIALS

- clock
- salty ice cubes (to be made the night before by mixing salt into warm water, pouring it into an ice cube tray and placing it in the freezer)
- non-salty ice cubes
- 2 pieces of paper
- pen

Did You Know?

In America during winter they put salt on snow to make it melt more quickly!

STEPS

1. Write an S on one piece of paper to make it easier to identify the salty ice cubes.
2. Place a salty ice cube on the S piece of paper.
3. Place a normal ice cube on the other piece of paper.
4. Start timing. Do you think they will melt at the same rate? If not, which one do you think will melt more quickly?

EXPERIMENT

254

Inside or Outside Ice?

5–12
AGES

SUPERVISED

ACTIVITY

AIM

To see if ice melts more quickly inside or outside.

MATERIALS

- 2 ice cubes
- 2 trays
- clock

STEPS

1. Place an ice cube in each tray.
2. Put one tray outside and leave one tray inside.
3. Start timing. Which ice cube do you think will melt more quickly, the one inside or the one outside?

Did You Know?

Air molecules slow down when they are cold: the colder the air, the slower the molecules, which means ice is less likely to melt in a cool place.

Shade or Sun?

AIM

To see if ice melts more quickly in the shade or in the Sun.

MATERIALS

- 2 ice cubes
- 2 trays
- clock

STEPS

Did You Know?

The enormous amount of heat from the Sun causes it to give Earth light!

1. Place an ice cube in each tray.

2. Put one tray outside in direct sunlight and put one tray outside in the shade.

3. Start timing. Which ice cube do you think will melt more quickly, the one in the shade or the one in the sunlight? Why?

EXPERIMENT

256

Heat Waves

AIM

To see what heat looks like when it is travelling from the Sun.

MATERIALS

- ribbon about 30 cm (12 in) long

STEPS

1. In one hand hold onto one end of the ribbon and then shake it in front of you. You should notice that the ribbon looks like a wave as it moves.

Did You Know?

In order to travel from one place to another, energy travels in waves. Light and heat are carried in short waves.

Making a Rainbow

AIM

To make your own rainbow.

MATERIALS

- glass of water
- white piece of paper

STEPS

1. Place the glass of water in front of the window.

2. Put the piece of paper on the floor in the path of the sunlight shining through the window and through the glass.

Did You Know?

Rainbows appear when sunlight shines through water droplets in the air at an angle of about 40 and 42 degrees.

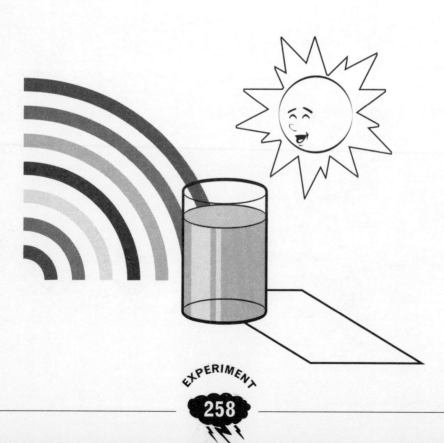

EXPERIMENT
258

Make Your Own Thunder

5–12
AGES

SUPERVISED ✓

✓

✓

ACTIVITY

AIM

To see what causes thunder.

MATERIALS

- balloon

STEPS

1. Blow up the balloon.
2. Put a hand on each end of the balloon and push your hands towards each other until the balloon pops.

Did You Know?

By popping the balloon you create your own thunder because the air inside the balloon moves so fast.

rrrrrrrRRRRRRRUUUUUUMMMMMBBBBBLLLLLLEEEE!!!!!!

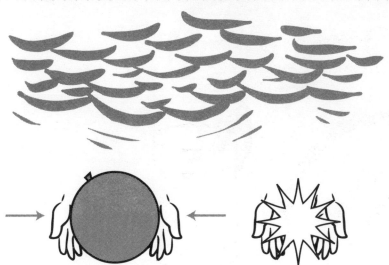

Which Evaporates Faster?

SUPERVISED

ACTIVITY

AIM

To see which container causes water to evaporate more quickly.

MATERIALS

- dish or bowl
- bottle
- measuring cup
- water

Did You Know?

Water is made up of molecules. Molecules escape from the surface of the water, so the bigger the surface area, the more escapees! The dish has a bigger surface area compared to the narrow hole at the top of the bottle.

STEPS

1. Pour the same amount of water into the dish or bowl and into the bottle.

2. Put them beside each other on a table and leave them overnight.

3. In the morning check both containers to see which one is holding the most water.

4. Pour the water from each container, one at a time, into the measuring cup. What did you discover?

EXPERIMENT

260

In and Out

AIM

To measure humidity (the moisture in air).

MATERIALS

- 2 bottles (one with a lid and one without)
- measuring cup

STEPS

1. Measure and pour the same amount of water into each bottle.
2. Put the lid on one of the bottles.
3. Leave the bottles overnight and see what happens. The open bottle allows the molecules to escape out of the bottle (evaporate) – just like a puddle drying out.

Did You Know?

Moisture in the air is called humidity.

Your Own Hurricane!

AIM

To experience your own hurricane.

MATERIALS

- a piece of string, about 1 m (40 in) long with an object tied securely to the end of it (a soft toy is a good choice)

STEPS

1. Spin the piece of string around your head. The toy will feel like it is pulling away from you the faster you spin it around.

Did You Know?

When a hurricane occurs, the wind tries to pull away from the middle, and when the wind pulls hard enough it makes a hole in the middle.

EXPERIMENT

262

Heat is in the Air

AIM

To see how much room warm air takes up.

MATERIALS

- balloon
- narrow glass jar
- saucepan
- water

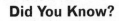

Did You Know?

The air that is inside the balloon gets bigger because the molecules are getting warmer and moving around more quickly!

STEPS

1. Ask an adult to help you boil water in the saucepan.

2. Stretch the balloon over the opening of the jar.

3. Take the saucepan off the stove and place the jar in the water.

4. Watch for a few minutes and see what happens to the balloon.

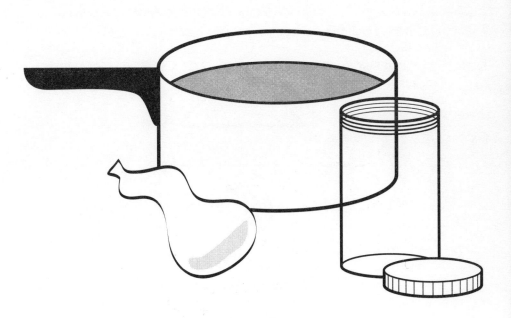

How Heavy is the Air?

AIM

To see how heavy air can be.

MATERIALS

- 2 balloons
- string
- stick about 20 cm (8 in) long
- a coat hanger

Did You Know?

Air on the top of mountains is very thin and it weighs less!

STEPS

1. Tie some string in the middle of the stick and then attach the other end of the string to the coat hanger.
2. Hook the coat hanger somewhere so that the stick can swing.
3. Tape some string onto each balloon.
4. Tie the other end of the string from each balloon loosely to the stick.
5. Balance the balloons.
6. Carefully take one of the balloons off the stick and blow the balloon up.
7. Put the blown-up balloon back onto the stick.
8. The stick should be unbalanced. Which end is heavier?

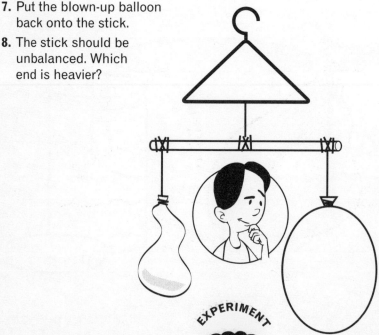

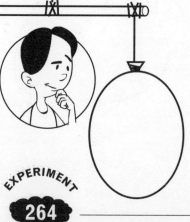

EXPERIMENT

264

What is the Greenhouse Effect?

 SUPERVISED

 ✓
 ✓

ACTIVITY ✓

AIM

To see what the greenhouse effect really is.

MATERIALS

- 2 thermometers
- see-through plastic bag

STEPS

1. Put one of the thermometers in the plastic bag and tie the bag so it is airtight.
2. Put the bag in direct sunlight for about 10 minutes.
3. Put the other thermometer beside the bag.
4. Wait for about 15 minutes and then look at the two temperatures. What do you notice?

Did You Know?

When the sunlight travels into the plastic bag the light turns into heat. The inside of the bag gets hotter because the air can't escape quickly enough. The sunlight does the same thing when it enters Earth's atmosphere. This is called the greenhouse effect.

Tracking the Sun

AIM

To see what happens to the Sun when Earth moves.

MATERIALS

- large piece of paper (1 m or 40 in long)
- sticky tape
- marker

STEPS

1. Sticky tape the piece of paper on the floor in front of a window the sun shines through.

Did You Know?

Earth moves around the Sun.

 SUPERVISED

 ✓

 ✓

✓ ACTIVITY

2. Draw a line with the marker exactly where the sunlight's edge appears on the floor through the window. Write the date and the time beside the line.

3. Each week, at the same time, mark the sunlight's edge on the paper and record the date.

4. Continue marking the sunlight's edge until you run out of paper. What do you notice?

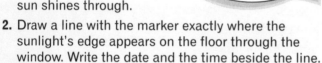

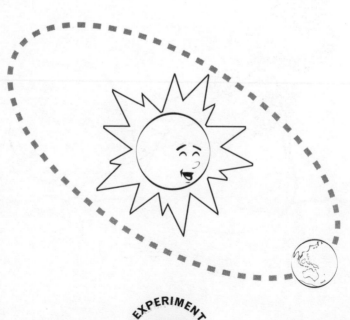

EXPERIMENT

266

Bags of Wind

AIM

To see the direction the wind is blowing.

MATERIALS

- plastic bag

STEPS

1. Go outside on a windy day.
2. Hold the handles of the plastic bag in each hand. The wind will fill the bag with air and blow the bag in the same direction as the wind.

Did You Know?

Windsocks are used to help pilots land their aeroplanes.

EXPERIMENT

267

Cool as Water or Air?

SUPERVISED

ACTIVITY

AIM

To see if air or water holds more heat.

MATERIALS

- 2 glasses, one filled with water and one empty
- freezer

STEPS

1. Place both of the glasses in the freezer.
2. Take them out of the freezer after 10 minutes. Which glass feels warmer?

Did You Know?

The glass with the water in it feels warmer because the empty glass, which is really full of air, lost its heat much more quickly than the water lost its heat. So we know water holds more heat than air!

Flying High

AIM

To see the direction of the wind.

MATERIALS

- flag or towel
- compass
- pegs

STEPS

1. Peg the flag or towel to the washing line.
2. Observe the direction the wind is blowing the flag.
3. Use the compass to work out which direction the wind is blowing from.

Did You Know?

Our bodies have air pressure pushing on us all the time. It's actually about 6.3 kg (14 lb) of air pressure!

Make Your Own Air Pressure

SUPERVISED

ACTIVITY

AIM

To see if you can make your own air pressure.

MATERIALS

- funnel
- ping pong ball

STEPS

1. Put the ping pong ball inside the funnel.

2. Tilt your head back and blow air into the funnel. Try to blow the ping pong ball out of the funnel. What happens?

Did You Know?

The fast rushing air travels around the edges of the ball, rather than just pushing it straight up!

Make Your Own Lightning

AIM

To make your own lightning.

MATERIALS

- comb
- piece of wool
- metal door knob

STEPS

Did You Know?

Lightning is a huge electric spark that jumps from the clouds to the ground.

1. Rub the comb with a piece of wool. This charges the comb with electricity.

2. Hold the comb near a metal door knob, which is uncharged. You should see a small spark because electricity is jumping from the charged object (the comb) to the neutral object (the door knob).

EXPERIMENT

271

Indoor Clouds

AIM

To see a cloud form inside.

MATERIALS

- kettle filled with water
- metal tray

STEPS

Did You Know?

Fluffy clouds are called cumulus clouds.

1. Boil the water in the kettle. (Ask an adult to help.)

2. As the water boils and steam begins to appear, place the tray above the spout. Droplets of water will begin to appear on the tray. These tiny droplets of water are what clouds are made of.

Which One is Faster?

AIM

To observe the speed of wind.

MATERIALS

- clothesline
- 2 wet dishcloths
- fan (or a piece of strong cardboard)
- pegs

Did You Know?

By fanning the dishcloth the evaporation process speeds up. The moist air gets replaced with drier air.

SUPERVISED

ACTIVITY

STEPS

1. Peg the two wet dishcloths on the clothesline.

2. Leave one dishcloth hanging on its own.

3. Fan the other wet dishcloth with the fan. (The one being fanned should dry more quickly.)

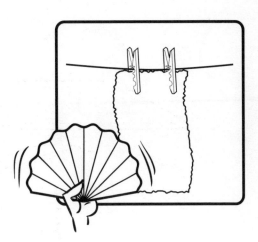

My Own Puddle

AIM

To see how long it takes for a small puddle to evaporate.

MATERIALS

- plastic container (an old take-away food container would be perfect)
- measuring cup
- pen
- paper

Did You Know?

When water evaporates it becomes invisible.

STEPS

1. Make a hole in your backyard and place the plastic container in it. If you don't have a backyard put the container on a windowsill.

2. Measure one cup of water and pour it into your bowl.

3. Record the day on your piece of paper.

4. Observe the container each day until all of the water has evaporated. How long did it take?

Make Your Own Frost

SUPERVISED

ACTIVITY

AIM
To see how frost forms.

MATERIALS
- rock salt
- crushed ice
- tin without a lid

STEPS
1. Crush two cups of ice and put it in the tin.
2. Add half a cup of rock salt.
3. Stir the ice and rock salt rapidly.
4. Leave the mixture for half an hour.
5. After half an hour the tin will have some dew on it.
6. If you wait a bit longer, the dew will turn into frost.

Did You Know?
The air we breathe has moisture in it. As the tin gets colder the moisture in the air condenses on its surface. This is why the dew on the tin turned to frost. Just like frost on the grass on a cold morning!

EXPERIMENT

275

Travelling By Air

SUPERVISED

ACTIVITY

AIM

To find out what gets carried by the wind.

MATERIALS

- vegetable oil
- cardboard about A4 size
- string
- scissors
- paintbrush

Did You Know?

The wind carries seeds from plants and spreads them around to new places.

STEPS

1. Take the piece of cardboard and put a hole in the top of it using the scissors.

2. Thread the string though the hole and tie it on.

3. Paint one side of the cardboard with the vegetable oil.

4. Hang the piece of cardboard outside for about an hour (longer if it is not a windy day).

5. Look at what is stuck to the cardboard and see what the wind is carrying!

Make Your Own Cloud

SUPERVISED

ACTIVITY

AIM

To watch how clouds form.

MATERIALS

- a clear plastic bottle with the cap
- warm water
- matches

Did You Know?

Clouds form when water vapour cools enough to form tiny droplets of water.

STEPS

1. Pour a little bit of warm water into the bottle, just enough to cover the bottom.

2. Ask an adult to light the match and let it burn for a little while.

3. Blow the match out and immediately let the smoke from the match fill the bottle. The smoke will clear quite quickly, but there will be invisible particles floating in the bottle.

4. Screw the cap onto the bottle and try to keep as much smoke in the bottle as you can.

5. Squeeze the bottle six or seven times.

Flouring Rain

SUPERVISED

ACTIVITY

AIM

To observe the 3D shape of rain drops.

MATERIALS

- bowl
- flour
- flour sieve
- plate
- rain (an eye dropper will work too)
- water

Did You Know?

The warmer the water is, the quicker it evaporates!

STEPS

1. Put one cup of flour into the bowl.
2. Either put the bowl outside in the rain for five minutes then bring it back inside or drip about five drops of water from the eye dropper into the flour.
3. Leave it to stand for about five minutes.
4. Sift the flour gently, allowing the loose flour to fall through to the plate.
5. The flour rain drops should be left in the sieve.
6. Gently place them on a piece of paper. Are they the same size and shape?

Measuring Thunder

AIM

To see how long it takes thunder to make a sound.

MATERIALS

- thunderstorm
- stopwatch

STEPS

Did You Know?

If you see lightning without thunder following it, the lightning is over 24 km (15 miles) away, which is too far away for you to hear the thunder.

1. Go to a safe dry place in your house where you can see outside.

2. Watch for a flash of lightning. As soon as you see the lightning, start the stopwatch. When you hear the thunder, stop the stopwatch.

   For every five seconds the storm is 1.6 km or 1 mile away. So …

   5 seconds: 1.6 km/1 mile

   10 seconds: 3.2 km/2 miles

   15 seconds: 4.8 km/3 miles

   20 seconds: 6.4 km/4 miles etc.

EXPERIMENT

279

Hair Dryer Wind

✓

SUPERVISED

✓

✓

ACTIVITY

AIM

To observe the wind.

MATERIALS

- few pieces of small paper
- some toys
- hair dryer

STEPS

1. Line the paper and the toys up.

2. Plug the hair dryer into the power point, and point it towards the paper and toys.

3. Turn it on so the air blows and watch what happens. The paper should start flying around the room and the toys should stay still.

Did You Know?

The hair dryer is acting just as the wind outside would, blowing light objects around and leaving the heavier objects alone.

Air, Air Everywhere

 ✓

 ✓

 ✓

✓

AIM

To see that air is everywhere even though we can't see it.

MATERIALS

- bucket of water
- plastic bottle

Did You Know?

Wind is moving air, and something has to make it move. Take a deep breath and then breathe out. Your body is making that air into wind!

STEPS

1. Put the plastic bottle into the bucket of water until it is completely covered with water and gently squeeze. Bubbles will come out of the bottle, which shows us that while the bottle appeared to be empty, it was actually full of air!

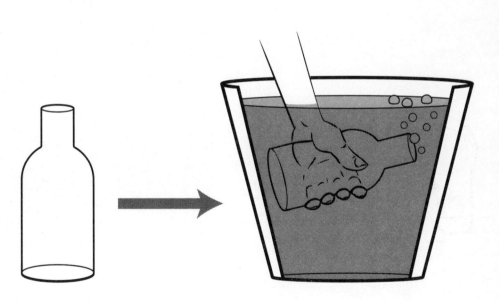

Flying Kites

SUPERVISED ✓

ACTIVITY ✓

AIM

To see if the wind pushes or pulls a kite.

MATERIALS

- kite
- windy day

STEPS

1. Go outside to a place where you can run with your kite.

2. Feel which way the wind is blowing. Try to fly your kite the same way the wind is blowing.

3. Now run into the wind so you feel the wind blowing in your face. Which way did the kite fly best?

Did You Know?

Earth's rotation affects the direction the wind blows!

Useful Wind Watching

AIM

To see the direction of the wind.

SUPERVISED

MATERIALS

- grass

STEPS

1. Go outside and use a piece of grass to show you which way the wind is blowing. How? Throw the piece of grass into the air and watch the direction it blows.

Did You Know?

There are many different types of winds. In Australia, a squall (strong gusts of cold air that don't last very long) is called a 'Cockeyed Bob'.

ACTIVITY

EXPERIMENT

283

Where is the Wind?

AIM

To see when the wind is blowing.

MATERIALS

- 2 sticks about 15 cm (6 in) long
- string
- 8 spoons
- sticky tape

Did You Know?

Monsoons (a wind that changes direction with the seasons) bring lots of rain with them.

STEPS

1. Sticky tape the two sticks together in a cross shape.
2. Cut nine pieces of string about 30 cm (12 in) long.
3. Tie one end of a piece of string to the centre of the cross.
4. Tie one piece of string to one spoon each.
5. Tie the other end of the string to the stick cross (two on each arm of the cross).
6. Using the string from the centre of the cross, go outside and tie the wind chime so it can hang somewhere.
7. You will know when it is windy because the spoons will clang against each other and you will hear a noise. Be prepared to give the spoons back!

SUPERVISED

ACTIVITY

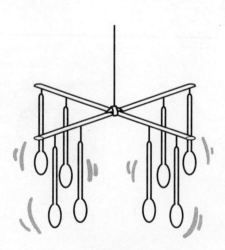

Slippery Skin?

SUPERVISED

ACTIVITY

AIM

To find out where air pressure is.

MATERIALS

- coin
- water

STEPS

1. Press the coin into your cheek. It falls off quite easily.
2. Put a little bit of water on one side of the coin.
3. Place the damp side of the coin on your cheek.

Did You Know?

Air is pressing all over the coin and when you add water to the coin it pushes out the air between the coin and your skin.

JUST ADD WATER!

Popping Air!

SUPERVISED

ACTIVITY

AIM

To see the pressure of air when it gets hot.

MATERIALS

- empty coffee tin (with a lid)
- very hot water

STEPS

1. Ask an adult to pour the hot water into the tin.
2. Put the lid on the tin.
3. Stand back (do not have your face close to the tin) and watch what happens. The lid will fly off. This is because the air inside the tin is getting warmer and it is expanding.

Did You Know?

When air is heated it expands and increases the air pressure!

DO YOU THINK IT'S GOING TO COME BACK DOWN AGAIN?

The Pressing Issue of Air

✓

SUPERVISED

✓

✓

ACTIVITY

AIM

To see what happens when water replaces air.

MATERIALS

- water
- coins

STEPS

1. Rub two coins together. They should rub very easily.

2. Put water between the two coins and try rubbing them together now. Do they rub easily?

Did You Know?

Air presses on the coins and when the water is put between the coins it replaces the air. This stops the coins from moving easily.

Tornado in a Bottle!

AIM

To see how a tornado moves.

MATERIALS

- 1 clear plastic bottle
- 5 small aluminium foil balls
- water
- blue food colouring
- teaspoon
- clear liquid soap

Did You Know?

The fastest tornado winds recorded, 457 km (286 miles), happened in 1958, in Texas, USA.

STEPS

1. Measure one teaspoon of the liquid soap and pour it into the bottle.
2. Drop the aluminium balls into the bottle.
3. Fill the bottle with water.
4. Add a couple of drops of blue food colouring.
5. Rotate the bottle and you should see a swirling motion. The swirling represents the motion of a tornado.

EXPERIMENT

288

Rising Hot Air

SUPERVISED

ACTIVITY

AIM

To see if hot air rises.

MATERIALS

- bubble solution (dishwashing liquid is fine)
- crushed ice
- plastic bottle
- dish

Did You Know?

As air gets warmer it expands and gets bigger. This is why hot air rises!

STEPS

1. Pour the bubble solution onto the dish.
2. Put the ice inside the bottle, put the lid on and shake it so the air inside the bottle cools down.
3. Take the lid off the bottle, tip the ice out and try to get out any water.
4. Dip the open end of the bottle into the dish so that it is covered with bubble solution.
5. Leave the bottle standing upright and watch what happens as the air inside the bottle begins to warm up again.

Air Pressure

 ✓

 ✓
 ✓

AIM
To see the pressure of air.

MATERIALS
- plastic cup
- piece of paper
- water

Did You Know?
In this experiment the air pressure is greater than the water pressure!

STEPS
1. Working over the sink or outside, fill the cup with water right to the top. Make sure the rim is wet!
2. Put the piece of paper on top of the cup.
3. Turn the cup over. The pressure of the air will push the piece of paper up to the cup and keep the water in the cup. (But not for too long!)

Watery Air

AIM

To see water in the air.

MATERIALS

- drinking glass
- water

STEPS

1. Put a dry glass (upside down) under a running (cold water) tap. This will make the glass cold.

2. Take the glass out from under the tap, and breathe heavily into the glass. A thin lining of water drops should form inside the glass. This water was in your breath.

Did You Know?

When rain falls from the clouds it is because the water droplets have become so heavy!

EXPERIMENT
291

Thirsty Dish?

AIM

To see how much water evaporates in 24 hours.

MATERIALS

- kitchen scales
- dish
- water

Did You Know?

Evaporation is an important part of the water cycle. The water in the air rises up to the clouds and returns back to the earth as rain.

STEPS

1. Put water in the dish.

2. Put the dish on the scales and write down its weight. Leave the dish uncovered for one day.

3. Look at the scales. Has the weight changed? It should weigh less because water has evaporated into the air – it is not being swallowed by the dish!

EXPERIMENT

292

Hot or Cold Balloons?

SUPERVISED

ACTIVITY

AIM

To see the effect temperature has on balloons.

MATERIALS

- 2 balloons
- hair dryer
- box (a cardboard box with a lid is good)
- freezer (or refrigerator)
- marker

Did You Know?

Hot air expands and cool air contracts!

STEPS

1. Blow the two balloons up.
2. Use the marker to mark one with H (for hot) and one with C (for cold).
3. Put the C balloon in the freezer (or refrigerator).
4. Put the H balloon in the box.
5. Gently blow warm air from the hair dryer into the box.
6. After about 10 minutes compare the balloons. What has happened?

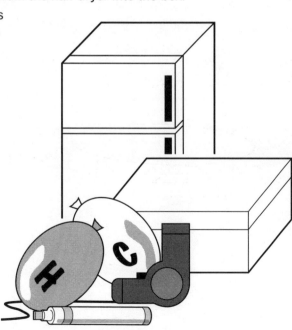

Air is in the Atmosphere

AIM

To see the force of hot and cold air and water in the atmosphere around us.

MATERIALS

- funnel
- hot water
- cold water
- large bowl
- plastic soft drink bottle
- ice

Did You Know?

The pressure of the air inside the bottle is not as great as the pressure in the atmosphere, which means the air pressure on the outside of the bottle crushes it!

STEPS

1. Ask an adult to fill about one third of the plastic bottle with very hot water (not boiling because the plastic will melt!).

2. Put the lid on the bottle.

3. Fill the large bowl with cold water and ice.

4. Put the plastic bottle in the bowl and make sure it is covered with the cool water and ice. What has happened to the bottle?

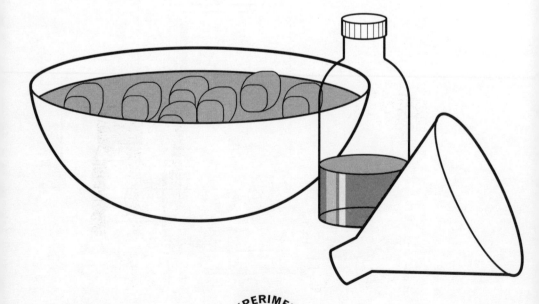

EXPERIMENT
294

Umbrellas!

AIM

To see the importance of waterproof materials.

MATERIALS

- real umbrella
- small paper umbrella (used as decoration in cocktails)
- water

Did You Know?

Umbrellas that keep the sun off your skin are called parasols!

STEPS

1. Sprinkle some water on the real umbrella. What do you notice happens to the water?

2. Sprinkle some water on the small paper umbrella. What do you notice happens to the water? The water on the real umbrella rolls down the side, whereas water on the small paper umbrella is absorbed.

EXPERIMENT

295

Patterns in the Frost

AIM

To see how frost forms.

MATERIALS

- a clean tin can
- ½ cup of rock salt
- 1 cup of crushed ice
- spoon
- small paper cut-outs of different shapes

Did You Know?

As the can cools down, the air molecules cool down and close in on the water (dew) outside the tin. The water (dew) gets cooler and frost forms.

STEPS

1. Pour the crushed ice and rock salt into the tin.
2. Stir it together quickly.
3. Slightly moisten the paper cut-outs and place them around the outside of the tin can.
4. Leave the tin for about half an hour. Dew will begin to form on the outside of the tin, and if you leave it for a bit longer the dew will turn into frost!
5. Peel off the paper cut-outs and see what patterns you have made!

In the Heat of the Sun

5–12
AGES

SUPERVISED

ACTIVITY

AIM

To feel how hot the Sun is.

MATERIALS

- a window with a blind or curtain

STEPS

1. Keep the blind or curtain drawn. Put your hand up to the glass. Can you feel any heat?

2. Put the blind or curtain up. Put your hand up to the glass. Can you feel any heat now? What happened?

Did You Know?

The Sun is a star that is 148 million kilometres (93 million miles) away!

Measuring Temperature

SUPERVISED

ACTIVITY

AIM

To make a device that measures temperature.

MATERIALS

- food colouring
- clear bottle
- markers
- cold water
- plasticine
- food colouring
- piece of cardboard
- sticky tape
- straw

Did You Know?

The device for measuring the temperature is called a thermometer.

STEPS

1. Fill the bottle until it is three quarters full of cold water.
2. Add a few drops of the food colouring.
3. Put the straw into the bottle so that it goes into the water.
4. Use the plasticine to secure the straw in the bottle. Make sure it is airtight.
5. Sticky tape the piece of card to the straw using two pieces of tape, one at the bottom and one at the top.
6. Suck the straw gently until the water rises to about halfway.
7. Use a marker to mark the water level in the straw on the cardboard.
8. Put the bottle in a warm place; the water will rise.
9. Use a different coloured marker and mark where the water has risen on the cardboard.
10. Now put the bottle in the fridge. The water level goes down when the temperature gets cooler.
11. Use a different coloured marker and mark where the water level is on the cardboard.

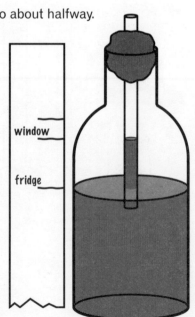

window

fridge

Evaporation

✓

✓
✓

AIM

To see how water evaporates.

MATERIALS

- 2 cups
- food colouring
- eye dropper
- paper towel

Did You Know?

Evaporation is how water gets into the clouds!

STEPS

1. Half fill the cups with water.

2. Add food colouring to one of the cups.

3. Use the eye dropper to get the clear water from one cup and drop a couple of drops onto the paper towel.

4. Use the eye dropper to get the coloured water from one cup and drop a couple of drops onto the paper towel.

5. Keep a watchful eye on the paper towel and observe what happens. The water will evaporate from the towel, leaving the food colouring behind but nothing will be left behind from the clear water droplets.

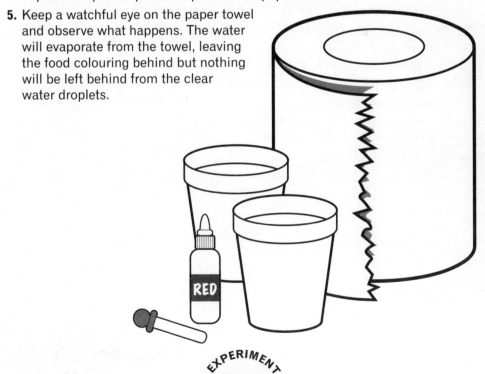

EXPERIMENT

299

Hot, Hot, Hot!

SUPERVISED

ACTIVITY

AIM

To store some heat.

MATERIALS

- 2 jars with lids (one smaller that will fit inside the big jar)
- sticky tape
- wide cork
- aluminium foil
- warm water
- scissors
- drinking glass

Did You Know?

By placing the smaller jar inside the big jar it acts just as a thermos would.

STEPS

1. Use the foil to wrap two layers around the small jar, with the dull side on the outside. Use the sticky tape to make sure it stays on.

2. Fill the small jar three quarters full of warm water and screw the lid on.

3. Fill the drinking glass three quarters full of warm water.

4. Put the cork inside the big jar and carefully place the small jar inside the big jar too, on top of the cork.

5. Wait 10 minutes.

6. Take the small jar out of the big jar and unscrew the lid.

7. Use your fingers to feel the temperature of the water in the glass and in the small jar. The water in the jar will be warmer because heat does not pass easily through the cork and the air in the big jar.

BIG AL'S AL-FOIL

EXPERIMENT

300

The Shape of Rain

AIM

To see the shape of rain when it lands.

MATERIALS

- eye dropper (to act as rain)
- marker or pen
- paper

Did You Know?

H_2O is the scientific name for water.

STEPS

1. Fill the eye dropper with clean water.
2. Hold the dropper about 30 cm (12 in) above the paper and drip one drop of water on the paper.
3. Trace around the edge of the drop with the marker or pen.
4. Repeat steps 1, 2 and 3. Are they the same shape?

EXPERIMENT

301

Raining at Sea

AIM

To see what might happen to a tin boat when it rains.

MATERIALS

- plastic cup (to act as a tin boat)
- bucket of water (to act as a lake or ocean)
- watering can (to act as the rain)

Did You Know?

Clouds change shape because as they come into contact with warm air, parts of them evaporate.

STEPS

1. Fill the bucket with water.
2. Make the empty plastic cup float on the water in the bucket.
3. Slowly drizzle water from the watering can into the plastic cup. What is happening to the plastic cup?

Puddles of Hail

AIM

To see what happens when ice melts.

MATERIALS

- small ice cube (to act as hail)
- plastic cup (to act as the puddle)

STEPS

1. Fill the plastic cup three quarters full with water.

2. Put the ice cube in the cup of water. What do you think will happen as the ice cube melts?

Did You Know?

Hailstones have been known to be the size of golf balls!

The Fading Sun

SUPERVISED

ACTIVITY

AIM

To see the effects of the heat from the Sun.

MATERIALS

- 2 pieces of newspaper
- 2 paper weights

STEPS

1. Lay a piece of newspaper down outside in direct sunlight using a paper weight to keep it still.

2. Lay a piece of newspaper down inside, out of the sunlight, using a paper weight to keep it still.

3. Leave the newspapers in their positions for one week.

4. After a week compare the two pieces of newspaper. What has happened to the paper?

Did You Know?

During the winter the Sun is 1,400,000 km or 90 million miles away from Earth.

EXPERIMENT

Classifying Clouds

AIM

To observe different types of clouds.

MATERIALS

- clouds
- paper
- pencils

STEPS

1. Go outside on a cloudy day and observe the clouds in the sky.

2. Identify the types of clouds that are in the sky from the list below.

3. Draw the clouds you can see.

- Cirrus are white and feathery (the highest clouds).

- Cumulus are puffy clouds that look like cotton balls.

- Stratus are flat, wide looking clouds (drizzle usually falls from these clouds).

- Nimbus are dark, grey rainy clouds.

You can observe clouds over a few days and comment on the similarities and differences. The weather may influence the types of clouds in the sky.

Did You Know?

Clouds are fog in the sky!

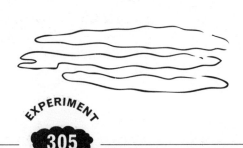

EXPERIMENT

305

Underwater Clouds

AIM

To observe the difference in the density of hot and cold water.

MATERIALS

- large clear bowl (or a glass vase)
- cold water
- small glass jar with a lid
- food colouring

STEPS

1. Pour cold water into the large glass bowl until it is three quarters full.

2. Fill the jar with very warm tap water – not hot enough to burn your fingers though.

3. Drip a few drops of the food colouring into the jar.

4. Put the lid on the jar and shake it so the water and the food colouring mix.

5. Put the jar into the glass bowl full of cold water.

6. Wait for the water to settle.

7. Put your hands in the water and gently undo the lid of the jar. Be very careful to try not to move the water.

8. Gently take your hands out of the water. What happens?

Did You Know?

The sea makes up 97 per cent of Earth's water.

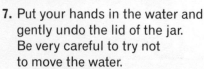
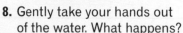

Sun or Lamp? Part A

AIM

To see the effects of heat from the Sun.

MATERIALS

- watch with a second hand
- small lamp
- 2 thermometers
- water
- 2 different coloured containers (one needs to be very dark)
- measuring cup

Did You Know?

The highest world temperature ever recorded was 58°C (136°F) in Al Aziziyah in Libya on 13 September 1922.

STEPS

1. Put one of the light coloured containers and one of the dark coloured containers in a sunny place.
2. Use the measuring cup and pour the same amount of water into each container.
3. Put a thermometer in each container and leave for 10 minutes. What happens?

EXPERIMENT

307

Sun or Lamp? Part B

SUPERVISED

ACTIVITY

AIM

To see effects of heat from a lamp, and how it compares to the Sun.

MATERIALS

- watch with a second hand
- small lamp
- 2 thermometers
- water
- 2 different coloured containers (one needs to be very dark)
- measuring cup

Did You Know?

The boiling point of water is 100°C (212°F).

STEPS

1. Put one of the light coloured containers and one of the dark coloured containers on a table where the lamp can shine directly onto the containers.

2. Use the measuring cup and pour the same amount of water into each container.

3. Put a thermometer in each container and leave for 10 minutes. What happens? How does this compare to Part A of the experiment (Experiment 307)?

EXPERIMENT
308

Walking Water

✓

✓

AIM

To observe the movement of water.

MATERIALS

- water
- 2 see-through plastic cups
- paper towel, cut into strips
- bowl

STEPS

1. Fill one of the cups
   with water.

2. Place the cup full of water
   on top of the upside down bowl
   (or something that will raise the cup!).

3. Place one end of the paper towel in the cup with water
   making sure it is touching the bottom of the cup.

4. Put the other end of the paper towel in the other cup.
   What happens?

5. Repeat the experiment, but
   this time change the width
   of the piece of paper towel.

Did You Know?

Paper has many tiny spaces. The
water fills these tiny spaces and
moves along the paper.

EXPERIMENT
309

Making an Eye Dropper

AIM

To observe the pressure of air and water.

MATERIALS

- straw
- water

STEPS

1. Suck up some of the water through the straw.

2. Cover the end of the straw with your finger (usually the end you have been sucking from, but it works if you use the other end).

3. Lift your finger off the straw for a second, then quickly replace it. Each time you let your finger go some water will be released.

Did You Know?

The more experiments you do the better you will get at releasing one small drop.

Salt to the Rescue

AIM

To see the effects of salt on ice.

MATERIALS

- ice cube
- cold water
- drinking glass
- string
- salt

Did You Know?

The largest piece of ice to fall to Earth was 6 m (20 ft) across. It fell in Scotland on 13 August 1849.

STEPS

1. Fill the drinking glass three quarters full with very cold water.

2. Put the ice cube in the water, in the drinking glass.

3. Put the piece of string in the drinking glass so one end is touching the ice cube and the other end is hanging over the side of the glass.

4. Sprinkle some salt on to the ice cube and leave it for about 10 minutes. The string should freeze to the ice cube, then you can pull the ice cube out and rescue it!

Bubbles of Rainbows

AIM

To see the different colours made by rainbows.

MATERIALS

- bubble mix (dishwashing detergent works well too)
- teaspoon
- sugar
- bubble blower
- fridge
- bubble stand (an upside down plastic cup will work!)

> ### Did You Know?
> In Australia, Darwin in the Northern Territory is the sunniest city. It has an average of 8.5 hours of sunshine a day, whereas Melbourne in Victoria has the dubious honour of being Australia's least sunny city, with an average of 5.7 hours of sunshine each day.

STEPS

1. Put one teaspoon of sugar into the bubble mix.
2. Put the mix into the fridge (it helps the bubbles last longer).
3. Dip the blower into the mixture.
4. Gently blow a bubble and try not to it let fly away.
5. Attach the bubble to the bubble stand. Wait a little while and you will be able to see different colours in the bubble!

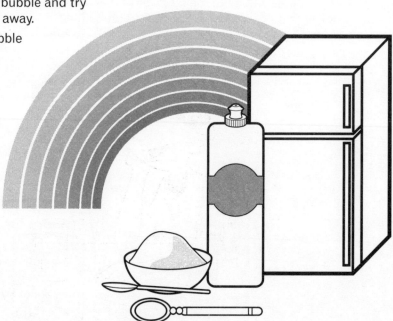

Hasty Hot Water

AIM

To observe the speed of hot and cold water.

MATERIALS

- 2 plastic cups
- 2 pins
- 2 clear drinking glasses
- cool water
- hot water from the tap
- ice cubes

Did You Know?

Molecules of hot water move much faster than the molecules in cold water.

STEPS

1. Make a pin hole in the middle of the bottom of the two plastic cups.
2. Put the plastic cups on top of the drinking glasses.
3. Put the ice cubes in one cup and add water.
4. Put hot water from the tap in the other cup. What happens?

Blowing Your Money

 ✓

SUPERVISED

AIM

To experience the strength of wind.

MATERIALS

- drinking glass
- coin

STEPS

1. Balance the coin on the edge of the glass.

2. Blow very fast on the rim of the coin. What happens?

3. If you keep trying you should be able to blow the coin right over the open glass and make it land on the other side of the table!

Did You Know?

The fastest winds on Earth are inside a tornado funnel. Winds have been recorded at 480 km/h (300 mph).

 ✓
 ✓

ACTIVITY

Wind Force

AIM

To observe the force of wind.

MATERIALS

- plastic bottle
- small piece of paper rolled up into the size of a pea

Did You Know?

The windiest place in the world is Port Martin, Antarctica, which has an average wind speed over a year of 64 km/h (40 mph). It experiences gale force 8 winds for over a hundred days a year!

STEPS

1. Put the bottle on its side on a table or bench.
2. Put the paper in the neck of the bottle.
3. Blow hard and fast into the bottle. What happens to the piece of paper? (The fast moving air should go straight past the piece of paper, hit the back of the bottle and then come out again, forcing the little ball of paper to come out!)

Sunlight Spotlight

SUPERVISED

ACTIVITY

AIM

To see how the Sun reflects its rays.

MATERIALS

- cardboard squares
- aluminium foil
- sunshine

STEPS

1. Cover the cardboard squares with the aluminium foil, shiny side up.

2. Find a stream of sunshine.

3. Put the aluminium foil in the path of the sunshine, and then reflect the sun in the direction you would like it to go. The reflection can then act as a spotlight!

Did You Know?

You should not stay in the sun for too long as the sun does not need to feel hot to damage your skin.

EXPERIMENT

316

Water Paintings

AIM

To learn more about the water cycle.

MATERIALS

- paintbrush
- water
- dry surface, such as concrete or asphalt

Did You Know?

The heat from the sun allows the water from your painting to evaporate. It then turns into water vapour and heads back up to the clouds!

STEPS

1. Wet the paintbrush with water.

2. Paint a picture using the water as 'paint'. When you have finished leave your water painting for a few hours. What happens?

Rainbows

AIM

To make your own rainbow using the garden hose.

MATERIALS

- garden hose

STEPS

1. Put the hose onto a fine spray setting (you can do this by placing you finger over the end of the hose and restricting the water flow) and stand with your back to the sun. You should see a rainbow in the spray of the water!

Did You Know?

A rainbow was once visible for 6 hours (from 9 am to 6 pm) at Wetherby, Yorkshire UK on 14 March 1994. This was very rare because most rainbows last for only a few minutes.

Sausage Sunburn

AIM

To see the effects of the heat from the Sun.

MATERIALS

- sunny day
- two sausages
- sunscreen

STEPS

1. Put two sausages outside in the sun.

2. Put sunscreen on one sausage. Observe what happens to each of the sausages throughout the day. (You may need to move the sausages so they stay in the sun.) The sausage without the sunscreen will cook, while the sausage covered in sunscreen won't!

Did You Know?

You should apply sunscreen at least 20 minutes before you go outside. Then you need to reapply it every two hours.

Disappearing Water

AIM

To see how quickly water evaporates.

MATERIALS

- frying pan
- teaspoon
- water
- an adult

STEPS

1. Heat a frying pan.
(Ask an adult to help you.)

2. When the pan is hot, carefully
spoon the water into the frying pan.
The water will sizzle and disappear.

Did You Know?

Less than one per cent of the
water on Earth is fresh enough
to use. Ninety-seven per cent
is too salty and two per cent
is ice.

EXPERIMENT

320

Coloured Ice

AIM

To see how colour is affected by heat.

MATERIALS

- ice cube tray
- food colouring
- water
- freezer

Did You Know?

The largest hailstone that has ever been recorded fell on 14 April 1986 in Bangladesh. It weighed 1 kg (2.25 lb).

STEPS

1. Fill the ice cube tray with water.
2. In each section of the tray drip one or two drops of food colouring – make sure you leave one with just plain water.
3. In one section drip in many different colours in order to make the ice cube as dark as possible.
4. Put the ice cube tray in the freezer and leave it to freeze.
5. Take the ice cubes out and watch them melt. What do you notice? (The darkest ice cube should melt the quickest!)

Absorbing Water Drops

AIM

To discover what sort of objects absorb water.

MATERIALS

- paper towel
- glossy magazine page
- aluminium foil
- cardboard
- wood
- plastic
- water
- watering can or a strainer

Did You Know?

Objects that absorb water are called porous, which means they have lots of tiny holes.

STEPS

1. Place all of the items in a row, outside or in the bath.
2. With your watering can or strainer gently pour the 'rain' over the different objects. Which objects absorbed the water? Which objects didn't absorb the water? Why didn't they all absorb the water?

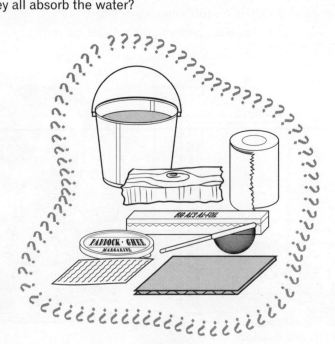

EXPERIMENT

Heavy Air

SUPERVISED

ACTIVITY

AIM

To show there is air pressure all around us.

MATERIALS

- folded sheet of newspaper
- old 30 cm (12 in) wooden ruler or flat stick
- bench

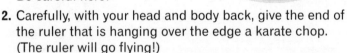

Did You Know?

The air is pushing down on the folded sheet of newspaper so hard that it weighs more than one tonne!

STEPS

1. Put the ruler on the bench with about a quarter of it hanging out over the edge. Be careful here!

2. Carefully, with your head and body back, give the end of the ruler that is hanging over the edge a karate chop. (The ruler will go flying!)

3. Retrieve the ruler and set it up the same way as step 1.

4. Now put the newspaper over the part of the ruler that is on the bench, leaving the overhanging section uncovered.

5. Give the ruler another karate chop. What happened this time? (The air pressure on top of the newspaper should be so great that it snaps the ruler!)

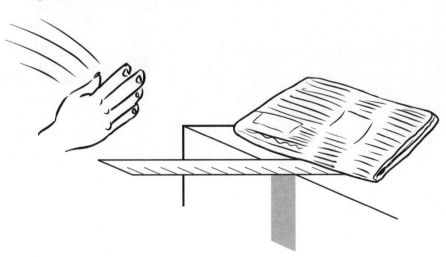

EXPERIMENT

323

Wet and Dry

AIM

To feel the difference between wet and dry clothing.

MATERIALS

- pair of socks
- bucket
- water

STEPS

Note: Ask an adult before you do this one!

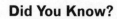

Did You Know?

Water can take on many different forms, such as liquid, solid or gas.

1. Put the socks on your feet.

2. Put one foot in the bucket of water, and keep the other sock/foot dry. How do your feet feel? Your wet foot should feel much colder than your dry foot. The dry foot is surrounded by air, and the wet foot is surrounded by water because it has pushed the air away.

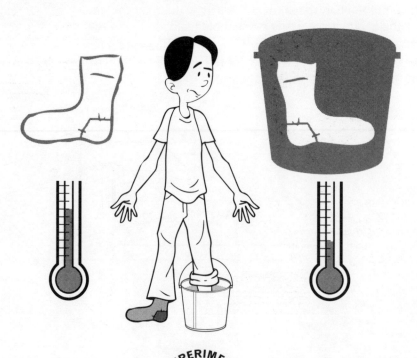

Heater or Refrigerator?

SUPERVISED

ACTIVITY

AIM

To feel the difference between cool air and warm air.

MATERIALS

- heater
- refrigerator

STEPS

1. Stand in front of your heater for a few minutes.

2. Stand in front of your open fridge for few minutes. When you stand in front of the heater you feel warm air and when you stand in front of the fridge you feel cold air.

Did You Know?

Hot air balloons were discovered in France in 1783.

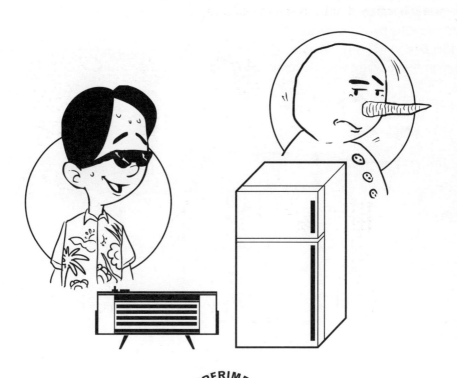

Daze in the Clouds

SUPERVISED

ACTIVITY

AIM

To see the effects humidity, temperature and air pressure have on the way clouds are formed.

MATERIALS

- large glass jar
- rubber band
- clear plastic bag
- water
- matches
- measuring cup
- water

Did You Know?

Vapour is the name for invisible evaporated water.

STEPS

1. Measure 20 ml (½ fl oz) of water and tip it into the jar.
2. Put the lit match into the jar. Ask an adult to do this.
3. Put the plastic bag over the jar as fast as you can and use the rubber band to secure it to the jar.
4. Push the bag into the jar.
5. Now pull the bag out of the jar. When you push the bag into the jar the pressure and the temperature in the jar goes up, and makes the jar look clear. When you pull the bag out the pressure and the temperature go down, so then the water vapour condenses, which makes the cloud in the jar.

Wind Watching

AIM

To observe the direction of the wind.

MATERIALS

• ball

STEPS

1. Go outside and throw the ball the same way the wind is blowing. The wind will help the ball to travel further.

2. This time throw the ball against the wind. The wind pushes against the ball and the ball will not travel as far.

Did You Know?

Hurricanes in Australia are called 'Willy Willies'.

SUPERVISED ✓

ACTIVITY ✓

EXPERIMENT
327

Rainbow in a Bottle

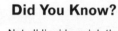

AIM

To make your own rainbow.

MATERIALS

- clear plastic bottle
- water
- food colouring (2 colours)
- methylated spirits
- cooking oil

Did You Know?

Not all liquids weigh the same. Some liquids are heavier than others.

STEPS

1. Pour water into your bottle so it is about one third full.
2. Add a few drops of one of the food colourings.
3. Very carefully pour some cooking oil into the bottle, about a third again.
4. Pour the methylated spirits into the bottle, about one third again.
5. Add a few drops of the other food colouring.
6. Put the lid on tightly. Try to turn the bottle upside down carefully!

Precipitation

SUPERVISED ✓

ACTIVITY ✓ ✓

AIM

To see how precipitation forms.

MATERIALS

- funnel
- plastic bag
- jar
- 250 ml (1 cup) hot tap water
- 50 ml (¼ cup) cold water
- ice cubes

Did You Know?

The world's water cycle is never ending. It travels on a journey from the sky to the land or sea and travels back up to the clouds again!

STEPS

1. Pour one cup of hot water into the jar.
2. Put the funnel in the jar.
3. Now put the plastic bag into the funnel.
4. Pour the cold water into the plastic bag and add the ice cubes. Watch the jar. What is happening?

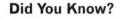

EXPERIMENT
329

Weighing Water

SUPERVISED

ACTIVITY

AIM

To see how the weight of flowing water compares with the weight of frozen water.

MATERIALS

- 250 ml (1 cup) of water
- open container (an old take-away food container would be ideal)
- kitchen scales
- freezer
- water

Did You Know?

Ice cubes float in water, just like ice on the top of a puddle on a very cold day in winter.

STEPS

1. Fill the container with one cup of water.
2. Place it on the kitchen scales and write down how much it weighs.
3. Put the container in the freezer and leave it to completely freeze.
4. When the water has completely frozen, weigh it again on the scales. What did you notice?

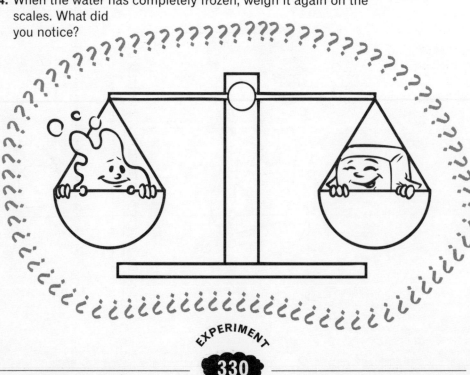

EXPERIMENT

330

Freezing Liquids

 ✓
SUPERVISED

 ✓
 ✓
ACTIVITY

AIM

To find out about freezing different liquids.

MATERIALS

- ice cube tray
- vinegar
- water
- cooking oil
- freezer

STEPS

1. Fill one ice cube mould with water.

2. Fill one ice cube mould with vinegar.

3. Fill one ice cube mould with cooking oil.

4. Put the ice cube tray into the freezer.

5. Record what time you put the tray in the freezer. Check the tray every hour and write down your findings. The water freezes into a hard block; the vinegar should freeze too; but what happens to the oil?

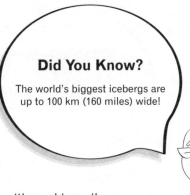

Did You Know?

The world's biggest icebergs are up to 100 km (160 miles) wide!

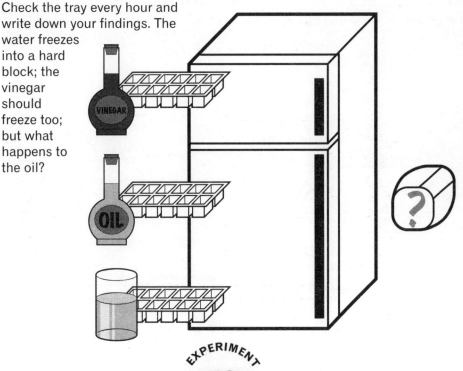

Colour and the Weather

SUPERVISED ✓

✓

✓

ACTIVITY

AIM

To see some of the principles of solar power.

MATERIALS

- 6 pieces of coloured paper about 10 cm × 10 cm (4 in × 4 in)
- 6 ice cubes
- newspaper
- clock

Did You Know?

Dark colours absorb heat and light, and light colours reflect heat and light.

STEPS

1. Spread the piece of newspaper outside in the Sun.

2. Place the different coloured squares on the newspaper.

3. Place an ice cube on each piece of paper.

4. Time how long it takes each ice cube to melt. What do you notice?

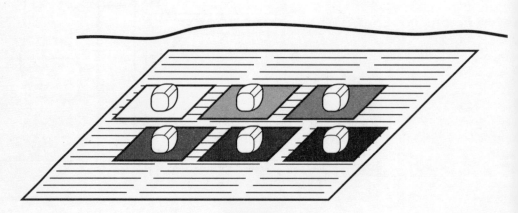

Water – Putting on Weight!

 ✓

 ✓
 ✓

AIM

To see how much water expands when it freezes.

MATERIALS

- film canister with a lid
- water
- freezer
- snap-lock bag
- bowl

Did You Know?

Snowflakes are tiny droplets of water that have frozen into crystals of ice in the clouds.

STEPS

1. Fill the bowl with water.
2. Put the film canister in the water and fill it with water. Make sure there aren't any air bubbles then put the lid on.
3. Take the film canister out of the water and put it in the snap-lock bag.
4. Put the snap-lock bag in the freezer for 24 hours. What happens to the film canister?

Salty Rain?

AIM

To see why salt water doesn't become salt rain.

MATERIALS

- 2 teaspoons of salt
- 500 ml (2 cups) warm water
- stove
- spoon
- saucepan with a lid
- cup

Did You Know?

The water from the sea gets heated by the Sun, evaporates to form water vapour, and eventually becomes salt-less water in the clouds.

STEPS

1. Taste the water (make sure it's not too hot to drink).

2. Add the salt to the water and stir it to help the salt dissolve. Taste the water now.

3. Place the salty water into the saucepan. Now ask an adult to help you boil the water on the stove. Keep the lid on.

4. Condensation will form on the lid. As it does, take the lid off and let the water drip off the lid into the cup.

5. When the water in the cup cools down taste it. How does it taste?

Shrivelled Potatoes

AIM

To make a potato shrivel.

MATERIALS

- 1 potato
- 2 saucers
- chopping board
- knife
- salt
- water

Did You Know?

The salt water draws the water out of the potato, causing it to shrivel and become dehydrated. Dehydrated means when the water is removed. This often happens to humans when they sweat a lot and don't drink enough water. Your body can be like the potato if you don't drink enough water to replace what you sweat out!

STEPS

1. Ask an adult to help you cut the potato in half.

2. Fill both saucers with water. Into one saucer mix some salt. Leave the other one with just plain water. Mark the one with salt water so you remember which one it is.

3. Place one half of the potato into each saucer, with the flat side facing down. Leave for about half an hour. What has happened after this time?

EXPERIMENT

335

Growing Both Ends

AIM

To grow roots and leaves from a potato.

MATERIALS

- 1 sweet potato
- toothpicks
- drinking glass
- water

Did You Know?

Potatoes are known as a root vegetable. This means that they grow from the roots of the plants under the ground. Do you know any other root vegetables? Carrots are another one.

STEPS

1. Fill the drinking glass with water.

2. Stick some toothpicks in the middle of the potato so that they poke out.

3. Place the potato into the drinking glass. The toothpicks will stop the potato touching the bottom of the glass. Make sure the bottom part of the potato is touching the water.

4. Leave it for a few days. The bottom part of the potato will sprout roots and leaves will grow out of the top.

EXPERIMENT

336

Breathing Plants

5–12
AGES

SUPERVISED

ACTIVITY

AIM

To observe how plants get nutrients from the soil.

MATERIALS

- plastic bottle
- flower with stem attached
- water
- small amount of clay or plasticine
- drinking straw

Did You Know?

Plants are like straws. In their leaves are tiny little pores or holes, so tiny that you cannot see them. These pores are used by plants to breathe air. When you are sucking on the straw and removing the air from the bottle, the pores in the plant are breathing and are bringing air into the bottle. Pretty clever!

STEPS

1. Fill the bottle three-quarters full with water.

2. Wrap the clay around the stem of the flower.

3. Place the flower in the bottle. Use the clay to seal and close the mouth of the bottle tightly.

4. Carefully push the straw through the clay. Do not let the straw touch the water. Make sure the clay is still sealed tightly around the straw and there are no leaks.

5. Check that the straw is not touching the water. Stand in front of a mirror and suck on the straw.

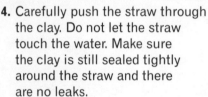

EXPERIMENT

337

Slippery Leaves

AIM

To examine if leaves lose their moisture.

MATERIALS

- 4 fresh large leaves with a small part of the stem still attached
- string
- scissors
- ruler or stick
- Vaseline

Did You Know?

The leaf with no Vaseline will shrivel and die first. This is because the water has 'evaporated' into the air. The Vaseline stops the water evaporating from the leaf pores as quickly. This is why the leaf with Vaseline on both sides stays fresh for the longest time.

STEPS

1. Tie a piece of string to the stem on each leaf. Then tie the other end of the string to the stick or ruler. Spread the leaves out so that they are not touching each other.

2. On the first leaf smear Vaseline on both sides. On the second leaf put Vaseline on the bottom side of the leaf and on the third on the topside of the leaf. Leave the last leaf without any Vaseline.

3. Leave for a few days and note the differences.

Mini Greenhouse

5–12
AGES

SUPERVISED

ACTIVITY

AIM

To create a mini greenhouse to grow plants.

MATERIALS

- clear plastic bottle
- soil
- small plant or seedling
- wide sticky tape
- scissors

Did You Know?

The sun causes the temperature inside the greenhouse to rise. Because the lid is sealed the air inside stays heated, even when air outside the greenhouse cools down. This means the air inside turns to water that feeds the plant to keep it alive.

STEPS

1. Wash the bottle carefully so that it is very clean. Don't worry if it is still wet inside.
2. Cut the bottle in half.
3. Take the bottom part of the bottle and half fill it with soil.
4. Plant the seedling in the soil, making sure you cover all the roots.
5. Place the top half of the bottle back onto the bottom half and use the sticky tape to seal them together, making sure there are no leaks.
6. Put a few drops of water into the bottle. Place the cap back on.
7. Leave your mini greenhouse in a window where it will get plenty of sun.
8. After a few days you will notice the bottle 'sweating'. If it is too moist open it up and let it dry out for a while.

Sweating Plants

SUPERVISED

ACTIVITY

AIM

To see the water vapour given off by plants.

MATERIALS

- potted plant
- clear plastic bag
- water
- jug
- large rubber band

Did You Know?

The moisture inside the bag is not sweat but water. This comes from the plant drawing in the water and giving off water vapour from its leaves. This is turned into water and stays on the inside of the bag.

STEPS

1. Water the pot plant first, making sure you fill the plant to the bottom so that the roots are well watered.

2. Cover the plant and the pot with the plastic bag. Secure the bag to the pot with the rubber band so that no air can escape.

3. Leave the plant overnight. The next day you will notice water in the bag.

Nocturnal Plants

AIM

To see if plants can grow in the dark.

MATERIALS

- 2 plastic cups
- 2 saucers
- soil
- water
- 2 seedlings
- scissors

Did You Know?

Plants need sunlight to survive. You can see from your plant in the window that it is healthy and growing in the light. Sunlight helps plants produce 'food' and stay healthy. Without sunlight they die.

STEPS

1. Ask an adult to help you poke some holes in the bottom of the cup. This will allow water to come into the cup.
2. Fill each cup with soil. Plant one seedling in each cup.
3. Place each cup on a saucer and water the plants.
4. Place one plant in a brightly lit place. Place the other cup in a dark cupboard and close it (make sure people know it's there and don't knock it over).
5. Leave for a few days and see what happens.

Mould Mania

 ✓

SUPERVISED

✓

✓

ACTIVITY

AIM

To grow different coloured moulds on different foods.

MATERIALS

- clear container – glass jar or plastic container with a lid
- sticky tape
- water
- food scraps such as bread, vegetables, fruit, cheese, and biscuits. (Do not use any meat, chicken or fish.)
- knife
- chopping board

Did You Know?

The mould that grows in the container is a type of fungus. Mushrooms are another type of fungus. Unlike plants that grow from seeds, mould grows from spores floating around in the air, which grow on damp food and turn into mould.

STEPS

1. Ask an adult to help you cut the food into pieces each about the size of a twenty cent piece.

2. Dip each piece of food in water.

3. Lay the container on its side and put the food inside. Make sure each piece is touching the others, but do not put all the food on top of each other.

4. Put the lid on tightly and seal the container with the sticky tape. Place the container of food scraps in a place where no one will knock it (or eat it!).

5. Observe the food everyday. In the first two or three days there will probably be very little change. Soon you will start to get mould of many different colours.

6. After a few days some of the food will start to rot. Leave it for two weeks and see what happens. After that you will need to throw the container and scraps out. Don't open it. Mould can be dangerous for some people to breathe in.

Spore Prints

 ✓

SUPERVISED

 ✓
 ✓

ACTIVITY

AIM

To record the print left by mushrooms.

MATERIALS

- mushrooms
- black and white cardboard
- notebook
- pencil
- cups or plastic containers
- hair spray
- magnifying glass (optional)

Did You Know?

Spores are like the seeds on plants. Mushrooms and other fungi produce spores that drop out of their gills. They fall to the ground or are carried by the wind and land in other places. These spores produce new mushrooms.

STEPS

1. Ask an adult to help you pull out the stems of the mushrooms so that you are left with the caps. If you have a magnifying glass look under the cap of the mushroom at the 'gills', or the frilly soft bits.

2. Place the caps with the gills facing down on the black and white cardboard and cover with the cups or plastic containers.

3. The next morning check under the mushrooms to see the spore prints. If there is nothing there leave it a little longer.

4. When you have your prints leave them for a day to dry. Afterwards stand at least 30 cm (12 in) away and spray the card with hair spray to preserve them.

EXPERIMENT

343

Making Ginger Ale

AIM

To make ginger ale.

MATERIALS

- measuring jug
- large saucepan with a lid
- water
- powdered ginger
- tablespoon
- ¼ lime
- 1½ cups sugar
- cream of tartar
- dried yeast
- sieve
- funnel
- mixing spoon
- 2 litre (12 cup) bottle with lid

Did You Know?

When mixed with sugar and heated, the yeast produces a gas called carbon dioxide that makes the mixture go fizzy. The gas is what makes the bubbles in the ginger ale. This is called 'carbonation' which is why they are called carbonated drinks.

STEPS

1. Ask an adult to boil 2 litres (12 cups) of water in a large saucepan. Add 1½ tablespoons of ginger, juice from the lime, 1½ cups of sugar and 1½ tablespoons of cream of tartar.

2. Leave the mixture to cool until it is just warm, then add the yeast and mix with the spoon until the yeast is dissolved. Place the lid on the saucepan and leave for six hours.

3. Have someone hold the sieve over the measuring jug and pour the mixture into the measuring jug. Throw away whatever is left in the sieve.

4. Place the funnel in the top of the bottle. Slowly pour the mixture into the bottle. Do not fill it all the way up.

5. Put the lid on tightly and place it in the refrigerator. Leave it for two days, and then it is ready to drink.

Magic Balloon

AIM

To blow up a balloon using gas made from yeast.

MATERIALS

- 1 packet of dried yeast
- warm water
- sugar
- teaspoon
- clear plastic bottle
- balloon

Did You Know?

This seems like a great trick but it is not really magic. By adding sugar and heat to the yeast, the yeast grows and produces a gas called carbon dioxide. The carbon dioxide in the bottle rises and fills up the balloon.

STEPS

1. Pour the dried yeast into the plastic bottle.

2. Add a little bit of warm water to the bottle. Then add a teaspoon of sugar and swirl the bottle around.

3. Place the balloon over the mouth of the bottle so that it is covered.

4. Place the balloon on a warm windowsill or keep the bottle in a bowl of warm water.

5. Watch the balloon magically blow up!

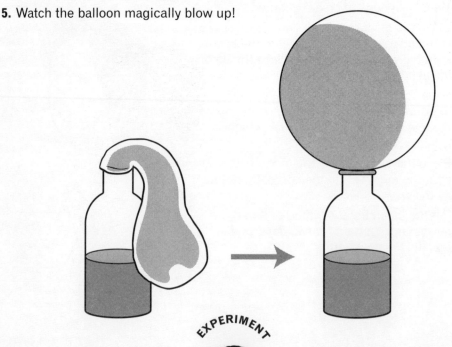

EXPERIMENT

345

Barney Banana

AIM

To trick your friends into thinking you have created a new type of banana.

MATERIALS

- banana
- long sewing needle

STEPS

1. Carefully push the needle into one of the edges of the banana. Push it all the way to the other side of the banana but do not push it through the skin on the other side.

2. Move the needle up and down. This will slice the banana inside.

3. Keep doing this all the way along the banana, leaving about a finger space between each hole. Only put the needle in one side of the banana or your friends may see even these tiny holes.

4. Now peel the banana for your friends. They will be amazed that inside is a beautifully sliced banana.

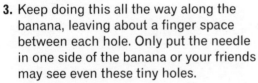

Did You Know?

This will not work with any other fruit. It is only because bananas are so soft that this works. Bananas are made up of thousands and thousands of tiny hairs and this is why they are so soft.

Fruit or Vegetable?

AIM

To classify some foods as either fruits or vegetables.

MATERIALS

- different foods – tomatoes, carrots, avocado, orange, potato, strawberries
- chopping board
- knife

Did You Know?

Because they have seeds, tomatoes and avocados are classed as a fruit not a vegetable. We usually think of fruits as sweet foods because of the natural sugar in them and not something we would eat with cheese in our sandwich.

STEPS

1. Ask an adult to cut all the foods in half for you.

2. Look at the inside and see if you can see a seed.

3. If there is a seed then the food is classified as a fruit. Any surprises?

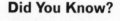

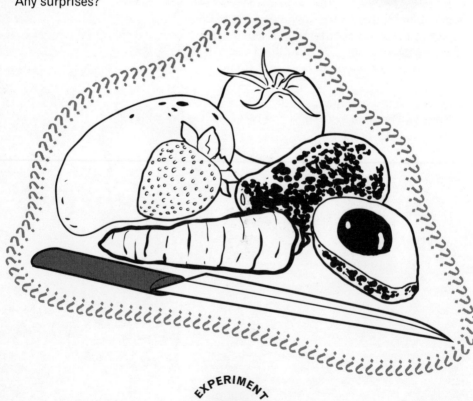

When is a Fruit a Berry?

SUPERVISED

ACTIVITY

AIM

To sort fruits into three groups.

MATERIALS

- different fruits – oranges, grapes, apricots, plums, apples and pears
- chopping board
- knife

Did You Know?

The three classifications of fruits are:
1) Drupes – which have one hard seed in the middle, such as peaches.
2) Berries – where the seeds are all through the fruit such as oranges and raspberries.
3) Pomes – which have many seeds in a core, such as pears and apples.

STEPS

1. Ask an adult to cut all the fruit in half for you.

2. Look very carefully at the inside of the fruit and find the seeds.

3. Sort the fruit into three groups – a group with one large hard seed in the middle; a group where there are many seeds throughout the fruit; and a group where there are some seeds surrounded by a core.

   These are the three groups used to classify fruits.

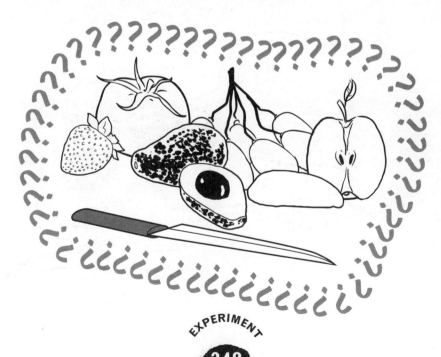

Lemon Floaties

SUPERVISED

ACTIVITY

AIM

To see if a lemon floats in water.

MATERIALS

- lemon
- bowl of water
- knife
- chopping board

Did You Know?

The lemon fills with water after it is cut and sinks because it is too heavy. The skin on the lemon is waterproof and protects the lemon when it is growing on the tree from the weather.

STEPS

1. Fill the bowl with water. Place the lemon in the water and watch it float.

2. Ask an adult to help you cut the lemon into pieces.

3. Now put the lemon pieces in the water. Watch what happens.

EXPERIMENT

349

Making a Compost Bin

 ✓

 ✓

SUPERVISED

✓

ACTIVITY

AIM

To make a compost bin to keep at home.

MATERIALS

- large plastic bin with lid and holes in the bottom
- moist old newspapers
- worms
- straw, sawdust, shredded leaves
- food scraps (see note below)

Did You Know?

Compost makes a great fertiliser for your plants. Fertiliser helps keep your plants healthy by feeding them extra nutrients.

STEPS

1. Make sure the bin has holes in the bottom. Fill the bin with the newspapers and other things, including the straw or leaves, making sure that it is moist.

2. Get some worms from your garden. Dig up the soil and find some worms to put in your compost bin.

3. You must feed the worms. They can have food such as fruit and vegetables and bread. NOTE: Do not use meat, chicken, milk (and other dairy foods) or eggs.

4. Put the lid on. If possible keep the bin outside, or in a spot where the water can drain out and not make a mess.

5. Make sure your compost bin is always moist. If not, add more water. Keep the lid on because it will get smelly.

Compost is My Home

AIM

To look at the creatures that live in compost.

MATERIALS

- rotting leaves from a compost bin
- large clear jar
- plastic funnel
- rubber gloves
- black paper
- sticky tape
- desk lamp
- magnifying glass
- pile of books, the same height as the jar

Did You Know?

Light from lamps causes heat. In this experiment the creatures can move and the leaves can't, so the bugs will try to move away from the light and further into the funnel where they fall down the slope into the jar.

STEPS

1. Put on the rubber gloves. Do not touch the leaves without the gloves. Collect some rotting leaves from the compost bin.

2. Place the funnel on top of the jar. Loosely place the rotting leaves inside the funnel.

3. Cover the jar with the black paper and use the sticky tape to keep it on. The whole jar must be covered to block out all the light.

4. Put the desk lamp on top of a large pile of books. Place the jar next to the books and move the light so it is directly shining onto the leaves.

5. Leave for about an hour then use the magnifying glass to examine what is in the jar.

The Oldest Tree

AIM

To find out which is the oldest tree.

MATERIALS

- large ball of string
- scissors
- sticky tape
- measuring tape
- pencil
- piece of paper
- a friend

Did You Know?

Every year trees grow a new layer of bark around them. Imagine every year that on top of the old layer of bark a new one grows. This means the more layers of bark the wider the tree becomes. The tree gets wider and wider as it gets older and older. If you ever see a tree cut down, look at the trunk. You can see a swirly pattern, starting with a small circle in the middle and lots of rings around this. These rings are the layers of bark. The more rings the trunk has, the older the tree.

STEPS

1. Find some big trees in the backyard or at the park.

2. Cut a piece of string about 1 m (3 ft) long (you may not need all of this or you might need a longer piece, depending how thick the tree trunk is).

3. Stick one end of the string on the tree and wrap it around the trunk. Match one end up to the end that is stuck to the tree. Use your scissors to cut it off.

4. Remove the string and use the measuring tape to measure the distance around the tree (called the girth). Record how big each tree is on your piece of paper.

5. Do this for as many trees as you can find. Ask the person with you if they can tell you what type of tree you are measuring.

6. After you have finished measuring, see which tree has the longest piece of string. Most of the time this is the oldest tree.

WHICH IS THE OLDEST?

Tree Hugger

5–12
AGES

AIM

To use your sense of smell and touch to identify trees.

MATERIALS

- blindfold
- partner
- trees

SUPERVISED ✓

☀ ✓

🏠

✂ ✓

ACTIVITY

Did You Know?

The type of bark depends on the age and type of tree. Usually younger trees have smoother bark. Older trees have rougher bark because as the tree grows older and wider the bark stretches and cracks around the tree.

STEPS

1. Secure the blindfold over your eyes. Ask your partner to spin you around and lead you to a tree.

2. You have to try and remember as much as you can about the tree from feeling and smelling it. Smell the bark. Ask your partner to lead you to the leaves and smell them. Feel for flowers, buds or nuts. Feel the bark. Hug the tree to feel how wide it is.

3. When you think you know the tree well enough to find it again, have your partner lead you away and spin you around in circles again.

4. Take the blindfold off and try to find the tree again by smelling and feeling the ones you can see.

5. Swap over.

How Many Plants to a Box?

5–12
AGES

 ✓

SUPERVISED

 ✓

✓

ACTIVITY

AIM

To make a list of plants in a set area.

MATERIALS

- metre (yard) ruler
- small sticks
- string
- scissors
- magnifying glass
- notebook
- pencil

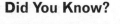

Did You Know?

The plants inside the box can vary greatly depending on where the area is located. The amount of sun, wind, water and animal life will affect the types of plants growing in the area.

STEPS

1. Measure a square the length of the ruler. Mark each corner by pushing a stick into the ground.
2. Tie the string to each of the sticks so that the string marks the square.
3. Sit outside of the square and use the magnifying glass to observe the plants inside the square. Use your notebook to write down what you see.
4. You may wish to do this at a park where you can compare different squares. You may find that the plants in the squares change depending upon what is near the area.

Grasses

AIM
To find the different types of grasses in a yard.

MATERIALS
- paper
- pencil

STEPS

1. Do this activity at a park or in your backyard.

2. Walk around and see how many different types of grass you can find. Remember if you are near a pond there will be different types near the water.

3. Sort them and then list them in order of the most common in the area to the least common.

Did You Know?
Grasses come in all different types. Like trees, some are soft and some are hard. Near water grasses tend to be a lot harder.

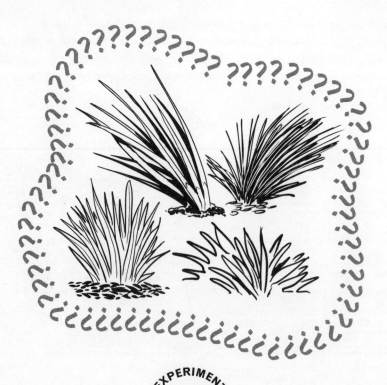

Bark Rubbing

AIM

To see the different patterns of bark on trees.

MATERIALS

- large white paper
- crayons

STEPS

1. Place the paper against the trunk of the tree.

2. Lay the crayon on its side and rub it on the paper. You should start to see a pattern appear on the paper. If it is not working you may need to press harder or you might be pressing too hard.

3. When you have finished with one tree, write on the paper with the rubbing what type of tree it is (if you don't know, ask someone).

   Try different trees and change your colours.

Did You Know?

Different trees have different bark. You can see from your rubbings that some trees have smooth bark and some have rough bark.

Bark Detective

SUPERVISED

ACTIVITY

AIM
To look at what is hiding in tree bark.

MATERIALS
- magnifying glass
- trees

STEPS

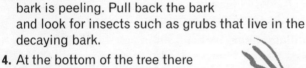

1. Find a tree with a thick trunk.
2. Look for cracks in the bark. Use the magnifying glass to look for insects hiding in the bark.
3. Find places on the tree where the bark is peeling. Pull back the bark and look for insects such as grubs that live in the decaying bark.
4. At the bottom of the tree there is often green, powdery moss where other creatures live.

Did You Know?
Bark is the home of many little insects. We know that birds often live in the branches of trees but bark makes a nice, sheltered home for little insects and grubs.

Leaf Rubbings

SUPERVISED

ACTIVITY

AIM

To look at the different parts of the leaf.

MATERIALS

- different types of leaves
- paper
- crayons

STEPS

1. Place the leaves on the table.
2. Put the paper on top of the leaves.
3. Lay the crayon on its side and slide over the paper. If this is not working try pressing harder or softer.
4. Use different leaves and different colours to make a colourful picture.

Did You Know?

Inside the leaf you will be able to see lines on the paper. Down the middle of each leaf you will see a bigger line. This is the vein that attaches each leaf to the stem of the plant and brings water into the leaves. The smaller lines move the water around the leaf.

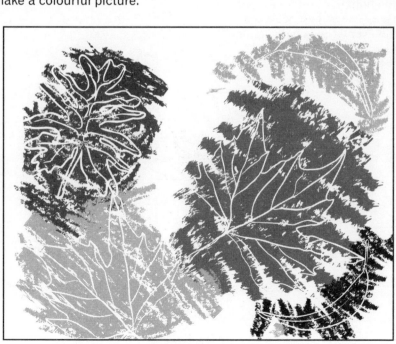

Crazy Leaves

AIM

To find different shaped leaves.

MATERIALS

- paper
- pencil
- sticky tape

Did You Know?

The maple leaf is so special that it appears on the Canadian flag. Not only is the leaf from this tree an interesting shape but the maple tree also produces that yummy maple syrup you put on your pancakes!

STEPS

1. Do this experiment at the park or in your backyard.

2. Pick leaves from trees. (If there are leaves on the ground under the tree, try to use those.) You may like to note the trees where you picked these leaves.

3. Sort the leaves into matching shapes and stick them to the paper.

4. You may like to find out if there are any similarities between the shapes of the leaves coming from big trees or small trees. Which leaves appear to have more insects living on them?

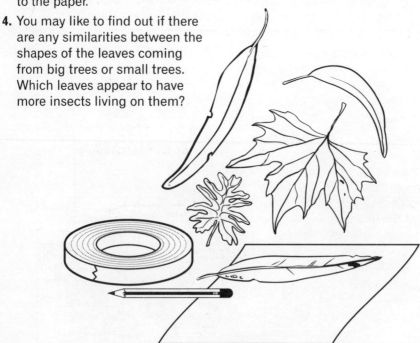

Tree Encyclopaedia

SUPERVISED ✓

ACTIVITY ✓

AIM

To make a book of photos of different trees in your yard or park.

MATERIALS

- camera
- small notebook
- pencil
- guidebook on trees
  (you can borrow this
  from your local library)
- large scrapbook
- glue

Did You Know?

The smaller lines on a leaf move
the water around.

STEPS

Note: This experiment is fantastic if you make bark and
leaf rubbings as well. You can find these at Experiments
356 and 358.

1. Walk around the backyard or the park with the camera. Choose a
   tree and make notes about it. This is a good chance to make a bark
   and leaf rubbing to add to your information.

2. Take a close-up photograph of the tree. Take some from different
   angles and some close-ups of the bark.
   When you have used up the film have
   the photographs developed.

3. Visit different places with different
   trees. Use your guidebook to help
   you identify each tree.

4. Stick the photographs into the
   scrapbook using the glue. Under
   the photograph write the
   name of the tree and any
   information you have
   found out. Sticking your
   bark and leaf rubbings in with
   the photographs looks fantastic.

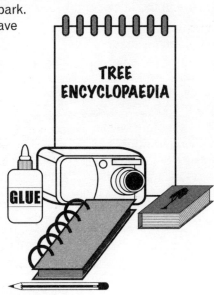

TREE
ENCYCLOPAEDIA

GLUE

Pressed Leaves and Flowers

5–12
AGES

SUPERVISED

ACTIVITY

AIM

To make a leaf and flower press to preserve flowers.

MATERIALS

- old newspaper
- heavy books
- freshly picked leaves
- fresh flowers

Did You Know?

The newspaper absorbs all of the water and moisture from the leaves and flowers. This stops them from rotting after all this time.

STEPS

1. Collect as many different leaves and flowers as you can from the one place. You might like to collect them from many locations to compare the differences.

2. Start with all the leaves and flowers from one place. Put a book on the bottom then cover it with a sheet of newspaper. Place some of the leaves or flowers on top of the newspaper. Make sure that they are not touching each other and are not on top of each other.

3. Place another sheet of newspaper and then a book on top of the flowers or leaves. Repeat layers of newspaper, flowers, newspaper and books, making a tower with the books, until you have run out of leaves and flowers.

4. If you have things from different places make another pile with the books and newspaper again and write where they came from.

5. Wait at least four weeks (if not longer) until the leaves are flat and dry.

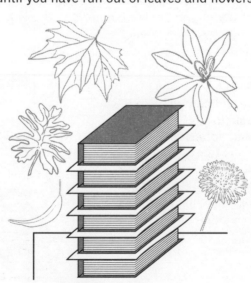

Making Pot-pourri

SUPERVISED

ACTIVITY

AIM

To make pot-pourri using all types of flowers.

MATERIALS

- different types of flowers (roses and lavender are great)
- scissors
- heavy books
- newspaper

Did You Know?

Flowers smell nice because of the oil they make. Every flower smells differently because they all produce different oils. These oils are often used in soaps and candles to make them smell nice. Visit your local florist and smell all the different flowers. Which ones do you like the best?

STEPS

1. Collect all the flowers you are going to use. If they have long stems cut the stem off, leaving about a thumb length below the flower.

2. Place a book on the ground or table. On top of the book place a sheet of newspaper and then some flowers. You must make sure that they are not touching each other and are not on top of each other or they will not dry out properly.

3. On top of the flowers place another sheet of newspaper and then a book. Repeat layers of newspaper, flowers, newspaper and books, making a tower with the books, until you have run out of flowers.

4. Place the 'flower press' you have made in a space where it will not be knocked over.

5. Wait at least four weeks until the flowers have dried out.

6. When the flowers are dried, pull the petals off all the flowers and mix them in a bowl. You will have a lovely smelling pot-pourri.

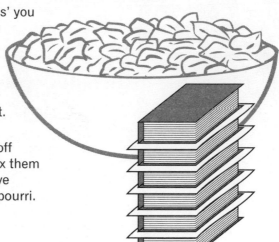

Coloured Flowers

AIM

To make flowers of different colours.

MATERIALS

- white flowers (such as carnations)
- food colouring
- water
- drinking glasses

Did You Know?

The flowers draw the water up the stem and into the petals. As this water is coloured the water that reaches the petals is also coloured and causes the petals to become that colour. If you cut the stem of the flowers you will also see the coloured water inside the stem.

STEPS

1. Fill the glasses with water.
2. Place three or four drops of food colouring in each glass. Mix colours to make new colours. This will give you different coloured flowers. For example, mixing red and blue will make purple; red and yellow will make orange; and yellow and blue will make green. Make as many different colours as you like.
3. Place a flower in each glass and leave overnight.
4. The next morning you will have flowers of all colours. They make a very interesting gift for someone special.

Multi-coloured Flowers

AIM

To make multi-coloured flowers.

MATERIALS

- 4 white flowers (such as carnations)
- scissors
- food colouring
- water
- 8 drinking glasses

Did You Know?

The flowers draw the water up the stem and into the petals. As half of the flower is in coloured water and half is plain water, half the water that reaches the flower is coloured, so half the petals will be coloured and the other half will still be white.

STEPS

1. Fill the glasses with water.
2. Leave four of the glasses with just water in them.
3. Colour the water in the remaining four glasses by adding three or four drops of food colouring to each glass. Mix the colours to make new colours.
4. Carefully cut the stems in half lengthways to about halfway up. The stem should still be together at the top where the flower is.
5. Place a glass of plain water and a glass of coloured water next to each other.
6. Place half of the stem in a glass of coloured water and the other half of the stem in a glass of plain water. Repeat with the other flowers.
7. Leave the flowers overnight.

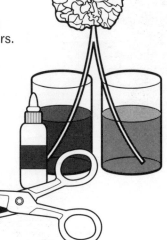

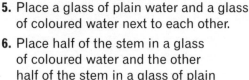

EXPERIMENT

364

Colourful Celery

AIM

To create purple celery.

MATERIALS

- 6 long pieces of celery
- chopping board
- knife
- red and blue food colouring
- 6 drinking glasses or small jars
- water
- vegetable peeler
- ruler

Did You Know?

Just like humans plants need water to survive. Plants get water from the soil through their roots. Inside the plants are capillaries that allow the water to travel through the plant. You can see from the celery that over a period of time the plant draws water up through its capillaries all the way through its system.

STEPS

1. Ask an adult to help you cut the celery into pieces of the same length. Chop off the bottom, and at 10 cm (4 in) below the leaves.

2. Fill each glass with an equal amount of water.

3. To each jar add 10 drops of red and 10 drops of blue food colouring.

4. Place one piece of celery in each glass and leave.

5. After one hour remove the first piece of celery from the jar. Has anything changed? Peel the round part and measure how far up the celery the colour has gone.

6. Remove the celery from the jars at different times – after two hours, four hours, six hours, eight hours and overnight (you have six glasses). Peel, and measure the colour. Observe the difference to the celery after each time interval and make notes in a journal.

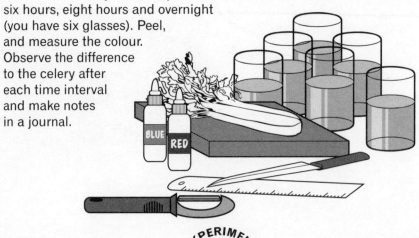

Stem-less Flowers

AIM

To see what happens to a flower with no stem.

MATERIALS

- 2 fresh flowers
- scissors

Did You Know?

The stem of the flower holds water. It draws water up when flowers are in a vase to keep the flower petals moist. Even when it is out of water the stem still holds some water. Without the stem the flower has no way of getting water and dies much faster than the flower with the stem.

STEPS

1. Use the scissors to cut the stem off one of the flowers.

2. Leave both flowers in a spot where they will not be knocked over.

3. Check after an hour and note the difference between them. What happens after a long period of time?

Plants and Air

AIM

To see if plants can grow without air.

MATERIALS

- 2 seedlings
- soil
- pot
- saucer
- jar with a lid
- rubber gloves
- water

Did You Know?

Without air, plants cannot survive. Plants need the gas called carbon dioxide from the air. We also need the plants to keep the air healthy for humans. Plants pass out oxygen from their leaves. Oxygen is the part of air that humans need to help them breathe. Without plants there would not be enough oxygen in the air for us!

STEPS

1. Wearing the rubber gloves, half fill the jar with soil.
2. Plant the seedling in the soil in the jar, making sure the roots are covered (you may need to put some more soil in the jar).
3. Lightly water the seedling and screw the lid on tightly.
4. Fill the pot with soil until it almost reaches the top.
5. Plant the seedling, covering the roots.
6. Place the pot on the saucer of water.
7. Put both the jar and the potted plant in a sunny place and leave for a few days.

SUPERVISED

ACTIVITY

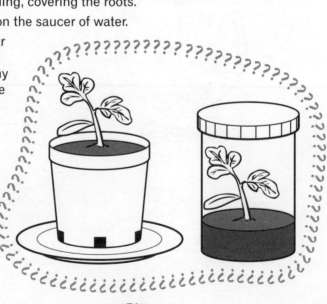

Plants and Soil

AIM

To see if plants can grow without soil.

MATERIALS

- 2 seedlings
- soil
- 2 small pots
- 2 saucers
- rubber gloves
- water

Did You Know?

Soil plays an important part in helping a plant grow. Soil contains lots of nutrients and minerals that help the plant grow. It also allows the roots of the plant to grow and hold the plant up which is especially important for the big old trees. Their roots are enormous and act like a boat anchor to hold the tree in place.

STEPS

1. Wearing the rubber gloves, fill one of the small pots with soil until it almost reaches the top.
2. Plant one of the seedlings in this pot with the soil, making sure the roots are covered.
3. Place the other seedling in a pot with no soil.
4. Put both pots on a saucer of water.
5. Place in a sunny spot and leave for a few days.

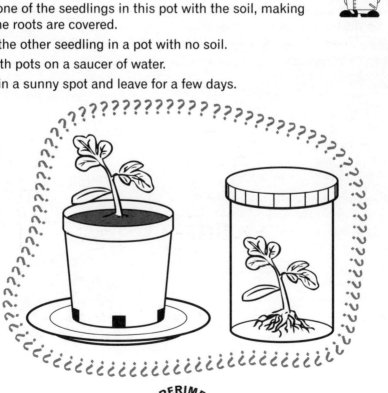

Plants and Water

SUPERVISED

ACTIVITY

AIM

To see if plants need water to grow.

MATERIALS

- 3 seedlings
- soil
- 3 small pots
- 3 saucers
- rubber gloves
- water
- carbonated drink (soft drink)
- permanent marker

Did You Know?

Water is good for you and for plants. Because water comes from under the Earth many minerals have been dissolved in the water. These minerals are necessary to help the plants grow. Without them plants will die. All the extra things in cola, like sugar and additives, are not good for the plant.

STEPS

1. Wearing the rubber gloves, fill all three pots with soil until they almost reach the top.

2. Plant one seedling in each pot, making sure the roots of the plant are well covered. Place a pot on each of the saucers.

3. On the first pot use the marker to write 'no water'. Place this pot in a sunny spot and do not water.

4. On the second pot write 'cola' (or whatever drink you are using). Fill the saucer with the drink and place in a sunny spot.

5. On the third pot write 'water'. Fill the saucer with water and place in a sunny spot.

6. Leave your plants. You will need to make sure they are damp and if they are not, add more water or cola, depending on which plant it is.

"NO WATER"

"WATER"

"COLA"

Brown light? Clear light?

 ✓

SUPERVISED

 ✓
 ✓

ACTIVITY

AIM

To see if plants can grow in different coloured light.

MATERIALS

- 2 small plants
- 2 small pots
- 2 saucers
- 2 plastic bottles – one clear and one brown (dry ginger ale comes in a brown plastic bottle)
- scissors
- soil
- rubber gloves
- water

Did You Know?

Although the plant in the brown bottle is getting light, the coloured plastic acts as a 'filter'. This means that some of the sunlight is blocked by the brown colour and this plant does not get as much sunlight as the one in the clear plastic bottle. This is why the one in the plastic bottle is growing faster and larger.

STEPS

1. Use the scissors to cut the top part of the bottles off.
2. Wearing the rubber gloves, fill the small pots with soil almost to the top. Put the plants in the pots, making sure you cover the roots.
3. Place the pots on the saucers of water, then put in a sunny spot.
4. Turn the two bottle bottoms upside down over the plants.
5. Keep watering your plants during this activity. Observe your plants every few days and take note of the differences.

Undercover Leaves

SUPERVISED

ACTIVITY

AIM

To observe how leaves change colour when they do not receive natural light.

MATERIALS

- small potted plant with large leaves
- black cardboard
- clingwrap
- sticky tape
- scissors
- water

Did You Know?

Sunlight is not only important to help plants grow but it also helps give plants their colours. It helps the leaves produce chlorophyll, which gives them their green colour.

STEPS

1. Count the number of leaves on the plant. You will cover half of them in the black cardboard and half in the clingwrap.

2. Using the scissors, cut the black cardboard into pieces that will cover the leaves. Use sticky tape to hold them in place. Leave space for air to get in and out.

3. Now use the clingwrap to cover the other leaves, again leaving space for the leaves to breathe.

4. Leave the plant in a sunny spot. Each day observe the changes to the colour of the leaves.

EXPERIMENT

371

Plants From Other Plants

AIM

To use a plant cutting to grow a new plant.

MATERIALS

- scissors
- plant cutting (with at least two leaves on it)
- small pot
- soil
- saucer
- water
- plastic bag

Did You Know?

The plastic bag acts like a greenhouse in this activity. It keeps the plant warm and damp and encourages it to grow more quickly.

STEPS

1. Ask an adult to help you cut the stem of another plant. Remember to make sure there are at least two leaves on the plant. If there are any flowers on your cutting take them off.

2. Wearing the rubber gloves, fill the pot with soil. Push a hole in the soil as deep as your thumb.

3. Place the cutting in the soil and carefully cover the bottom.

4. Leave the plant on a saucer and cover with the plastic bag. Keep it in a sunny place and remember to water it.

Carrot Top

 ✓

 ✓

 ✓

AIM

To grow carrots, observing that carrots are the roots of the plant.

MATERIALS

- carrot seeds
- small pot or an empty milk carton
- scissors
- soil
- rubber gloves
- water
- saucer

Did You Know?

The carrot grew under the soil. What you can see above the soil are the leaves and the stems. The part of the carrot that you eat (the orange part) is actually the root of the plant.

STEPS

1. If you are using the milk carton, cut it in half. Ask an adult to use the scissors to poke some holes in the bottom.

2. Wearing the rubber gloves, fill the container until it almost reaches the top. Plant the seeds in the soil, and then cover them with a little bit more soil.

3. Place the pot or carton on the saucer. Fill the saucer with water and leave it in a sunny spot.

4. Don't forget to keep watering it.

Leaves Galore

SUPERVISED

ACTIVITY

AIM

To see which leaves we can eat.

MATERIALS

- magnifying glass
- different types of leaves – spinach, lettuce types, watercress

STEPS

1. Examine each of the leaves under a magnifying glass. You will be able to see small lines throughout the leaf. These are the veins that bring water.
2. Rip the leaves into small pieces and mix together.
3. Serve for dinner – a leaf salad!

Did You Know?

We eat all different parts of the plant. This salad shows you different leaves you can eat. When you eat celery you eat the stem of the plant. Potatoes and carrots are the root of the plant. Tomatoes and chillies come from the flower of the plant.

Salty Bean Sprouts

SUPERVISED

ACTIVITY

AIM

To see the effects of salt in the soil when trying to grow plants.

MATERIALS

- 2 clear plastic cups
- cotton wool
- salt
- water
- bean sprout seeds
- marker

Did You Know?

Salt comes from water and because there is water in the soil there is also salt in the soil. Salt makes it very difficult for plants to grow (you can see this in your experiment). In some places if the water underground comes up too high, the salt level in the soil is also too high, making it impossible to grow plants, even for farmers.

STEPS

1. Cover the bottom of each cup with cotton wool.

2. In one cup sprinkle the cotton wool with salt. Write on the cup 'salt added'.

3. Put about five bean sprout seeds on top of the cotton wool in each cup, then add a little water.

4. Place in a brightly lit window and leave for a few days. Observe the cups and make note of which one is growing first and faster.

Grass Heads

 ✓

SUPERVISED

 ✓

 ✓

ACTIVITY

AIM

To turn old stockings into creatures.

MATERIALS

- grass or alfalfa seeds
- old stockings
- scissors
- cotton wool
- saucer
- ribbon, old buttons, wool

Did You Know?

Grass seeds and alfalfa seeds do not need soil to grow like a lot of other plants. Unlike other plants these seeds grow quickly and do not need the nutrients provided by soil. They do need to be kept moist in order to germinate or they will not grow.

STEPS

1. You will only need the end of the stocking where the toes go. Cut the stocking, leaving about 30 cm (12 in).

2. Pour grass seeds into the stocking so they fill the part where the toes would normally be, then fill the stocking with cotton wool until the stocking is a ball shape.

3. Tie the stocking tightly around the cotton wool. Use the scissors to cut off any extra stocking material.

4. Turn the stocking so that the grass seeds are on the top.

5. You can now decorate the stocking to make it look like a face. When the grass grows it will become the hair.

6. Place the stocking on a saucer of water. Place in a sunny spot.

7. The seeds will take a few days to start growing. Make sure the stocking is always damp and if not, water it.

Growing Sprouts

AIM

To grow alfalfa sprouts to eat.

MATERIALS

- alfalfa seeds
- old stockings
- scissors
- rubber band
- small jar
- water

Did You Know?

Alfalfa seeds grow very quickly and are healthy for you. Put them in a sandwich with cheese, in a salad or just pick them and eat them!

STEPS

1. Leave the alfalfa seeds soaking in water overnight in the jar.

2. Remove the seeds from the water.

3. You will only need the end of the stocking where the toes go. Cut the stocking so that it hangs over the top of the jar.

4. Attach the stocking to the top of the jar with the rubber band.

5. Sprinkle the seeds on top of the stocking.

6. Pour water over the seeds so that they are all wet. Let the extra water go into the jar.

7. Place the jar in a dark spot to grow.

8. Let the sprouts grow and pull them off, ready to eat!

EXPERIMENT

377

Growing Seeds

AIM

To grow seedlings.

MATERIALS

- seeds from a packet
- small pots
- soil
- water
- jug
- rubber gloves

Did You Know?

Plants need both water and sun to grow. To test this you can try growing a plant in a dark place or instead of watering the plant with water use cola or cordial and see what happens. The results are not very good!

STEPS

1. You can use whatever seeds you like. It depends what you would like to grow.

2. Wearing the rubber gloves, fill the pot with soil until it almost reaches the top. Put in one or two seeds so that they are not next to each other. Do not put in too many seeds.

3. Cover the seeds with a thin layer of soil (about the thickness of your thumbnail).

4. Place the pot on a saucer of water using the jug.

5. Place the pot in a sunny place and wait for the seeds to grow.

Is a Spider an Insect?

5–12
AGES

 ✓

 ✓

SUPERVISED

 ✓
 ✓

✓

ACTIVITY

AIM

To classify insects and spiders.

MATERIALS

- dead spider (ask an adult to make sure) or a toy spider. Do not pick up a live spider. It may be poisonous.

Did You Know?

An insect is a creature with six legs. Although a spider is not an insect they do share some of the same body parts. Both insects and spiders do not have a separate head. Their head is part of their body called the 'thorax'. The bottom part of their body is called the 'abdomen'.

STEPS

1. Carefully count the number of legs on the spider.

2. There should be eight (if there is less some may have fallen off).

3. Insects have six legs. So a spider is not an insect.

EXPERIMENT

379

Buzzy Bees

SUPERVISED

ACTIVITY

AIM

To see what attracts bees.

MATERIALS

- 5 pieces of strong cardboard, 1 black, 1 white and 3 colours
- drinking straws
- water
- scissors
- sticky tape
- 4 plastic milk caps
- sugar
- cordial
- salt
- notebook
- pencil

Did You Know?

Bees are attracted to the sweetness of the sugar and the cordial. A bright colour also brings more bees to the flowers. You should have observed the bees being drawn towards the coloured flowers rather than the black cardboard and to the caps with the sugar and cordial.

STEPS

1. Cut the cardboard into the shape of flowers with large petals. Make five different coloured flowers.

2. Using the scissors, cut four small slits in one end of the drinking straw. Push this end onto the back of the flowers so it makes a star shape. Use the sticky tape to attach the straw to the cardboard. Repeat so that you have four flowers on the straws.

3. Mix a tiny amount of sugar with water so that it forms a thick paste and place in one of the milk caps. Repeat with the salt. Do not mix the cordial. Just place a tiny amount in a milk cap.

4. Roll up balls of sticky tape and place one ball in the middle of four of the cardboard flowers.

5. Stick the milk caps on the sticky tape. One flower will not have a cap.

6. Place the flowers outside. Observe and record which coloured flower the bees are most attracted to and what is in the cap on that flower.

7. Now swap the caps over to another colour flower. Record the results again.

EXPERIMENT

380

Mosquito Bites

SUPERVISED

ACTIVITY

AIM

To watch what happens when a mosquito bites.

MATERIALS

- magnifying glass
- lamp
- piece of paper
- itchy bite cream (for afterwards)

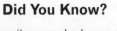

Did You Know?

Mosquitoes are also known as 'blood suckers'! When they land on your skin they use their long noses to prick your skin and suck up your blood. The small prick they make to suck up the blood becomes itchy afterwards.

STEPS

Note: Do not try this experiment if you are allergic to mosquitoes!

1. You will need to do this activity at night. Wear a T-shirt so that the mosquito can get onto your skin.

2. Sit outside near a light or have a lamp on.

3. Wait until the mosquito lands on one of your arms. Quickly pick up the magnifying glass in the opposite hand and bring it up close to the mosquito.

4. Watch closely how it bites you.

5. While it is still there squash it with the piece of paper. What happens?

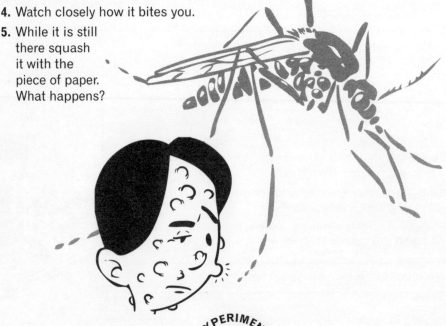

EXPERIMENT

381

How Slow Is a Snail?

 ✓

SUPERVISED

 ✓

 ✓

ACTIVITY

AIM

To work out the speed of a snail.

MATERIALS

- at least one snail (snails come out after the rain or at night)
- measuring tape
- watch or stopwatch
- calculator (or paper and pencil)
- small rock

Did You Know?

Snails leave a slimy trail behind them when they move. This slime helps them move along the ground.

STEPS

1. Place the small rock on the ground. This marks where the snail starts.

2. Put the snail next to the rock and start the stopwatch.

3. Time for two minutes. After two minutes use the measuring tape to measure from the small rock to the snail and record the result.

4. To work out how fast a snail moves per hour multiply how far the snail travelled in two minutes by thirty.

5. If you have more than one snail you may like to repeat the experiment and compare them. Are some snails faster than others?

How Strong is a Snail?

SUPERVISED

ACTIVITY

AIM

To test how strong a snail is.

MATERIALS

- snails
- empty matchboxes
- scissors
- cotton or fine wool
- small rocks

Did You Know?

If you shine a torch on concrete at night, you may see some shiny trails left behind by snails.

STEPS

1. Ask an adult to help you poke some small holes in each side of the matchbox.

2. Cut a small piece of cotton. Thread one end through a hole and tie. Repeat on the opposite side. You now have a cart with a handle.

3. Carefully loop the cotton over the snail's shell so the matchbox is behind the snail.

4. See if the snail can still move and pull the matchbox.

5. Add one rock at a time, seeing how many the snail can pull.

6. If you have many snails you might compare which is the strongest by seeing which snail can pull the most rocks.

Wriggling Worms

AIM

To study what makes worms wriggle.

MATERIALS

- worms in a container of soil
- dry soil
- small lamp or torch
- icy-pole stick
- ice cubes
- newspaper

Did You Know?

Worms always live underground.
They like a damp, dark
environment to live in. Although
they like moisture, the ice is
much too cold for them.

STEPS

1. Spread the newspaper out on
   a table and put all the materials
   on top.

2. Tip the worms out of their container. Pick them out
   of the soil.

3. You are going to use the different materials to see how the worms respond.
   First, push them gently with the icy-pole stick to see their response.

4. Next, shine the torch on them. Then put
   them on the dry soil and see what
   happens. Finally, place them on top
   of the cube of ice.

5. When you have finished
   put the soil back into
   the container and
   watch the worms
   crawl back into the soil.

Blind Ants

AIM

To test if your sense of smell is as strong as an ant's.

MATERIALS

- range of different foods
- blindfold
- partner

STEPS

1. Have your partner blindfold you.
2. Ask them to place the food in different places around the room.
3. Walk around the room using your hands and your nose to see if you can find any of the food. When you find something, pick it up and see if you can work out what it is.
4. This is especially fun if you have not seen the food your partner has chosen. It makes it that little bit harder when you don't know what the foods are.

Did You Know?

Ants live under the ground where it is dark. They have a very strong sense of smell because they cannot see in the dark. They find food by smelling around for it and they bring it back to the queen ants.

EXPERIMENT

385

Catching Ants

AIM

To see what food attracts the most ants.

MATERIALS

- small piece of apple
- piece of bread
- potato
- chopping board
- knife

Did You Know?

Ants are most attracted to the apple. The sweetness of the apple gives off a strong scent that attracts the ants. Even ants know what is good for them!

STEPS

1. Ask an adult to chop the food into pieces.

2. Place a piece of each one in different places around the garden.

3. Observe which one of these foods has the most ants on it.

Making an Ant Colony

 ✓
 ✓

 ✓

SUPERVISED

ACTIVITY

AIM

To build an ant colony.

MATERIALS

- glass jar
- soil
- black paper
- sticky tape
- old stocking material
- scissors
- spoon
- honey
- leaves
- rubber gloves

Did You Know?

Ants live in colonies. Each of the ants has a special job. The queen ant lays the eggs and the other ants find food and bring it to the nest of the queen ant. When they find food they drag it back to the nest, leaving a scent behind, so that the other ants can follow the smell to find more food.

STEPS

1. Wearing the rubber gloves, fill the jar with soil. Lightly water the soil and place the leaves on top.

2. Wrap the black cardboard around the outside of the jar and secure it in place with the sticky tape.

3. Go outside and put some honey on the spoon. Put the spoon on the ground near some ants and wait for the ants to come to the honey. When you have ants on the spoon, gently tap the spoon on top of the jar so that the ants and honey fall on top of the leaves.

4. Place the old stocking over the top of the jar and use the rubber band to hold it in place.

5. Feed the ants each day with fresh fruit and leaves. Make sure the soil is damp.

6. Keep the ant colony in a cool place, away from the sun.

7. After a few days remove the cardboard and look at the jar. You will see winding tunnels through the soil.

Insect Encyclopaedia

AIM

To make a book of photos of different insects in your yard.

MATERIALS

- camera and film (if you have one with a zoom lens this is especially good for magnifying the insects)
- small notebook
- pencil
- guidebook on insects (you can borrow this from your local library)
- large scrapbook
- glue

Did You Know?

Try taking your photographs at different times of the day. For example, moths are easier to find around bright lights at night, as are mosquitoes. Changing weather also affects the insects that are around.

STEPS

1. Walk around the yard with the camera. Go up close to the grass, leaves, flowers, bark and branches looking for different insects. If you have a zoom lens on the camera ask an adult to help you practise using it first.

2. Take a close-up photograph of the insect. Visit different places with different trees and flowers and find different insects.

3. When you have used up the film have the photographs developed.

4. Use your guidebook to help you identify each insect. Stick the photographs into the scrapbook using the glue. Under each photograph write the name of the insect pictured and any information you have found out, such as where you found it and anything interesting you find in the guidebook.

5. This becomes your own encyclopaedia on insects. You can keep adding to it every time you find a new type of insect.

Mini-beasts in a Box

✓

SUPERVISED

 ✓

 ✓

ACTIVITY

AIM

To make a list of living things in a set area.

MATERIALS

- metre (yard) ruler
- small sticks
- string
- scissors
- magnifying glass
- notebook
- pencil

Did You Know?

The creatures inside the square may change, depending upon what is near the area. If it is close to a river, or in the shade, or near a big tree, the living things in the square will be different to those in a square in the middle of a football ground.

STEPS

1. Measure a square with the length of the ruler. Mark each corner by pushing a stick into the ground.

2. Tie the string to each of the sticks so that the string marks the square.

3. Sit outside of the square and use the magnifying glass to observe the mini-beasts inside the square. Use your notebook to write down what you see.

4. You may wish to do this at a park where you can compare different squares. You may find that the insects in the squares change depending upon what is near the area.

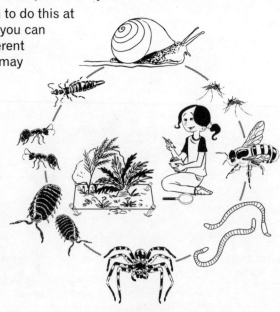

EXPERIMENT

389

Create a New Insect

AIM

To use your knowledge of insects to create a new insect.

MATERIALS

- old boxes and containers from food items
- sticky tape
- paint
- markers
- newspaper
- scissors
- glue
- buttons, pipe cleaners, icy-pole sticks

Did You Know?

Using your imagination is a vital part of science!

STEPS

1. Think about all the things you know about insects – their body parts, their colours used for camouflage and the number of legs they have.

2. Stick the boxes and containers together with the sticky tape to create a new insect.

3. Spread the newspaper on the floor and paint the creature.

4. Leave the paint to dry and then decorate it with the markers and other things that you have collected.

THE PATAGONIAN FLYING TIGER ANT!

Leaf Eaters

 ✓
SUPERVISED

 ✓

 ✓
ACTIVITY

AIM

To observe which animals eat particular leaves.

MATERIALS

- 3 small jars
- clingwrap
- 3 rubber bands
- insects from your backyard or park
- different kinds of leaves (3 each) – if you already know which ones are being eaten pick some of these

Did You Know?

Different insects will eat different leaves. Insects are a bit like humans – we don't all like the same foods and nor do they.

STEPS

1. Collect the insects in a jar and take them home.
2. Place an insect in each jar. Choose one type of leaf at a time. Place one leaf in each jar.
3. Cover the jars with clingwrap and secure with a rubber band. Make sure there are small holes in the cover so that the animals can breathe.
4. Leave the jars for a while. Observe which animals are eating the leaf.
5. Change the leaves over and choose a different type. You can keep repeating this experiment until you have tried all the leaves.

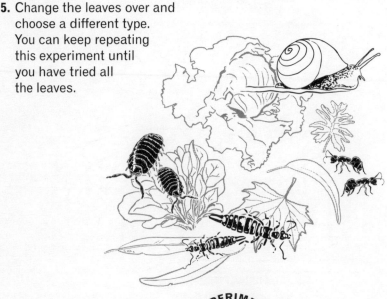

Attracting Moths

AIM

To attract moths with food.

MATERIALS

- sugar
- warm water
- piece of ripe fruit – apricots, peaches or plums
- mixing bowl
- spoon
- fork

Did You Know?

Moths are attracted to the sugar. The ripe fruit has a strong aroma and the moths like the sweetness of both the sugar and the fruit.

STEPS

1. Pour some sugar into a bowl.
2. Ask an adult to add some warm water and stir to dissolve some of the sugar.
3. Add the fruit and use a fork to mash it into the mixture.
4. Go outside and rub the mixture onto some trees.
5. When it is dark, go outside and observe the places you put the mixture.

Moth or Butterfly?

SUPERVISED

ACTIVITY

AIM

To classify butterflies and moths.

MATERIALS

- bug catcher
- magnifying glass
- butterflies and moths

STEPS

1. You may need to do this activity in parts because once you have one butterfly in the bug catcher it is difficult to open it to catch another one without the other escaping.

2. You might also like to use the mixture for attracting moths (Experiment 392) or by planting a butterfly garden (Experiment 394) to help find them.

3. When you catch a butterfly or moth do not be tricked into thinking that just because it has colourful wings that it is a butterfly.

4. Use a magnifying glass to look carefully at its antennae. Butterfly antennae have a thick end, which almost looks like a cotton bud in the magnifying glass. Moths have straight antennae, some with little feathers.

> ### Did You Know?
> There are over 12,000 different species of butterflies and 150,000 species of moths.

Attracting Butterflies

 ✓

SUPERVISED

 ✓

 ✓

ACTIVITY

AIM

To grow a beautiful garden to attract butterflies.

MATERIALS

- small flowers such as pansies
- watering can
- large pot (if you don't have a garden)
- soil
- rubber gloves

Did You Know?

Butterflies and birds are attracted to flowers because they feed off them. They are attracted by the nectar on the plant which you can see them drinking. The nectar on these plants is very sweet for the animals.

STEPS

1. Wearing the rubber gloves, fill the pot with soil until it almost reaches the top.

2. Plant the flowers in the pot, making sure you leave lots of room between each flower so that they can grow.

3. Make sure that the roots are covered.

4. Place the pot outside in a sunny spot and make sure to keep watering it.

5. The flowers will attract beautiful butterflies.

Making a Butterfly

AIM

To hatch caterpillars into butterflies.

MATERIALS

- glass aquarium with a glass lid
- wide sticky tape
- glass jar
- water
- leaves on branches
- caterpillars

Did You Know?

The correct name for the caterpillar in this process is the larva. It produces the pupa (the cocoon) and from this hatches a butterfly. Butterflies lay eggs. Can you guess what hatches from a butterfly's egg? Yes, that's right, a caterpillar!

STEPS

Note: When choosing leaves for this experiment look for ones that have been eaten by caterpillars already. This way you know they are leaves the caterpillars like to eat.

1. Stand the aquarium lengthways.
2. Fill the jar with water and place the branches in the jar and put it inside the aquarium.
3. Place the caterpillars on the leaves.
4. Ask an adult to help you put the lid on and use the sticky tape to hold it in place.
5. Leave the aquarium. This experiment will take a long time to complete. You will need to watch the leaves. When they are eaten replace them with fresh branches from the same plant. When the caterpillars become fat they will make their cocoon. The cocoon will begin to move when the butterfly is ready to come out.

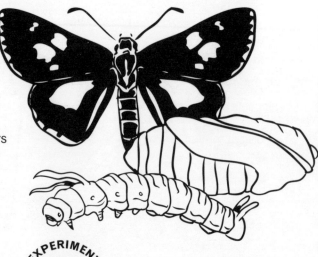

Colour Control

SUPERVISED

ACTIVITY

AIM

To see if growing caterpillars in different coloured environments results in different coloured pupa.

MATERIALS

- caterpillars on their leaves
- leaves on the branches
- 3 small bowls of water
- 3 empty shoe boxes
- brown and green paint
- paintbrushes
- newspaper
- scissors

Did You Know?

The colour of the butterflies is not related to the colour of the home it is brought up in. The colours are due to the type of butterfly it is, rather than the colours around it. Like humans not being able to choose the colour of their skin, butterflies cannot choose their colours.

STEPS

1. Make sure that you collect all the caterpillars from the same type of tree. The leaves should also be from that tree. This way you know that these are leaves the caterpillars like.

2. Put the newspaper down on the floor. Paint the inside of one of the shoe boxes and its lid brown. Paint another one green. Leave one as it is.

3. When the paint is dry, place the branches and water inside the boxes.

4. Place the caterpillars on the leaves inside each of the boxes.

5. Ask an adult to help you put the lid on and use the sticky tape to hold it in place. Use the scissors to poke a few holes in each box.

6. This activity will take a long time to complete. You will need to watch the leaves and when they are eaten replace them with fresh branches from the same plant.

7. Observe any differences between the caterpillars, pupa, and butterflies produced in each box.

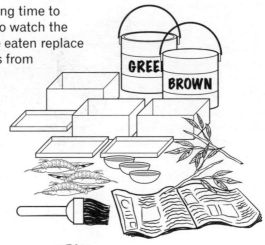

EXPERIMENT

396

Growing Silkworms

 ✓

 ✓

 ✓

AIM

To watch silkworms hatch.

MATERIALS

- shoe box with a lid
- scissors
- mulberry leaves
- silkworms

Did You Know?

Silkworms are very fussy eaters. They will ONLY eat mulberry leaves. So if you want this experiment to work do not try and feed them anything else. They will not touch other leaves and will starve. Are you this fussy with your food? Imagine only eating one thing all day everyday!

STEPS

1. Use the scissors to poke small holes in the lid of the shoebox. Do not make them too big or the silkworms will crawl out!

2. Put the silkworms and mulberry leaves inside the box.

3. Place the lid back on the box.

4. The experiment will take a few weeks so you will need to continually replace the leaves.

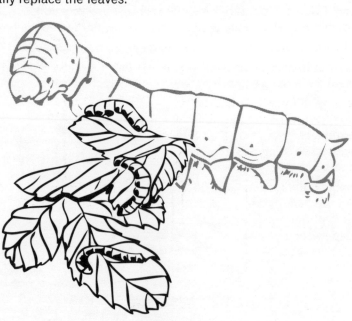

Pond in a Jar

✓

SUPERVISED

✓

ACTIVITY

AIM

To observe living things from a pond.

MATERIALS

- large jar with a lid
- stick, slightly shorter than the jar
- small spade
- measuring jug or plastic bottle
- magnifying glass
- pond (go with an adult)

Did You Know?

The stick is there because some of the creatures that live in ponds don't always stay in the water. Can you think of any animals that you know of that live on land and water? Frogs are one of them and you may find them at the pond.

STEPS

1. Use the spade to fill the bottom of your jar with mud from the pond.
2. Carefully take some plants from the water (ask an adult to help you) and plant them in the mud.
3. Fill the bottle or measuring jug with water from the pond. Pour it against the side of the jar. Fill to a little less than halfway.
4. Place the stick in the jar and seal the lid.
5. Leave in a shady place and add water if you notice your 'pond' drying up.
6. Use your magnifying glass to observe what is growing and moving inside the jar and see if you can identify some of the living things.

EXPERIMENT

398

Growing Tadpoles

5–12
AGES

✓

SUPERVISED

✓

✓

ACTIVITY

AIM

To watch tadpoles grow into frogs.

MATERIALS

- large clear plastic container or aquarium
- large plastic sheet (to cover the container)
- large jar with a lid
- pond water and some pond plants
- tadpoles (you can get these at the pond)
- small sticks

Did You Know?

The tadpoles do not change straight from a tadpole into a frog overnight. The first thing you will notice is that they lose their tails, then start to grow legs. Watch very carefully because once they have front and back legs they can jump and get away.

STEPS

1. Look for tadpoles in the water at the pond. (Take an adult with you.) Use the jar to scoop them up in the water. Make sure your jar is filled with water. You may even need more to fill your container (it is really important to use only pond water and not water from a tap).

2. At home pour the water and the tadpoles into the large plastic container or aquarium. Put the pond plants in the water. Place the sticks in the container so that they lean against the side and poke out of the water.

3. Cover the top of the container with the lid, leaving a small space for the tadpoles to breathe.

4. Watch the changes over time as the tadpoles change into frogs. Remember to keep the lid on or one day your frogs might escape.

EXPERIMENT

399

Feeding the Birds

AIM

To make food to attract the birds.

MATERIALS

- animal fat
- oats
- breadcrumbs
- chopped nuts
- seeds such as pumpkin seeds
- long piece of string
- plastic cup
- mixing bowl
- spoon

Did You Know?

This bird cake will attract different types of birds. Find a book with different birds and see which ones are eating your food.

Note: You can use packet birdseed in this experiment in place of the breadcrumbs, seeds and nuts. You will still need the oats to make it thick.

STEPS

1. Ask an adult to melt the fat for you in the microwave oven or a saucepan.

2. In the mixing bowl put half a cup of each ingredient. Mix them together, then add the lard. The mixture should be like soggy cereal, but not too runny. If there is too much liquid from the fat, add more oats.

3. Tie a big knot in the end of the string and put the knotted end in the bottom of the cup. Hang the string over the side of the cup.

4. Make sure the string does not fall into the cup. Pour the oat mixture into it, then push down hard so that there is no air.

5. Move the string into the middle of the cup and put it in the refrigerator to set.

6. When the mixture is solid push on the bottom of the cup and the mixture should come out as a 'bird cake'. If you cannot get it out, try pulling on the string or get an adult to run the cup under warm water for a minute.

7. Tie the string to a branch in a tree and wait for the birds to come.

Making a Bird Feeder

AIM

To build a bird feeder to attract birds.

MATERIALS

- empty milk carton
- string
- scissors
- birdseed

Did You Know?

You may find that some birds are too big for your bird feeder. Next time you could use something heavier or get an adult to build one out of wood.

STEPS

1. Cut the top half off the milk carton. You must make sure that the bottom part (that you are going to use) is clean and dry.

2. Use the scissors to poke a hole in each side of the carton. The holes must be near the top of the carton and in the middle of each side.

3. Cut two pieces of string the same length. Thread one end of the string through a hole and tie it tightly. Now take the other end of this piece of string and tie it to the hole on the opposite side of the carton. Repeat with the other piece of string, tying it to the other holes.

4. Now fill your bird feeder with birdseed and take it outside. Hang the feeder over a branch on a tree and watch the birds come to feed. Make sure it is high enough off the ground so that cats cannot jump at the birds.

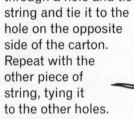

Observing Birds Feeding

 ✓

 ✓

 ✓

AIM

To observe how birds use their beaks to feed.

MATERIALS

- pencil
- notebook

STEPS

1. Sit in your backyard or park and watch the birds.

2. Observe how they eat. Some birds will open their beaks first while some will stick their beaks into the food.

3. Draw a beak on your paper and write how a bird with a beak that shape eats.

Did You Know?

Birds in different places will have different shaped beaks based on the food available. Over time the beaks have changed so that they can eat to survive in their environment.

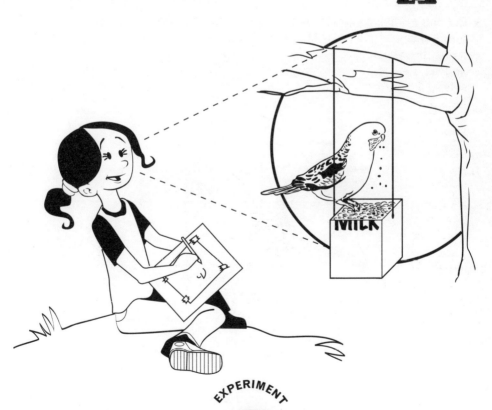

MILK

EXPERIMENT

402

Making a Birdbath

AIM

To make a birdbath.

MATERIALS

- large plastic container (an old ice-cream container is fine)
- permanent markers
- water
- old bread crusts

Did You Know?

Rainbow Lorikeets only have one mating partner for life!

STEPS

1. Use the permanent markers to decorate your container or birdbath. Draw flowers and insects so that your birdbath looks pretty in the yard.
2. Fill the container with water.
3. Put some small pieces of bread in the water. This will give the birds something to eat.
4. Place the container outside, in a tree if you can. Wait and see who visits.

EXPERIMENT

403

Identifying Birds

5–12
AGES

 ✓
 ✓

SUPERVISED

 ✓

 ✓

ACTIVITY

AIM

To sketch and make notes about birds to identify them.

MATERIALS

- small notebook
- pencil
- colouring pencils
- guidebook on birds
  (you can borrow this
  from your local library)

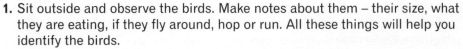

Did You Know?

There are about 9000 different kinds of birds. Can you imagine seeing all of them?

STEPS

Note: This is a good experiment to do if you have built the bird feeder (Experiment 401). If not, you can just observe birds in the park.

1. Sit outside and observe the birds. Make notes about them – their size, what they are eating, if they fly around, hop or run. All these things will help you identify the birds.

2. Draw pictures of the birds you see. Use your colouring pencils to show the colours. This helps you match the pictures in the book.

3. Match your drawing and notes to find the birds in the guidebook. You might even find out some more interesting facts about the birds.

4. Try doing this at different times of the day, in different weather and in different seasons. What things do you notice? Are there different birds at different times?

5. Change the food in the feeder and see if different types of birds come.

6. If you visit new places far from your home, see if you notice other types of birds.

Bird Encyclopaedia

 ✓

SUPERVISED

 ✓

 ✓

ACTIVITY

AIM

To make a book of photos of different birds.

MATERIALS

- camera and film
- small notebook
- pencil
- guidebook on birds (you can borrow this from your local library)
- large scrapbook
- glue

Did You Know?

This encyclopaedia is especially useful after you have returned the guide to the library. You are left with your own special book with information and photographs to easily identify the birds that visit your yard. You can do this for the insects that visit your yard as well.

STEPS

Note: You might like to make a bird feeder (see Experiment 401) to attract birds to your yard.

1. Sit outside and observe the birds. Make notes about them – their size, what they are eating, if they fly around, hop or run. All these things will help you identify the birds. Make notes about the colours to help you identify the photographs.

2. Take photographs of the birds.

3. When you have used up the film (you might like to go to lots of different places and find different birds), have the photographs developed.

4. Match your photographs and notes. Use your guidebook to identify the birds.

5. Glue the photographs into the scrapbook. Write the name of the birds and any information you have found out under the photos.

6. This makes your own encyclopaedia on birds. You can keep adding to it every time you find a new type of bird.

Bird Calls

AIM

To record the sounds of birds.

MATERIALS

- small tape recorder
- batteries
- tape
- notebook
- pencil

Did You Know?

Some birds can talk. Birds such as a cockatoo can be taught to say some words, like humans. Say 'hello cocky' to a cockatoo and more than likely it will say 'hello cocky' back!

STEPS

1. Ask an adult to help you put the batteries in the tape player and show you how to record on it.

2. Walk around outside and record the bird sounds you hear. Make notes in your notebook of any birds you know. This helps you remember which birds were making the sounds.

3. This is a fun experiment to do with a friend to see if they can recognise the sounds of any birds. It is quite tricky.

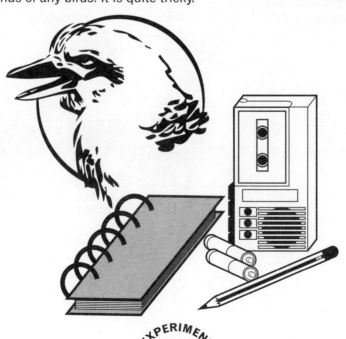

EXPERIMENT

406

Making a Bird Caller

5–12
AGES

✓

SUPERVISED

✓

✓

ACTIVITY

AIM

To make a bird caller to attract birds.

MATERIALS

- drinking straw
- scissors

STEPS

Did You Know?

A bird's diet is related to the things it not only likes, but also what it is able to pick up with its beak.

1. Squeeze one end of a drinking straw flat.

2. Use the scissors to cut this flattened end into a point. (For this to work the pointed end must be very flat.)

3. Put the pointed end in your mouth and blow hard. A very funny noise should come out.

4. You may notice birds looking at you wondering what type of bird you are!

Bird Beaks

AIM
To look at different types of bird beaks.

MATERIALS
- kitchen tongs
- tweezers
- pegs
- toothpicks

STEPS
1. Go into the backyard or the park to do this experiment.

2. Using each of the materials ('beaks') see what things you can pick up.

3. Make a list of the things you were able to pick up with each 'beak'.

Did You Know?
It is impossible for a small sparrow to pick up a fish, whereas a pelican, which has a large beak, can take a whole fish in its mouth.

Design a Beak for You!

SUPERVISED

ACTIVITY

AIM

To design and make a beak to pick up your favourite food with.

MATERIALS

- old boxes and containers from food items
- sticky tape
- scissors
- your favourite food

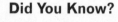

Did You Know?

Humans don't need beaks. We are lucky enough to have arms and hands to help us to pick up food and eat. Other animals, like squirrels, also pick up their food and hold it to nibble on. They also have strong teeth so they can eat hard foods, like acorns.

STEPS

1. You will need to think carefully about your favourite food – is it soft, crumbly or hard? If you poke something into it will it fall apart? Is it big or small? Is it wet or dry? All these things will change how you design your beak.

2. Come up with a design in your head. You may like to draw it on paper first.

3. Use the materials to design your beak. Use lots of tape so that it is really strong.

4. When it is finished, test your beak by trying to see if you can pick up your favourite food. Yummy!

Animal Behaviour

AIM

To observe what animals do all day.

MATERIALS

- notebook
- pencil
- watch or a stopwatch
- animals – observing a pet is a good experiment. If you do not have a pet ask someone you know if you can observe his or her pet.

Did You Know?

Cats spend most of their day sleeping. In fact, most cats spend around 14 hours a day sleeping.

STEPS

1. Sit where you can see the animal but will not disturb it.
2. Start timing the animal when it begins a new activity. List the activity and how long it did it for in your notebook.
3. The animal may move quickly from one activity to another (like a bee) or it may spend a long time doing one activity (like cats do sleeping).
4. Observe as many animals as you can.
5. Compare your results. Which animals spend more time sleeping? Eating? Running? Flying?

SOME ANIMAL BEHAVIOUR ISN'T TOO EXCITING

Guard Dogs

SUPERVISED

ACTIVITY

AIM

To see if you can hear as well as a dog.

MATERIALS

- blindfold
- partner or group of people

STEPS

1. Secure the blindfold around your head.

2. If you are playing with a group of people have them hide around the room. If there is only one other person have them move to a space in the room.

3. Each person must make a small sound so you can find them. They can also move around the room as you get closer to them.

4. See if you can catch each person.

5. You may play this game where the person hiding does not make a sound at all. You will have to see if you can hear them walking in order to find them.

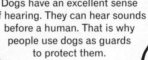

Did You Know?

Dogs have an excellent sense of hearing. They can hear sounds before a human. That is why people use dogs as guards to protect them.

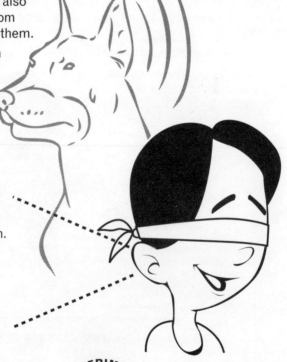

EXPERIMENT

411

Farm Animals

SUPERVISED

ACTIVITY

AIM

To sort and classify farm animals.

MATERIALS

- packet of plastic farm animals or magazine pictures

STEPS

1. Place all the animals on the floor.
2. Sort them into different groups. Ask the following questions:
   - how many legs do they have?
   - where do they live on a farm?
   - what do they eat?
   - do they provide us with food?
   - do they provide us with anything else, such as leather or wool?
3. Can you think of other ways to sort these animals?

Did You Know?

Animals give us food – beef, lamb, pork, chicken and eggs. We use the wool from sheep to make nice warm clothing and blankets, and the leather from a cowhide to make shoes and belts. Farms are very important to us.

Smelling Like a Shark

AIM

To test if your sense of smell is as strong as a shark's.

MATERIALS

- 3 large drinking glasses
- measuring jug
- water
- perfume (essential oils such as lavender work well also)
- marker

Did You Know?

Sharks have an amazing sense of smell that helps them hunt their prey. Even the glass marked '1 drop' is still 50 times the minimum a shark could smell.

STEPS

1. Label the glasses – '10 drops', '5 drops' and '1 drop'.

2. Fill the glasses with 500 ml (2 cups) of water.

3. In the glass marked '10 drops' place 10 drops of perfume. Repeat with the other glasses (5 drops and 1 drop).

4. Swirl them around to mix the water and the perfume.

5. Now smell each glass. Which has the strongest smell?

EXPERIMENT

413

Balloon Lungs

AIM

To build a model showing how human and animals breathe.

MATERIALS

- 2 bendable drinking straws
- sticky tape
- 2 balloons

Did You Know?

Humans and animals breathe using their lungs. The balloons in this experiment represent your lungs. When you breathe in (inhale) they fill with air and when you breathe out (exhale) they push the air back out. Your mouth and throat are linked to a pipe, which leads to your two lungs.

STEPS

1. Stand the two straws side by side so that the bendable sections are next to each other.

2. Use the sticky tape to stick half of the straws together, not going past the bendable section. Sticky tape them lightly so as not to block or squash the straws. You should now be able to bend part of each straw away from the other so that the make the shape of the letter 'Y'.

3. Seal a balloon to the end of each straw with the sticky tape. Make sure there are no holes or the air will escape.

4. Now blow into the top of the two straws. The balloons should inflate (blow up). If they do not, you may not have sealed the balloons to the straws tightly enough.

5. Breathe in. The balloons should deflate.

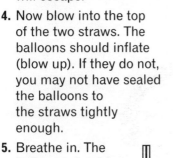

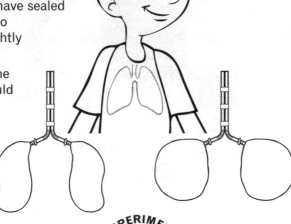

Footprint Detectives

AIM

To find and identify different animal footprints.

MATERIALS

- nothing – just your eyes!

STEPS

1. You can do this experiment at the beach or in a park.

2. Carefully walk around, looking at the ground. See if you can find some footprints.

3. Try to identify the animal these footprints belong to.

4. Look to see whether the footprints are closer or further apart in some places. Can you guess if the animal was walking or running?

Did You Know?

Not all animals leave footprints. Some animals move by sliding and it is harder to know where they have been. When snails slide they leave behind a shiny trail. See if you can come up with a list of animals that slide.

Footprints

AIM

To make plaster casts of animal footprints.

MATERIALS

- plaster of Paris (ready to pour)
- cardboard
- stapler
- beach or park

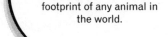

Did You Know?

Elephants have the largest footprint of any animal in the world.

STEPS

1. Make some cardboard strips and staple the two ends of each together so they make rings.

2. Go to the beach or park. Ask an adult to go with you.

3. Carefully walk around, looking at the ground. See if you can find some footprints.

4. Place the cardboard ring around the footprint. Pour the plaster into the ring.

5. You will need to wait until the plaster is almost set, then using a stick, write on the back of the plaster the animal the footprint belongs to.

6. When the plaster has set hard, remove the cardboard, lift the plaster up and dust off any extra dirt or sand.

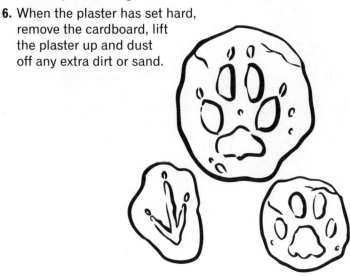

EXPERIMENT

Is It Alive?

5–12
AGES

 ✓

SUPERVISED

 ✓
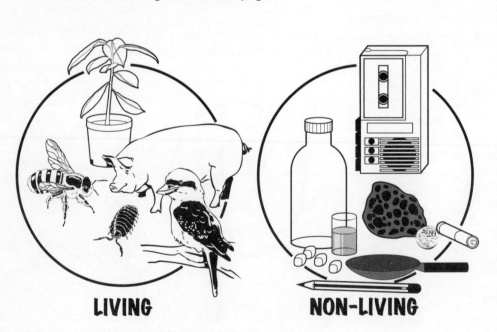 ✓

ACTIVITY

AIM

To classify things as living or non-living.

MATERIALS

- large sheets of paper
- scissors
- glue
- old magazines
- markers

Did You Know?

Although we can't see them breathing, plants and trees are living things. Try Experiment 367 where you test to see if plants breathe if you don't believe it!

STEPS

1. Draw a line down the middle of your page. On the top of one half write 'living' and on the other half write 'non-living'.

2. Cut out pictures from magazines and decide if they are living or non-living things. Stick them onto the right half of the page.

LIVING   NON-LIVING

Classifying Animals

AIM

To classify animals into groups.

MATERIALS

- old magazines
- scissors

STEPS

Did You Know?

Every animal is unique in some way, just like humans. And just like humans, there are some things the same, such as their likes and dislikes and the number of legs they have.

1. Cut out all the pictures of animals you can find in the magazines.

2. Decide how you are going to sort and classify these animals. You can choose to sort them by the number of legs they have; where they live; what country they are from; whether they are carnivores or herbivores; whether they are fast or slow, land or sea animals and so on. There are hundreds of ways you could sort these animals.

3. Play this game with a friend. Sort them and ask your friend to guess how you classified the animals. Swap over. See if you can trick your friend with something like marsupial or monotreme.

Physics

A Home-made Stethoscope

AIM

To see how sound waves can travel through enclosed spaces.

MATERIALS

- 2 funnels
- length of garden hose about 40 cm (16 in) in length
- plasticine

STEPS

1. Place one of the funnels into one end of the garden hose. If it doesn't fit tightly, secure it with some plasticine.

2. Repeat this process with the other end of the hose.

3. Place one end of the funnel over your heart and the other over your ear. What can you hear?

Did You Know?

A stethoscope can measure the rate of your heart and find out if you are healthy. It is a sound amplifier that carries the sound along the pipe to your ears.

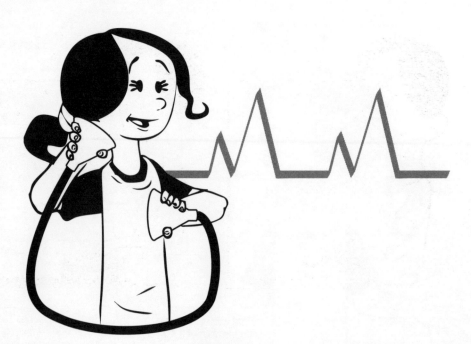

Who's got the Fastest Car?

5–12
AGES

SUPERVISED

ACTIVITY

AIM

To look at the effects of friction on different surfaces.

MATERIALS

- long strip of sandpaper
- long smooth piece of wood
- long stretch of smooth carpet
- small toy car

Did You Know?

Cars skid on wet roads because the water on the surface creates less friction between the wheels and the road.

STEPS

1. Take the toy car and push it along the surface of the wood.
2. Now push the toy car along the strip of sandpaper.
3. Now push the toy car along the carpet. On which surface does your car run the smoothest?

EXPERIMENT
420

Which Parachute?

AIM

To look at how different materials affect air resistance.

MATERIALS

- plastic bag
- 12 pieces of string, each 35 cm (14 in) long
- plasticine
- handkerchief
- piece of paper, the same size as the handkerchief
- scissors
- hole punch
- stopwatch

Did You Know?

Very strong nylon makes the best parachute material because it is light and flexible. The material that makes up the top of the parachute is called the canopy.

STEPS

1. Take the plastic bag and cut it into a 30 cm (12 in) square. Tie four pieces of string to each corner of the square. Attach the string to a large blob of plasticine.

2. Take the handkerchief and tie four pieces of string to each corner. Attach the string to a large blob of plasticine.

3. Take the paper, punch a hole in each corner and tie four pieces of string to each corner. Attach the string to a large blob of plasticine.

4. Stand on a chair and drop each parachute. Record the times for each parachute from letting go until it hits the ground.

EXPERIMENT
421

What's That Noise?

AIM

To see how sound waves can be collected and directed.

MATERIALS

- large piece of paper
- sticky tape
- radio
- friend

Did You Know?

In the past, instead of using hearing aids people who had trouble hearing would use ear trumpets. If someone wanted to say something to them, they would speak into the large end of the ear trumpet. This way they could be heard by the person who had trouble hearing. Today we use hearing aids to help with hearing.

STEPS

1. Roll the paper to make one large opening and one small opening. Tape the paper to make a sound funnel.

2. Put the small end of the sound funnel to your ear. (Do not put it in your ear.) What can you hear?

3. Now stand near the radio with the funnel to your ear. What do you notice? Take the funnel away. Is the sound different?

4. Ask your friend to make some soft rustling and moving noises while you hold the funnel to your ear. Can you hear the very soft sounds? (It is important that no loud sounds are put through the sound funnel as it could damage your hearing.)

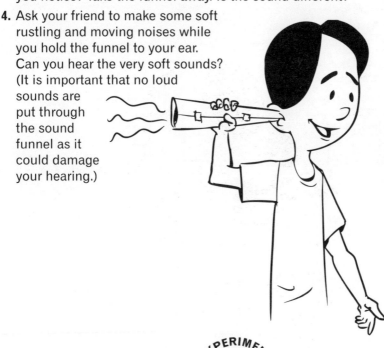

EXPERIMENT 422

My Magnetic House?

SUPERVISED

ACTIVITY

AIM

To discover everyday magnetic objects.

MATERIALS

- any items around your house such as forks, spoons, paper clips, aluminium foil, pencil, toy cars, soft toys
- magnet

Did You Know?

There are five planets with magnetic fields in our solar system. They are Earth, Neptune, Jupiter, Uranus and Saturn.

STEPS

1. Organise your testing items into two groups: items that you think are magnetic and those you think are not magnetic.
2. Test the items. If the magnet attaches to the object, it is magnetic.
3. Write a list of the items that are magnetic.

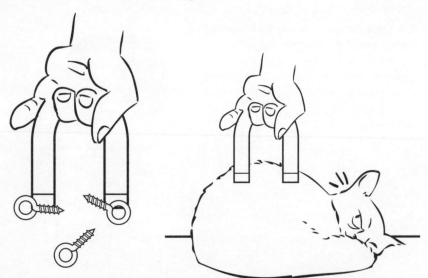

SCREWS = MAGNETIC   CAT = NOT MAGNETIC
(AND PROBABLY NOT A GOOD IDEA)

EXPERIMENT
423

Watch This!

AIM

To demonstrate the quality of inertia (keeping still, unless something is pushing or pulling you).

MATERIALS

- a piece of cloth with no hems to cover a table with straight edges
- heavy spoons, forks and knives
- plates and cups with smooth bases
- table on a carpeted floor

Did You Know?

Isaac Newton investigated the qualities of inertia and found that objects must have force applied to them to move. The objects on the table don't move because the force is not acting on the objects but rather on the cloth.

STEPS

1. Lay the cloth on the table.
2. Set the table with the utensils, plates and cups close to the edge of the cloth.
3. Hold the cloth with two hands and pull quickly down and away. Keep the cloth parallel and don't pull one side more than another.
4. Keep trying until you get the cloth out from under the objects. Try adding more objects after this.

EXPERIMENT
424

Unusual Pendulum

SUPERVISED

ACTIVITY

AIM

To see how pendulums move.

MATERIALS

- string
- plasticine
- sunglasses
- friend

STEPS

1. Attach the string to a good sized blob of plasticine.

2. Hold the string in your hand and let the pendulum swing.

3. Ask your friend to hold the sunglasses over their right eye. Ask them to tell you what is happening.

4. Now ask your friend to hold the sunglasses over their left eye. Ask them to tell you what is happening.

Did You Know?

This is an illusion. Did you notice that when the sunglasses are held over the left eye the pendulum appears to be moving in a clockwise direction, and opposite for the right eye?

RIGHT EYE COVERED   **LEFT EYE COVERED**

EXPERIMENT
425

Turning Inside a Balloon

SUPERVISED

ACTIVITY

AIM

To see how an object turns within a confined space.

MATERIALS

- clear balloon
- 5 cent coin

STEPS

1. Place the coin inside the balloon and blow the balloon up. Be careful not to overblow the balloon and make it too stretched. Tie the end of the balloon.

2. Hold the tied end of the balloon like a bowling ball.

3. Start to turn the balloon around quickly in a circle.

4. Feel the coin starting to move around in a circular path. Then hold the balloon still and let the coin keep moving. Why do you think this is happening? Why does the coin have this kind of path?

Did You Know?

The spinning coin is like a spinning top. A spinning top stays upright because of the forces of energy that keep it there. The same effect is happening with the coin inside the balloon. An inward force is making it travel in a circular way.

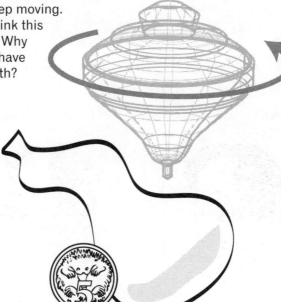

Turn It Up

 ✓

 ✓

 ✓

AIM

To see how sound can be amplified.

MATERIALS

- large piece of strong cardboard
- friend
- sticky tape

Did You Know?

The sound that came out of the cone is amplified – that is, increased in volume. This is how megaphones work.

STEPS

1. Roll up the piece of cardboard so that you have a large hole at one end and a small hole at the other end about the size of your mouth.

2. Tape the cardboard together so that it stays in place.

3. Now ask your friend to stand at a distance so that you have to shout for them to hear you. Say something nice to your friend.

4. Put the small end of the cardboard cone to your mouth. Shout something to your friend. Can your friend hear you better? Why do you think this happened?

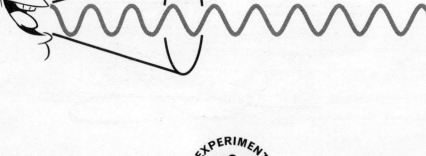

Tinkling

AIM

To show how sound vibrates.

MATERIALS

- coat hanger
- string about 60 cm (2 ft) in length
- metal objects, e.g. fork, spoon, metal ruler

STEPS

1. Take the string and make a loop.

2. Tie the string to the coat hanger so that the coat hanger is in the middle of the string and you have two strands to tie to your fingers.

3. Wrap the strands around a finger on each hand.

4. Knock the coat hanger on a table. What sound can you hear?

5. Now put your hands over your ears (not in your ears). Knock the coat hanger against the table. What can you hear now? Try this with other metal objects.

Did You Know?

When you put your hands over your ears, you create a path for the sound waves to travel. The sound you heard when you had your hands over your ears was more resonant than the sound you made before.

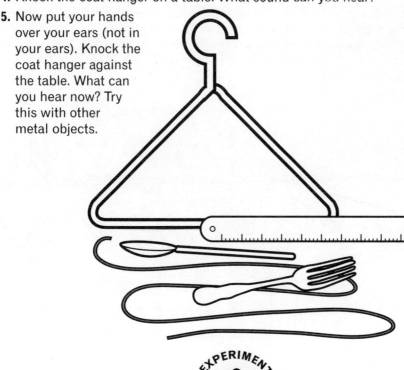

The Matchbox Guitar

5–12
AGES

✓

SUPERVISED

✓

✓

ACTIVITY

AIM

To see how stringed instruments work.

MATERIALS

- empty matchbox
- 4 rubber bands
- small piece of balsa wood
- craft knife

Did You Know?

Traditionally, guitar strings were made from cat intestines. These days they are made from nylon, bronze and steel.

STEPS

1. Cut the piece of balsa wood into a flat triangular shape so that its length is a little longer than the width of the matchbox.

2. Place the triangle across the width of the matchbox so that the pointed end is hanging over. You don't need the piece that is hanging over, so cut it off. Now you have what is called the 'bridge'.

3. Lay the bridge on the closed matchbox and open it up so that it is about three-quarters open.

4. Put the rubber bands over the matchbox lengthways and space them evenly. Make sure the rubber bands are tight. This can be done by opening the matchbox a little more.

5. Raise your bridge so that it stands up. Play your guitar.

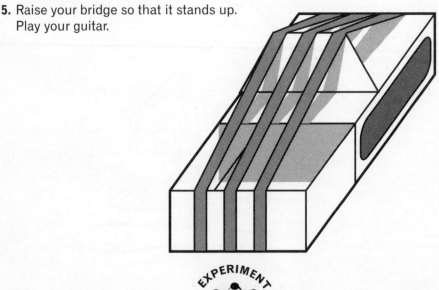

The Boxing Kangaroos

AIM

To see how heat rises and is a force.

MATERIALS

- large piece of thin cardboard
- ruler
- 2 bamboo skewers
- string
- sticky tape
- pencil
- scissors
- oil heater or radiator

Did You Know?

Electricity is produced by a similar method. Coal is burnt which heats water. The heated water creates steam and heat, which turns huge turbines and by further process produces electricity.

STEPS

1. Draw four kangaroos on the cardboard and cut them out.

2. Take the bamboo skewers and make a cross. Sticky tape the skewers together in the middle.

3. Cut four equal lengths of string about 10–15 cm (4–6 in). Attach each kangaroo to a piece of string with sticky tape. Then tie the other end of the string on each of the bamboo arms.

4. Cut a length of string about 10 cm (4 in) long and attach one end to the ruler and tie the other end to the middle of the bamboo sticks.

5. Hold the mobile over a heater in your home. Can you see evidence of the way the air is moving?

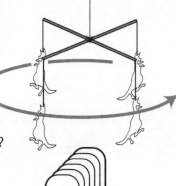

The Amazing Jumping Men

AIM

To see the relationship between electricity and magnets.

MATERIALS

- large long screw
- insulated wire
- C-cell battery
- pliers
- box of paperclips
- coloured lightweight paper
- scissors
- coloured pens

Did You Know?

Electromagnets are different to other magnets because the magnet is created by the electric current. If the electric current is taken away, it stops the metal from being magnetic.

STEPS

1. Draw some small people on the coloured paper. Cut them out and attach a paperclip to each one.

2. Cut a piece of insulation wire and strip about 15 cm (6 in) insulation from the wire then twist the exposed wires into one.

3. Wrap it around the screw 10–15 times.

4. Connect the two ends of the wire to the two ends of the battery. Now you have made an electromagnet.

5. See if you can get the paperclips to attach to your electromagnet.

Stickin' to the Outline

SUPERVISED

ACTIVITY

AIM

To draw an outline of a friend's face using light and shadow.

MATERIALS

- bright torch
- large piece of stiff paper
- dark room
- friend
- marker pen
- chair

Did You Know?

This kind of shadow, which shows the outline around an object, is called a silhouette.

STEPS

1. Put the chair against a wall.
2. Ask your friend to sit in the chair sideways.
3. Tape paper to the wall behind your friend's head.
4. Set up the torch so that it shines on the paper to make a crisp shadow.
5. Use the marker pen to trace the outline of your friend's head.

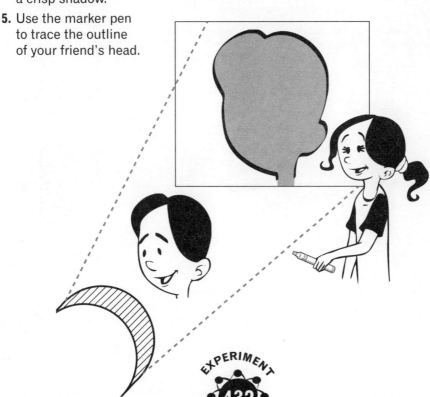

EXPERIMENT
432

Standing in the Shadows

 ✓

SUPERVISED

 ✓
 ✓

ACTIVITY

AIM

To investigate shadows and see how they work.

MATERIALS

- torch
- white wall
- dark room
- 2 friends

STEPS

1. Darken the room.
2. Set up the torch so that it shines onto the white wall.
3. Invite your two friends to stand in the light. Ask one to stand close to the wall and the other to stand closer to the light. Whose shadow is bigger?
4. Ask them to change positions. What happens to the shadows on the wall? Whose shadow is bigger now? Why do you think this is happening?

Did You Know?

A shadow is made when light cannot pass through an object. The closer the object is to the light, the larger the object becomes.

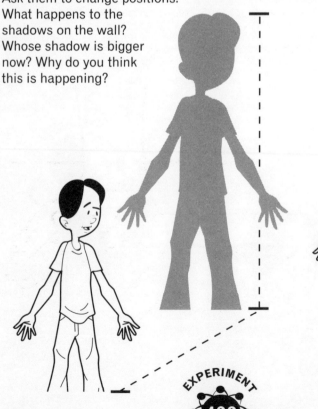

Snappy Ruler

AIM

To see how simple objects can make interesting sounds.

MATERIALS

- plastic or metal ruler
- table edge

STEPS

1. Take the ruler and place it so that half is on the table and half is off the table.

2. Firmly hold the part of the ruler that is on the table. Use your other hand to pull down on the part of the ruler that is off the table.

3. Let go and listen to the sound. Keep repeating this action. Can you make higher sounds and lower sounds by moving the ruler? Why is this happening?

Did You Know?

When an object vibrates through the air, particles bang into each other and sound is produced. Pitch is how high or how low a sound is. When the ruler vibrates at a slower speed, the air particles around it are not so agitated and so the sound is at a lower pitch.

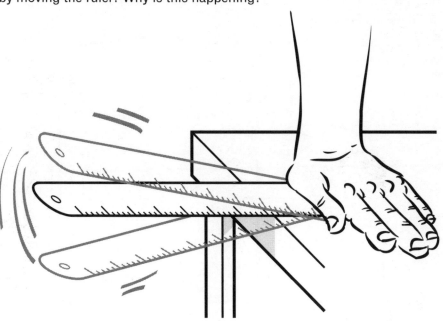

EXPERIMENT 434

Slippery Snake

 ✓
 ✓

AIM

To show how magnets work through glass.

MATERIALS

- paperclips
- plasticine
- large glass jar
- magnets

STEPS

Did You Know?

Magnets have two poles, a north and south pole. Each pole is on the end of the magnet.

1. Use the plasticine to make a colourful snake about 5–6 cm (2–2½ in) long.

2. Place two paperclips, one on top of the other, into the back of the snake.

3. Place the snake in the glass jar so that the paperclips are close to the inside wall of the jar.

4. Make your snake slither by holding the magnet on the outside of the jar and moving the magnet up and down.

5. What is happening?

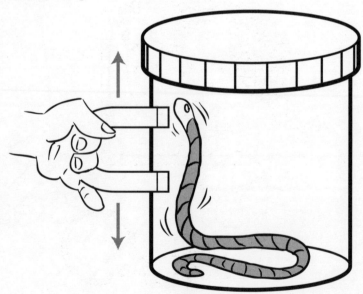

Seeing Double

SUPERVISED

ACTIVITY

AIM

To observe multiple images made with reflection.

MATERIALS

- hand-held mirror
- bathroom mirror

STEPS

1. Stand in front of the bathroom mirror.

2. Face the bathroom mirror and hold up the hand-held mirror.

3. Count the images you can see.

4. Now turn the hand-held mirror a little. What do you notice?

5. Put your face very close to the hand-held mirror. What happens?

Did You Know?

Reflection is a powerful tool. There is an infinite number of images as each image reflects itself.

EXPERIMENT

436

Save Your Money

SUPERVISED

ACTIVITY

AIM

To see how water reflects light.

MATERIALS

- bowl
- drinking glass
- coin
- water

STEPS

1. Fill the bowl with water.
2. Put the coin in the glass.
3. Put the empty glass in the water so it is standing upright.
4. Now look at the glass from the side. Where has the coin gone?
5. Tip water into the glass. Now look at the glass from the side. How much money have you made?

Did You Know?

Light can be reflected in water as well as refracted. The glass was made into a mirror in this experiment.

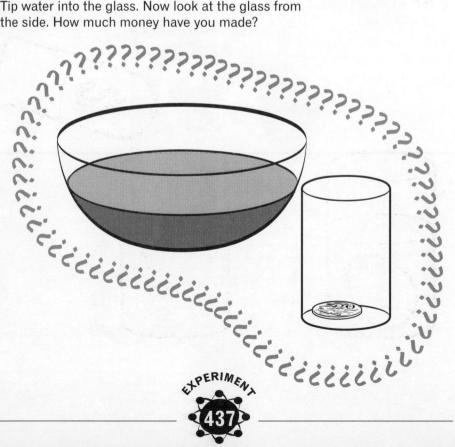

Salt With Your Eggs?

AIM

To see how salt affects the way things sink or float.

MATERIALS

- egg
- glass
- tablespoon
- salt
- water

STEPS

1. Fill the glass with water and place the egg in it.
2. Add a tablespoon of salt. What happens?
3. Keep adding more salt. What happens now? Is the egg floating?

Did You Know?

Salt in water helps things to float. Have you heard of the Red Sea? It is a sea full of salt where it is very easy to float.

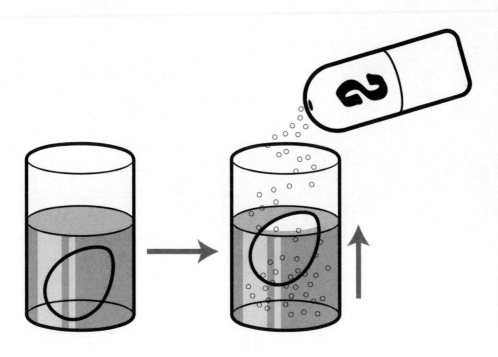

EXPERIMENT
438

Sailing the High Seas

AIM

To see how the shape of objects helps them float.

MATERIALS

- plasticine
- bucket
- water

Did You Know?

How dense an object is depends on whether it will float or not. Ships float because even though they are heavy, they have less density than water.

STEPS

1. Fill the bucket with water.
2. Take the plasticine and shape it into a ball. Put the plasticine in the water. What happens?
3. Take the plasticine and make it into the shape of a bowl. Put it into the water. What happens?

EXPERIMENT
439

Reverse

SUPERVISED ✓

 ✓

 ✓

ACTIVITY

AIM

To see how mirrors reflect light.

MATERIALS

- small rectangular mirror
- sheets of paper
- coloured marker pens

Did You Know?

Emergency services such as the ambulance use this idea. The word AMBULANCE is written in reverse on the front of an ambulance vehicle so that drivers can read it correctly in the rear-vision mirror while driving.

STEPS

1. Write your name in large letters on a sheet of paper.

2. Now hold the mirror on the edge of the paper so that you can see your writing reflected.
   How do the letters look in the mirror? Do any of them look the same in the mirror as they do on the paper?

3. Now, with another sheet of paper, try to write your name in reverse. Hold up the mirror and check your writing. Does it look the right way around? Keep improving your reverse writing to see if you can make the writing in the mirror look the right way around.

Rainbow Light

5–12
AGES

SUPERVISED

ACTIVITY

AIM

To observe refraction of light with sunlight.

MATERIALS

- drinking glass
- large sheet of paper
- box about 50 cm (20 in) high
- sunny window
- water

Did You Know?

There are many folk stories about rainbows, including the idea that there is a pot of gold at the end of the rainbow. A rainbow is made up of water and light, so a person cannot go under a rainbow or stand at the end of a rainbow.

STEPS

1. Early on a clear and bright sunny morning, set up the box about 4 m (4 yds) away from a window with strong sunlight.

2. Fill the glass with water and place it on the box.

3. Look down on the floor for a rainbow. Move the paper around on the floor to capture the rainbow. What colours can you see? How long will this rainbow last for?

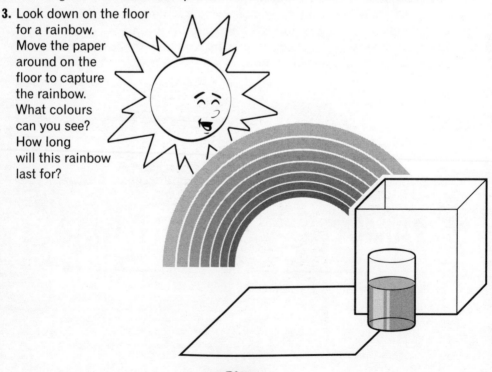

Colour Your Life

AIM

To see how primary colours make secondary colours.

MATERIALS

- torch
- red, blue and yellow cellophane

Did You Know?

Red, yellow and blue are called primary colours. When combinations of these colours are put together they make secondary colours, such as green, purple and orange.

ACTIVITY

STEPS

1. Shine the torch onto a white wall.

2. Cover the torch with red cellophane. Now cover the torch with yellow cellophane. What colour is made on the wall?

3. Now cover the red cellophane with the blue cellophane. What colour is made on the wall?

4. Cover the torch with blue cellophane. Now cover the torch with yellow cellophane. What colour is made on the wall?

5. Using the cellophane, what other colours can you make? Can you make black?

Pull It Up

AIM

To investigate how levers use force.

MATERIALS

- nails
- small hammer
- piece of wood

STEPS

1. With an adult's help, use the hammer to hit a nail into the wood.

2. Now try and pull out the nail with your hands. What happens?

3. Ask the adult with you to try and pull out the nail using their hands only. What happens?

4. Now use the end of the hammer to pull the nail out of the wood. What is the science that makes this work?

Did You Know?

Levers are machines that help by giving more strength. The end of the hammer made the lever to lift out the nail. When you pulled out the nail with the hammer, you put in the same amount of effort as the load of the nail, and so were able to pull it out.

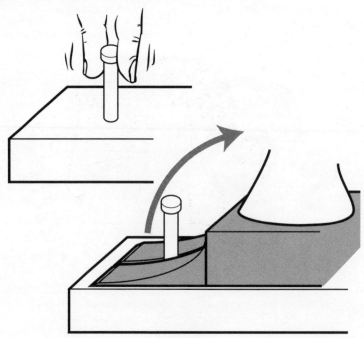

EXPERIMENT
443

Playful Paper

 ✓
SUPERVISED

 ✓

✓

ACTIVITY

AIM

To examine the effects of air pressure.

MATERIALS

- 2 long pieces of paper
  10 cm × 30 cm
  (4 in × 12 in)

STEPS

1. Take the pieces of paper, one in each hand.

2. Hold them close to your face.

3. Blow between the pieces of paper. What happens to the pieces of paper? Did they do what you expected?

4. Next take the end of one of the pieces of paper in your hand so that the length of the paper falls over your hand.

5. Now blow over the sheet of paper. What happens to the paper now? Did it do what you expected?

Did You Know?

This experiment explains part of the way that aeroplanes fly. Aeroplanes fly by means of air pressure.

Opposites Attract

SUPERVISED

ACTIVITY

AIM

To discover how magnetic poles attract and repel.

MATERIALS

- toy boats
- magnets with north and south marked on them
- sticky tape
- shallow tray
- water

Did You Know?

There is a difference between the geographic North Pole, where Father Christmas is said to live, and the magnetic north pole of Earth. The magnetic north pole of Earth is moving approximately 40 km (65 miles) a year.

STEPS

1. Fill the tray with water.
2. Attach the magnets to the top of the toy boats.
3. Put the boats on the water and push them towards one another.
4. What happens when opposite poles on the boats are close to each other? Do the boats come together or pull apart? Try this with the same poles close to each other. Do the boats come together or pull apart?

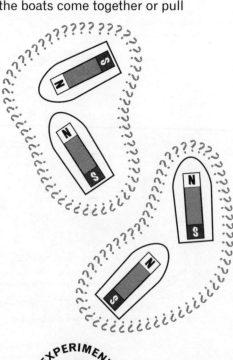

EXPERIMENT
445

North Pole or South Pole?

SUPERVISED ✓

ACTIVITY ✓ ✓

AIM

To discover the poles of magnets.

MATERIALS

- compass
- string
- sticky tape
- magnets
- marker pen

Did You Know?

The magnetism is strongest in the poles of magnets. The poles react differently when like poles are together and when opposite poles are placed together.

STEPS

1. Put the string around the centre of the magnet.

2. Attach the string to a table or ledge.

3. When the magnet is still, use the compass to find out the north pole.

4. Mark the north pole 'N' and the south pole 'S'.

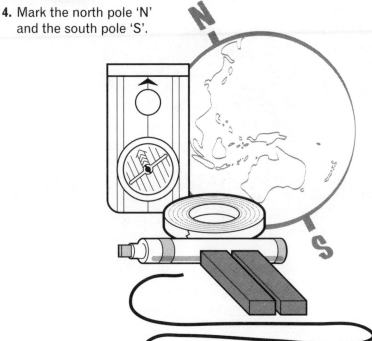

EXPERIMENT
446

Need Your Lenses Fixed?

SUPERVISED

ACTIVITY

AIM

To show how lenses work.

MATERIALS

- magnifying glass
- piece of white paper
- window

STEPS

1. Take your magnifying glass and stand with your back to a bright window.

2. Hold the paper in your other hand. Hold the magnifying glass up so that the light from the window shines onto the paper. What can you see on the paper?

Did You Know?

This experiment is demonstrating a lens. A lens is a curved piece of glass. Convex lenses are curved inwards and concave lenses are curved outwards. When you look in a camera you see a small image. This is because there is a lens in the camera.

EXPERIMENT
447

Am I Upside Down?

5–12
AGES

SUPERVISED ✓

 ✓

✓
ACTIVITY

AIM

To see how light is reflected off different surfaces.

MATERIALS

- shiny spoon

STEPS

1. Hold the spoon up to your face with the curve pointing away from you.

2. Move it away from your face. How does your face change? Does it change as you expected?

3. Now turn the spoon around. What do you see? Do you see what you expected?

Did You Know?

The magical mirrors that you see at amusement parks work by turning light in different directions.

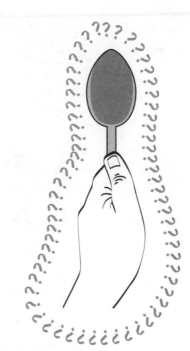

Musical Wine Glasses

AIM

To see how sound resonates.

MATERIALS

- 2 household wine glasses
- water

STEPS

1. Put the two wine glasses on a table.

2. Run your finger around the rim of one of the wine glasses. What happens?

Did You Know?

Did you realise sound has a property called resonance? That means a sound, even if it is soft, when contained in something like glass or wood, bounces off the various surfaces and increases in volume. A guitar sounds as loud as it does because of resonance.

3. Now, wet your finger with water and run it around the rim of the other wine glass. You may have to run your finger around it more than once. Keep going until something happens. Can you hear something?

4. Put some water in the glass and repeat step 3.

EXPERIMENT
449

Musical Bottles

SUPERVISED

ACTIVITY

AIM

To see how sounds of different pitch are made.

MATERIALS

- between 5 to 8 bottles
- water
- spoon or fork

STEPS

1. Put the bottles in a line.

2. Add water to the bottles filling the first bottle with a little water and the next one with a little more than the first, until you have filled all the bottles with different but increasing amounts of water.

3. Now take the spoon and strike the bottles one after the other.

4. Then strike the bottles in any order. Can you make a tune?

Did You Know?

If you want to make a musical scale, place each of the bottles from lowest to highest. See if you can make up a tune or play one that you know.

EXPERIMENT
450

Mighty Whites

AIM

To see how white light is made.

MATERIALS

- 3 torches
- red, blue and green cellophane
- sticky tape

Did You Know?

You can see a white centre and three surrounding colours. The pinkish colour that is produced when the blue overlaps the red is called magenta. The colour that is produced when the green overlaps the blue is cyan. What other colour is there?

STEPS

1. Attach each cellophane colour over the light of each torch.

2. Turn on the torches.

3. Place the torches about 10 cm (4 in) apart on a table and shine them at a white wall.

4. Arrange the torches so that the light from each torch overlaps with the other torches.

5. What can you see on the wall?

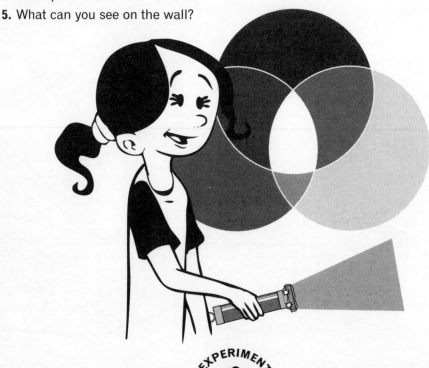

Melting Ice Hands-free

SUPERVISED

ACTIVITY

AIM

To see how light is intensified through a magnifying glass.

MATERIALS

- direct sunlight
- magnifying glass
- ice cubes

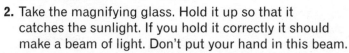

Did You Know?

When light passes through a magnifying glass it is intensified because the glass is shaped in a certain way.

STEPS

1. Take two pieces of ice straight from the freezer. Put each of them in a shallow bowl. Place the bowls in the sunlight.

2. Take the magnifying glass. Hold it up so that it catches the sunlight. If you hold it correctly it should make a beam of light. Don't put your hand in this beam.

3. Direct the beam onto one of the ice cubes. Is it melting more quickly than the other ice cube?

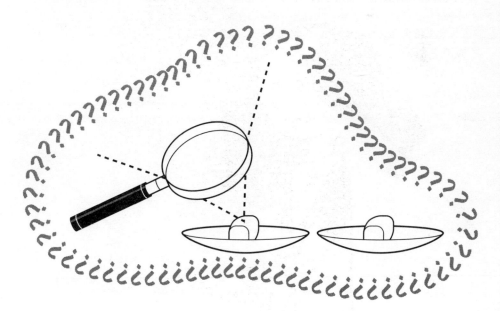

Matchbox Cars

SUPERVISED

ACTIVITY

AIM

To show how magnets work through solid objects.

MATERIALS

- paperclips
- empty matchboxes
- coloured pencils or markers
- stick about 30 cm (12 in) long
- magnets
- A4 cardboard
- sticky tape
- 2 stacks of books

Did You Know?

Magnets are very strong and can ruin watches, clocks, computers, television screens and videos if they are placed too close.

STEPS

1. Decorate the matchboxes to make them into racing cars.
2. Tape a paperclip inside each box.
3. Make the piece of cardboard into a racetrack for two cars.
4. Attach a magnet to the stick.
5. Lift the racetrack off the table by resting it on two stacks of books.
6. Move the magnet under the cardboard to make the race cars on top of the cardboard racetrack move.
7. Make another stick with a magnet so a friend can play with you.

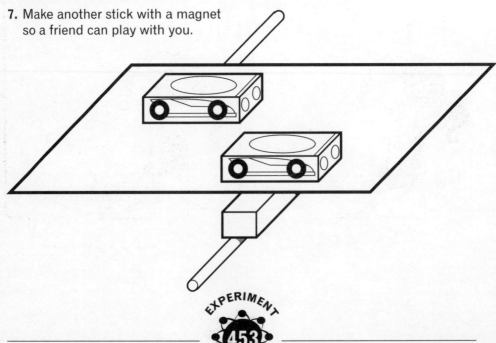

EXPERIMENT
453

Making the Distance

AIM

To see how sound waves affect different objects.

MATERIALS

- pan
- large metal spoon
- friend
- park

Did You Know?

Sound travels at a certain speed which is slower than the speed at which light travels. Sound waves are affected by the quality of the air they are travelling through. This is why it is hard to hear in windy weather.

STEPS

1. Go out to the park.
2. Ask your friend to stand 20 large footsteps away from you. Bang the pan with the spoon.
3. Ask your friend to take 40 more large footsteps away from you. Bang the pan.
4. Keep getting your friend to move back further. What does your friend notice the further he or she moves away from you?

EXPERIMENT
454

Making a Siphon

AIM

To see how water pressure works by making a siphon.

SUPERVISED

MATERIALS

- 2 empty soft drink bottles with openings big enough for a garden hose
- piece of garden hose about 60–80 cm (24–32 in) long
- water

Did You Know?

This experiment shows how water pressure works. In your home, water comes out of the taps because of water pressure.

ACTIVITY

STEPS

1. Fill one soft drink bottle with water and put one end of the hose into it.

2. Use your mouth to suck the other end of the hose until water comes through. Don't drink the water.

3. Quickly put your thumb over the end.

4. Now raise the full soft drink bottle so that it is higher than the empty soft drink bottle.

5. Put the end of the hose you are holding into the empty soft drink bottle. What do you notice?

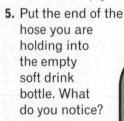

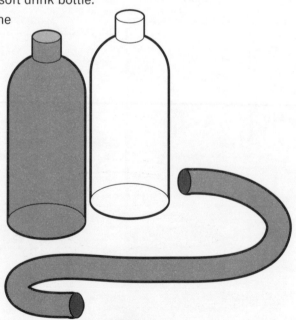

EXPERIMENT
455

Make Your Own Compass

AIM

To make a compass that tells north and south direction.

MATERIALS

- pin
- cork
- magnet
- bowl
- water

Did You Know?

Magnetism is important to Earth as it has a magnetic field. This is how compasses line up the north and south poles.

STEPS

1. Take the pin and run the magnet along the pin once.
2. Do not rub the magnet back the opposite way. Instead, rub the pin with the magnet the same way as the first time at least 20 times.
3. Put the pin in the cork.
4. Put the cork in the bowl with water. What is happening? Can you find the north–south direction?

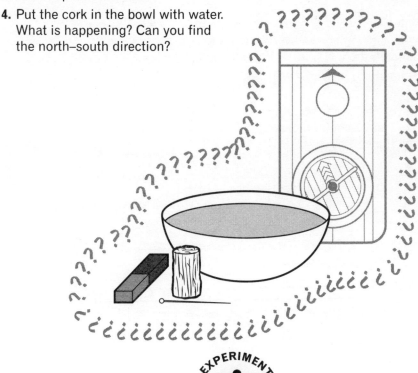

My Own Aeroplane Wing

AIM

To see how wing design works.

MATERIALS

- piece of paper 15 cm × 50 cm (6 in × 20 in)
- sticky tape
- bamboo skewer
- length of string 20 cm (8 in) long
- friend
- ruler
- pencil

Did You Know?

This is the same design as an aeroplane wing. When planes fly, they rush forward at a high speed and the wind rushing over the wings helps the plane to rise.

STEPS

1. Measure 10 cm (4 in) from one end of the paper on each of the long sides. Draw a line across the width.

2. Take the other end of the paper and fold it over to the drawn line. Don't crease the paper.

3. Hold your thumb over the end while you sticky tape it in that position.

4. Gently press a bamboo skewer through both layers of paper at the centre approximately 4 cm (1½ in) in from the fold. Take the skewer out.

5. Thread the string through the holes. Ask your friend to hold both ends of the string tight.

6. Blow on the fold of the paper from the front. Can you get the paper to rise up the string?

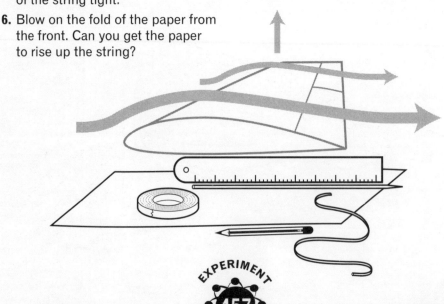

Make a Mini Rocket

 ✓
 ✓

AIM

To see how forces can propel objects.

MATERIALS

- long piece of string
- drinking straw
- balloon
- sticky tape

STEPS

1. Tape the drinking straw to the outside of an uninflated balloon.

2. Thread the string through the drinking straw.

3. Tie each end of the string between two points making sure the string is on an incline.

4. At the highest point of the string, carefully inflate the balloon.

5. Hold the end of the balloon, but don't tie it. Now let the balloon go. What happens?

6. Now try it again, inflating the balloon and letting go from the lowest point of the string. What happens now?

Did You Know?

Rockets are sent into space using the same idea as this experiment. Instead of using air, hot gases propel the rocket upwards at a very high speed.

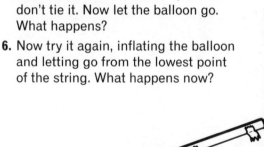

Magnetic Field

5–12
AGES

 ✓

SUPERVISED

 ✓
 ✓
ACTIVITY

AIM

To investigate magnetic field.

MATERIALS

- iron filings
- paper
- magnets

STEPS

1. Place the magnet on the table with the paper placed on top.
2. Put the iron filings on the paper.
3. Move the paper over the magnet and see what happens.

Did You Know?

People have known about the power of magnets for a long time. Magnets were originally known as magnetite and lodestone.

EXPERIMENT
459

Magic Floating Objects

SUPERVISED

ACTIVITY

AIM

To see the how an object travels in the air.

MATERIALS

- hair dryer
- light balls, e.g. table tennis (ping pong) balls or balloons
- toilet roll or aluminium foil roll

Did You Know?

This is how aeroplanes fly! Wings on aeroplanes are designed to have less pressure on the top of the wings than under the wings. This is how aeroplanes stay up and seem to defy gravity.

STEPS

1. Turn the hair dryer on high and turn it upwards so that the air is shooting straight up.
2. Put the balloon or table tennis ball in the stream of air. Hold the hair dryer as still as you can.
3. Watch the objects floating in the air.
4. Try tilting the hair dryer to each side. What happens?
5. Add more objects. How many can you have floating at one time?
6. Put the toilet roll over the stream of air so that the air is funnelled. What happens to the floating balls now? What is happening? The air flows around the balls evenly and while the pull of gravity draws the balls downwards, the air pressure pushes the balls up. The objects can float because the forces on them are equal.

EXPERIMENT
460

Lost My Marbles

5–12
AGES

✓
SUPERVISED

 ✓
 ✓
ACTIVITY

AIM

To show how push and pull can make objects move or stop.

MATERIALS

- marbles of different sizes
- sticky tape
- cardboard lid
- skateboard

STEPS

1. Tape the cardboard lid to the skateboard.

2. Put the marbles in the lid so that they are not close to each other.

3. Give the skateboard a gentle push. What is happening to the marbles?

4. Stop the skateboard by pulling it back. What is happening now?

Did You Know?

Once you start an object moving it will keep going by itself until it is stopped by something. This is called inertia. Have you noticed that you are pushed forward in the car when it stops suddenly? What is acting on you is inertia.

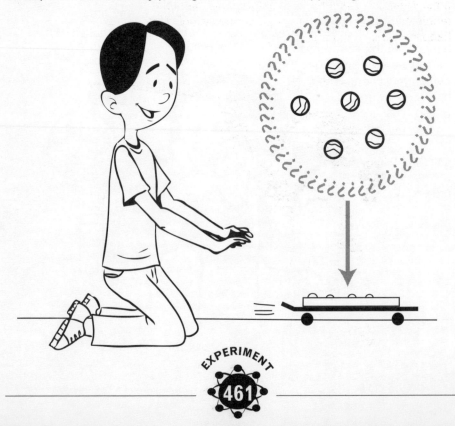

EXPERIMENT
461

Lifting Higher

AIM

To see how sideways force affects objects.

MATERIALS

- table tennis (ping pong) ball
- string
- sticky tape
- scissors
- tape measure

> ### Did You Know?
>
> This sideways force is called centrifugal force. This force is working against gravity and stops the table tennis ball from falling to the ground. Spinning rides at amusement parks use centrifugal force to keep people up off the ground.

STEPS

1. Cut a piece of string about 1 m (3 ft) long.

2. Attach the string to the table tennis ball with sticky tape.

3. Stand in an open outdoor space and start to spin the string around your head. Keep turning it for a short time. What is happening to the string and the table tennis ball? Can you feel any pull on the string? What happens when you let go of the string?

Jumping Up

AIM

To investigate static electricity.

MATERIALS

- hundreds and thousands cake decoration
- small plastic container with a lid
- cloth made of wool

STEPS

1. Place the hundreds and thousands in the plastic container with the lid on.

2. Rub the lid to charge it.

3. Carefully rub your finger across the top of the lid.

4. Do the hundreds and thousands stay up or fall down? What can you observe?

Did You Know?

Charged hundreds and thousands fall down or are repelled. Hundreds and thousands that are neutral stay attached to the lid.

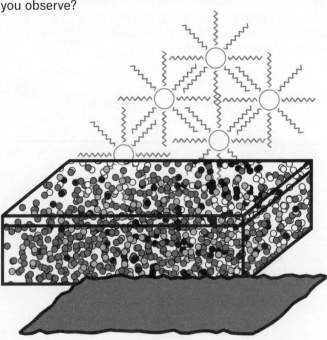

I've Found It!

5–12
AGES

SUPERVISED

ACTIVITY

AIM

To investigate the bending of light.

MATERIALS

- bowl
- friend
- 20 cent coin

STEPS

1. Place the bowl on the table.
2. Put the coin in the bowl and stand aside. Can you see the coin?
3. Ask your friend to fill the bowl with water while you are standing to the side.
4. What happens? Can you see the coin now?

Did You Know?

An image of the coin is visible because light rays refract to create an illusion.

EXPERIMENT 464

How to Make a Parachute

SUPERVISED

ACTIVITY

AIM

To look at the way pressure affects falling objects.

MATERIALS

- plastic bag
- 4 pieces of string, each
  35 cm (14 in) long
- spoon
- scissors

Did You Know?

To make parachutes easier
to control, a hole is made in the
top. This hole lessens the
air resistance.

STEPS

1. Take the plastic bag and cut
   it into a 30 cm (12 in) square.

2. Tie the string to each corner of the square.

3. Tie the other ends of the string to the spoon.

4. Stand on a chair and drop the parachute. What happens?

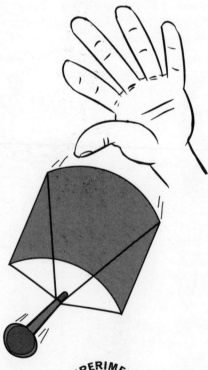

Like Them Lemons?

AIM

To make a battery.

MATERIALS

- 2 lemons
- 2 flat strips of zinc
- 2 flat strips of copper
- 9-volt light bulb
- insulated wire
- pliers

STEPS

1. Put a lemon on the table and place a strip of copper in one end and a strip of zinc in the other. The strips should be parallel to each other.

2. Repeat this for the other lemon.

3. Take the insulated wire and cut off two pieces 20 cm (8 in) long. Take one of the pieces and cut it in half. Trim the plastic insulation from the ends of the wire so that there is some wire visible.

4. Take the long piece of wire, attach it to one of the points of the light bulb and attach the other end to one of the pieces of zinc on one of the lemons.

5. With the shorter piece of wire, connect the piece of copper on the same lemon to the zinc on the other lemon.

6. Holding the last piece of wire on the insulated section, connect one end to the final piece of copper. With the other end connect it to the other point on the light bulb.

Did You Know?

Thomas Edison, 1847–1931, invented the first light globe.

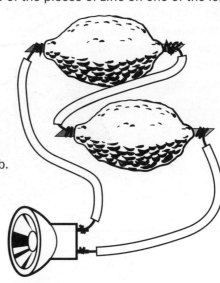

Hot or Cold?

 ✓

SUPERVISED

 ✓

 ✓

ACTIVITY

AIM

To see how temperature affects how objects move with force.

MATERIALS

- 6 new tennis balls
- tape measure
- chair in an outside space with a hard ground surface
- cardboard box
- masking tape
- small sealable (zip-lock) plastic bags
- thermometer

Did You Know?

A bouncy ball that is cold does not bounce as high as a warm ball because it is less flexible and therefore gives less bounce.

STEPS

1. Make two tennis balls hot by putting them inside the cardboard box in the sun for two hours.

2. Make two tennis balls cold by putting each inside a sealable plastic bag and placing them in the refrigerator for two hours.

3. Leave two tennis balls at room temperature.

4. Arrange the outside space where you will conduct this experiment. Measure a height of 2 m (6 ft) on a nearby wall and mark with masking tape. Place the chair beside this.

5. When the tennis balls are ready, test and record the temperature of each with the thermometer by placing it against the tennis balls.

6. Test what happens when you drop the tennis balls from the height marked on the wall.

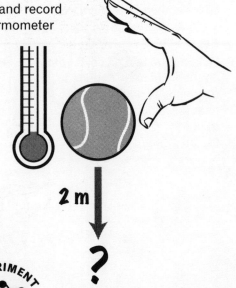

2 m

?

EXPERIMENT
467

Rainbow in Your Hand

5–12
AGES

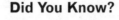

SUPERVISED

ACTIVITY

AIM

To observe different prisms that can create rainbows.

MATERIALS

- shallow pan
- small mirror
- water
- strong sunlight

STEPS

1. Pour the water in the pan.
2. Place the mirror against the side of the pan.
3. Place your hand in front of the mirror but not in front of the sunlight.
4. Where is the rainbow reflected? What is creating the prism for the light to travel through?

Did You Know?

A rainbow is seen on your hand. *Ray* is the word used for the stream of light. When rays of light pass through prisms, they create rainbows.

High Tides

 ✓

 ✓
 ✓

AIM

To see how water is affected by different objects.

MATERIALS

- glass jar with a lid
- water
- bucket

Did You Know?

There was an ancient philosopher called Archimedes. One day when he was having a bath he noticed that the water level rose. He discovered the law that the volume of water displaced equals the volume of the object placed in the water.

STEPS

1. Fill the bucket with water so that it is three quarters full.

2. Place the jar, with its lid tightly fixed, into the water. What happens?

3. Now slowly push the jar to the bottom of the bucket. Look at the level of the water on the sides of the bucket. What happens? Does it rise, fall or stay the same?

4. Fill the jar completely with water. Now place it in the bucket of water. Does the level of the water rise, fall or stay the same?

5. What would happen if you got into a bath?

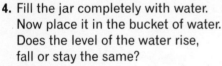

EXPERIMENT
469

Hey, Stand up Ruler!

AIM

To see how objects can be suspended.

MATERIALS

- ruler
- length of string twice the length of the ruler
- sticky tape
- table

Did You Know?

There are bridges that are held up in this way. They are called suspension bridges. One of these bridges is the Golden Gate Bridge in the USA.

STEPS

1. Tape one end of the string to the table.

2. Hold the ruler on the table vertically and run the piece of string over the top so that it is tight. The ruler should stand without you needing to hold it.

3. Now tape the other end of the string to the table.

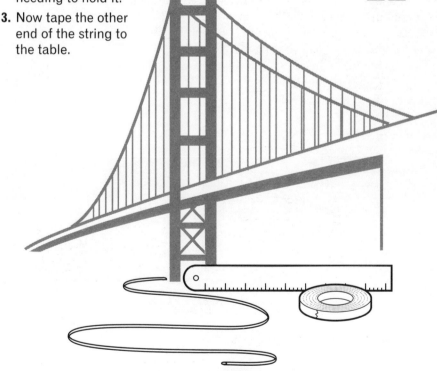

EXPERIMENT
470

Hangin' out for Answers

5–12
AGES

SUPERVISED

ACTIVITY

AIM

To see how weights can balance each other.

MATERIALS

- coat hanger
- 2 empty plastic containers of the same type
- 4 pieces of string 20 cm (8 in) in length
- household objects, e.g. pencil, eraser, sharpener, fork, spoon etc.

Did You Know?

The force pulling down on an object is called gravity. We walk on the Earth because of gravity. Without gravity people would float off into space.

STEPS

1. Take one of the plastic containers and tie a piece of string on each side.
2. Repeat for the other container.
3. Attach one container to each end of the coat hanger.
4. Now hang the coat hanger from a table or ledge so that it can move freely.
5. Put various objects into the containers. What happens?
6. Can you get two containers to hang at the same level?

The Swing of Things

AIM

To show how for every action there needs to be an equal and opposite reaction.

MATERIALS

- chair with wheels, e.g. a swivel chair
- space

STEPS

1. Place yourself comfortably in the chair.

2. Without letting your feet touch the ground, see if you can move yourself. Can you move yourself as easily as you thought you could?

Did You Know?

It is difficult to move because you are not pushing against anything. The wheels on the chair cause your pushing energy to go into the air. If you pushed against something solid, you would move because the solid object would not move back.

EXPERIMENT
472

Funny Funnel

5–12
AGES

SUPERVISED

ACTIVITY

AIM

To see the effects of changes in air pressure.

MATERIALS

- funnel
- piece of card the size of a postcard

STEPS

1. Place the card on the table.
2. Hold the funnel close to the card with the small end pointing upwards.
3. Use your mouth to suck air through the funnel.
4. With the funnel in the same position, blow hard. What happens?

Did You Know?

Air pressure presses on our bodies, but we don't feel it because our bodies press back with equal force.

Fun to Spin

AIM

To see how designed objects can move through the air.

MATERIALS

- paper (normal weight), thin paper and thick card
- ruler
- scissors

Did You Know?

Aerodynamics is the word used for understanding how objects move through air. This study includes kites, aeroplanes, paper planes, rockets and how objects like balls move through the air.

STEPS

1. Take the normal weight paper and make a strip of paper 20 cm (8 in) long and 2 cm (¾ in) wide.

2. Measure 1.5 cm (⅝ in) from each end and make a cut halfway across the strip. The cuts should be on opposite sides of the strip.

3. Turn the paper strip and use the cuts near the ends to make a closed shape. The shape should hold together and not undo.

4. Hold your flying machine over your head and drop it. Watch how it spins quickly as it falls.

5. Make another fun spinner with the thin paper then the thick card. What happens?

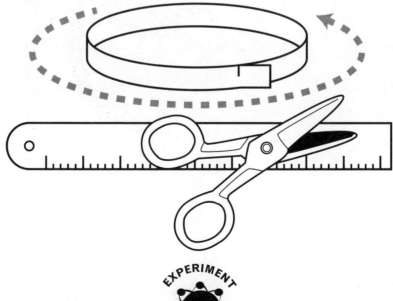

EXPERIMENT
474

Friction Around the Edges

 ✓

SUPERVISED

 ✓
 ✓

ACTIVITY

AIM

To see how motion is affected by friction.

MATERIALS

- piece of cardboard 30 cm (12 in) wide and very long
- coin
- eraser
- pen
- ice cube
- other household objects
- ruler
- a chair

Did You Know?

Friction is the force that happens when two objects move against one another. Notice the difference between riding your bike on the road and on the grass. The reason it is harder to ride on the grass is because of friction.

STEPS

1. Take the piece of cardboard and rest it on a chair so that one end is raised and the other end is on the floor.

2. Place each of the objects on the cardboard at the top. Use the ruler as a barrier to keep the objects from falling.

3. Take the ruler away. Which objects fall more quickly?

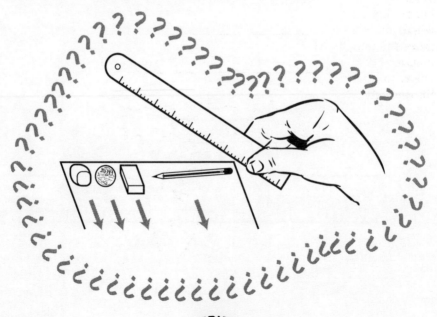

EXPERIMENT
475

Floating Leaves

AIM

To show the pull of magnets.

MATERIALS

- paperclips
- magazines
- scissors
- coloured pencils or markers
- string
- magnets
- sticky tape
- ledge nearby

Did You Know?

The steel in the paperclip is attracted to the magnet. Magnets attract other metals besides steel such as iron and nickel.

STEPS

1. Draw some pictures of autumn leaves. Cut them out.

2. Tie the string to a paperclip and attach the paperclip to the back of a leaf. Do this for each leaf.

3. Attach the other end of the string to a ledge with the sticky tape.

4. Hold your magnet and move close to the leaves and then away again.

5. What is happening when you move the magnet closer to the leaves?

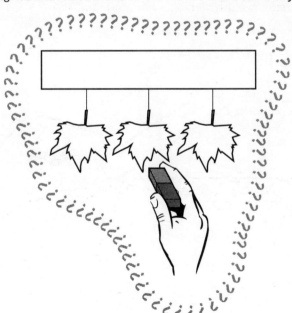

EXPERIMENT
476

Fish

AIM

To show how magnets work through solid objects.

MATERIALS

- paperclips
- empty matchboxes
- coloured pencils or markers
- stick about 30 cm (12 in) long
- magnets
- A4 cardboard
- sticky tape
- string

Did You Know?

It is important not to drop magnets as they will not be as strong.

STEPS

1. Decorate the matchboxes to look like fish.
2. Tape a paperclip inside each box.
3. Make the piece of cardboard into a pool for the fish and scatter the matchbox fish on it.
4. Attach some string to the stick and tie a magnet onto the other end. This is your fishing rod.
5. Now fish. How many fish can you catch at once?

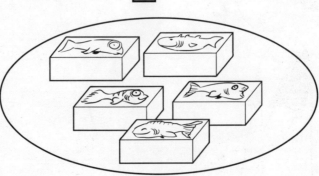

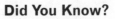

EXPERIMENT
477

Filter Fun

AIM

To see the effect of coloured light on objects of different colours.

MATERIALS

- torch
- red, blue and green cellophane
- objects of different colours, especially red, green and blue
- sticky tape

Did You Know?

When light hits a coloured object some of the light is absorbed and some reflected. The colour that you see is the colour that is reflected. Objects look black because they absorb all the light that shines on them.

STEPS

1. Tape the piece of red cellophane over the torch. Now shine the torch on the different coloured objects. What happens?

2. Take off the red cellophane and tape the piece of blue cellophane over the torch. Now shine the torch on the different coloured objects. What happens?

3. Take off the blue cellophane and tape the piece of green cellophane over the torch. Now shine the torch on the different coloured objects. What happens?

EXPERIMENT
478

Feeling Fruity

AIM

To see how some objects float and others don't.

MATERIALS

- apple
- carrot
- potato
- orange
- water
- bucket

Did You Know?

Some objects float better than others because they have more air in them. Rotten eggs float better than fresh eggs because they have more air in them. So, test your eggs next time you make an omelette!

STEPS

1. Fill the bucket with water.
2. Put all the fruit and vegetables in the water.
3. What happens? Are some floating and others sinking?

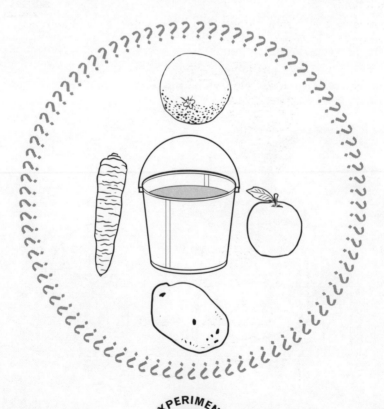

EXPERIMENT
479

Feeling a Little Tense?

SUPERVISED

 ✓
 ✓
 ✓

ACTIVITY

AIM

To see how some objects float some of the time.

MATERIALS

- metal lid from a jar
- bucket
- water

STEPS

1. Fill the bucket with water.
2. Gently place the lid with the sides facing up in the water. Does it float?
3. Now turn the lid upside down and place it gently in the water. What happens now? Does it float?
4. Now place the lid gently sideways into the water. Can you get it to float?

Did You Know?

Water has a quality called surface tension which means it can keep some objects afloat when placed in a certain way on the water. So, some insects can stand on water because of surface tension.

EXPERIMENT
480

Feelin' the Pressure

AIM

To see how air pressure works.

MATERIALS

- drinking glass
- water
- piece of card the size of a postcard

Did You Know?

Air has a quality called pressure. This is a force that pushes in all directions, even upwards.

STEPS

1. Fill the glass to the top with water.
2. Take the card and put it on top.
3. Warning! Do the rest of this experiment over the sink.
4. Holding the card in place turn the glass upside down.
5. Now take your hand away from the card. What happens?

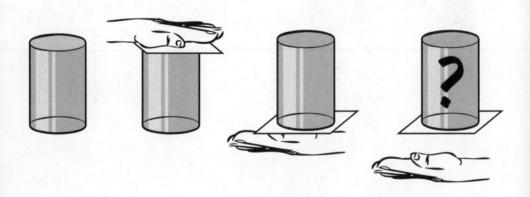

EXPERIMENT
481

Falling Over

AIM

To show how energy can be transferred from one object to another.

MATERIALS

- 2 packs of dominoes
- large flat area, e.g. table

STEPS

1. Stand the dominoes up on end on the table.
2. Set the dominoes about 2 cm (¾ in) apart.
3. Tap the first domino and watch what happens.

Did You Know?

This is called the *domino effect*. This term is used to describe how one action can cause a chain of events. This can be seen in storms when trees fall.

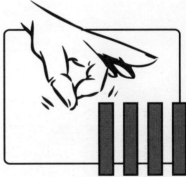

EXPERIMENT
482

Turning to White

AIM

To see how the colour white is made up of many colours.

MATERIALS

- coloured pencils
- piece of white cardboard
- compass
- protractor
- pencil
- scissors

Did You Know?

Isaac Newton discovered that white light was made up of many colours by shining white light through a prism.

STEPS

1. Draw a circle with the compass on the cardboard. Cut out the circle.

2. Use the protractor to mark out six equal sections.

3. Colour each section with the following colours – red, blue, green, yellow, orange and violet.

4. Push the pencil through the centre of the circle so that you can spin it like a top. Spin the circle. What happens?

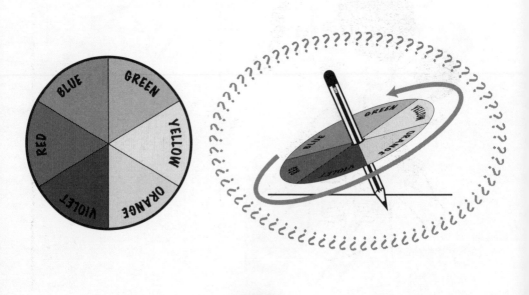

EXPERIMENT
483

Echo, Echo

 ✓

 ✓
 ✓

AIM

To discover how sound reflects off surfaces.

MATERIALS

- 2 blocks of wood
- enclosed corridor with a bare floor
- carpeted area

STEPS

1. Go to the enclosed area.

2. Bang the wood together softly. Now increase the volume and bang them together louder. What do you notice is happening?

3. Now go to a carpeted area. Repeat step 2. What happens?

Did You Know?

An echo is produced when sound reflects off a hard surface. The sound is duller in a carpeted area because carpet absorbs the sound waves.

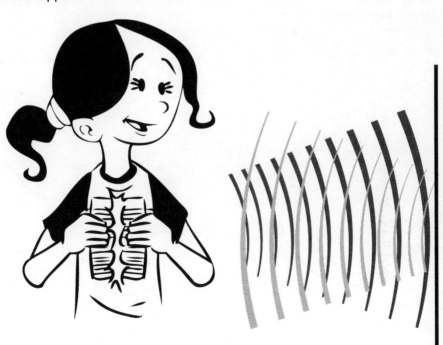

Double Magnetism

 ✓

 ✓
✓

AIM

To investigate magnetic field and opposite poles of magnets.

MATERIALS

- iron filings
- paper
- pencil
- magnets

Did You Know?

Lodestone (a magnet) was very useful to sailors when they needed to navigate. They discovered that when the lodestone was hung on a string, it showed a north–south direction.

STEPS

1. Place the magnet on the table with the opposite poles about 5 cm (2 in) apart.

2. Place the paper on top and gently scatter the iron filings on top of the paper.

3. Move the paper gently. 'Draw' a picture with the iron filings.

4. Try this again with the same poles facing each other. Do the iron filings look different?

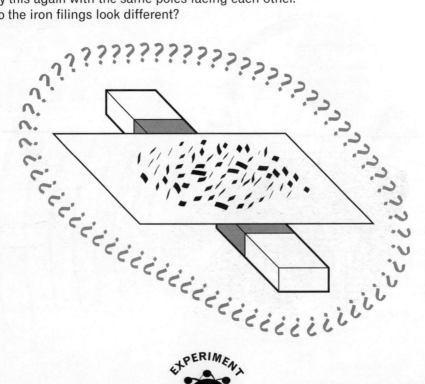

EXPERIMENT

485

Double Balloon Static

SUPERVISED

ACTIVITY

AIM
To make static electricity showing electricity attracting and repelling.

MATERIALS
- balloons
- string
- jumper (preferably wool)
- thick paper

Did You Know?
Electricity can repel, which means to push away. When the two balloons are charged they repel each other. The paper attracts the balloons.

STEPS
1. Blow up the balloons and tie the ends.
2. Attach the string to the ends of the balloons.
3. Rub the balloons on the jumper.
4. Hold them up by the string. What happens?
5. Now place the paper between the balloons. What happens now?

Don't Sink the Boat

AIM

To investigate the energy of static electricity.

MATERIALS

- corks
- plastic pens
- shallow tray
- water
- cloth (preferably wool)

Did You Know?

Lightning is a very strong form of static electricity. No one knows how it is formed.

STEPS

1. Use the corks as boats and place them in the tray of water. Push them under the water so that they are wet.

2. Rub the pen on your clothing quickly.

3. Use the pen to drag the boats across the water. Be careful not to touch the water or the cork with the pen. If this happens recharge the pen by rubbing it on your clothes again.

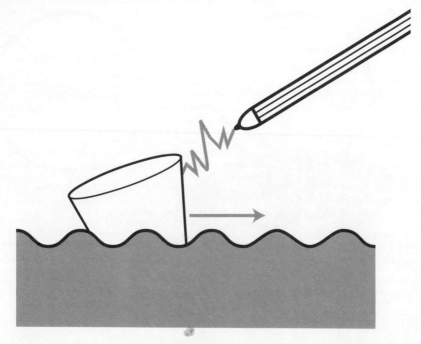

Don't Cheat

SUPERVISED

ACTIVITY

AIM

To look at the effects of air pressure.

MATERIALS

- soft drink bottle
- small piece of paper scrunched up into a ball

Did You Know?

On the ground the air pressure is at a certain level. The further you go away from Earth, the higher the air pressure gets.

STEPS

1. Lie the bottle sideways on the table with its mouth slightly over the edge of the table.

2. Place the small ball of paper a little inside the neck of the bottle.

3. Can you get the paper out without using your hands?

4. Try blowing into the bottle. What happens?

5. Tip out the paper and put it back in the starting position.

6. This time blow across the top of the bottle. Did you get the paper out without using your hands?

Doing Things by Halves

5–12
AGES

 ✓

SUPERVISED

 ✓
 ✓
 ✓
 ✓

ACTIVITY

AIM

To look at how the length of a piece of string affects sound.

MATERIALS

- hard string or thick fishing line, 1.8 m (6 ft) long
- 2 heavy bricks
- marker pen
- scissors
- ruler

Did You Know?

Sound is produced by vibrations through the air. A similar experiment to this was carried out by Pythagoras, an ancient Greek philosopher. He created a music scale from it.

STEPS

1. Take the string and wrap some of it around one of the bricks as tightly as possible.

2. Measure out three ruler-lengths of string and tie the rest of the string around the other brick.

3. Now put the bricks apart so the string is tight. Pluck the string. What kind of sound does it make?

4. Roll more string onto one of the bricks so that you are shortening the distance between the bricks, but keeping the string tight. Pluck the string. What kind of sound does it make now?

5. Repeat step 4. Pluck the string. What kind of sound does it make now?

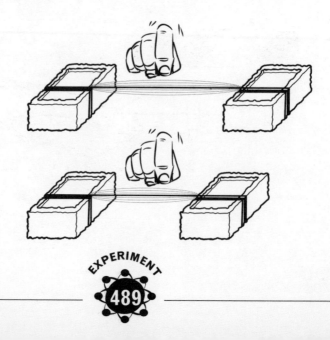

EXPERIMENT

489

Demagnetise Me

 ✓

SUPERVISED

 ✓
 ✓

ACTIVITY

AIM

To show how magnets can destroy magnetic materials.

MATERIALS

- unwanted audio cassette tape
- magnet
- tape player

Did You Know?

The magnet has wiped the recording on the audio cassette tape. These tapes are called magnetic tapes. This means the sound that you hear is stored on the tape by small magnetic particles. The magnet used in this experiment is more powerful than the magnetic particles of the tape and therefore destroys the stored information.

STEPS

1. Play the audio cassette tape. Stop it after a few minutes.
2. Take the audio cassette tape out of the tape player and pull out the brown tape.
3. Wave the magnet closely over the brown tape.
4. Wind the audio tape back into the cassette cover.
5. Play the tape again. What do you notice?

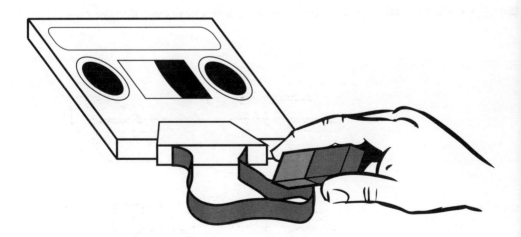

EXPERIMENT
490

Crater Than Thou

5–12
AGES

 ✓

SUPERVISED

 ✓

 ✓

ACTIVITY

AIM

To see the effect of falling objects.

MATERIALS

- large bowl
- flour
- large marble
- small marble
- tennis ball

Did You Know?

Craters are formed in a similar way to this experiment. The larger the crater, the greater the force with which it hits Earth. When asteroids hit Earth, they act in the same way as the marble did in the flour.

STEPS

1. Fill the bowl with flour and pat it down gently. Make it smooth on top.

2. From a height, drop a large marble into the middle of the flour. What do you notice?

3. Now smooth the flour again and repeat step 2 with a smaller marble. What do you notice?

4. Now smooth the flour again and repeat step 2 with a tennis ball. What do you notice?

Combing the Shadows

AIM

To look at how sunlight works.

MATERIALS

- comb

STEPS

1. Find a clear window with sunlight shining through.
2. On a flat surface hold the comb upright in the sunlight so it makes a shadow.
3. Incline the comb away from the Sun. What happens to the shadow? What kind of shadow is made by the Sun?

Did You Know?

Some light rays fan out but the Sun's rays hit Earth at a parallel angle, making shadows that are straight.

Ceiling Rainbows

AIM

To observe how rainbows are made.

MATERIALS

- torch
- clear plastic cup
- clear square container
- water in a jug

Did You Know?

The rainbow shape is determined by the container shape. The water creates a prism through which the light travels. Rain drops are also prisms that create rainbows.

STEPS

1. Darken a room.

2. Switch on the torch and place the cup in front of the torch.

3. Gently pour the water into the cup and watch the ceiling for rainbows.

4. Now do the same with the square container.

5. What kind of rainbows did you see? Did you notice any difference when using the different containers?

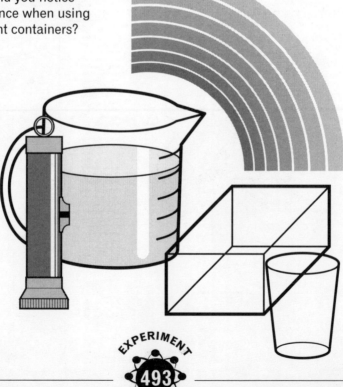

EXPERIMENT

493

Catch Me, I'm Falling!

5–12
AGES

 ✓

 ✓

SUPERVISED

 ✓
✓

ACTIVITY

AIM

To see how air resistance affects different objects.

MATERIALS

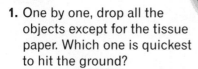

- sheet of paper
- feather
- leaf
- book
- 2 pieces of tissue paper

STEPS

Did You Know?

High-speed drag races are designed the way they are to reduce the amount of air resistance. The less resistance, the faster they will go.

1. One by one, drop all the objects except for the tissue paper. Which one is quickest to hit the ground?

2. Now take the tissue paper. Scrunch up one of the sheets.

3. Stand on a chair and drop both sheets of tissue paper. Which one hits the ground first?

EXPERIMENT
494

Burning Water

AIM

To investigate some ways light is reflected.

MATERIALS

- candle
- matches
- sheet of glass about
  30 cm (12 in) or A4 size
  (glass from an old
  picture frame works well)
- drinking glass
- water

Did You Know?

When light travels into glass some
of it is reflected. That means in the
glass you see an image of what is in
front of the glass. You could try this
again with one lit candle and
one unlit candle.

STEPS

1. Fill the glass with water and
   place it towards the middle of a table.

2. Ask an adult to help you light the candle and put it
   towards the edge of the table.

3. Now put the sheet of glass
   between the candle and
   the glass of water.

4. Look through the sheet of
   glass at the glass of water.
   What do you see? Can you
   see the candle burning
   in the water?

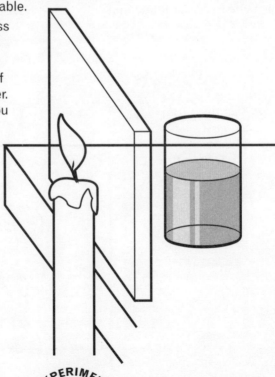

EXPERIMENT
495

Bounce Higher!

SUPERVISED ✓

 ✓

 ✓

ACTIVITY

AIM

To see bouncing energy.

MATERIALS

- 3 tennis balls
- tape measure
- chair
- outside space with a hard ground surface
- masking tape
- friend

Did You Know?

When a ball is bounced it conserves its energy. That is why it bounces up close to the height from which it was dropped.

STEPS

1. Use the tape measure to measure 40 cm (16 in), 80 cm (32 in) and 120 cm (48 in) on a wall. Mark these with masking tape.

2. Drop a tennis ball from the 40 cm (16 in) height and ask your friend to watch what happens. How high did the ball bounce? Do this two more times and record how high it bounces each time.

3. Do the same using the height of 80 cm (32 in).

4. Repeat the experiment at the 120 cm (48 in) height. Why do you think the ball bounces at different heights?

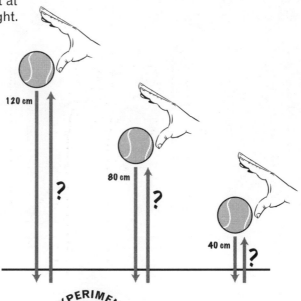

Bounce Factors

AIM

To see how different surfaces affect the bounce of balls.

MATERIALS

- basketball
- tennis ball
- carpeted floor area
- hard floor area

STEPS

1. In the hard floor area bounce the basketball and then bounce the tennis ball. What happens?

2. Now go to a carpeted area and bounce the basketball and the tennis ball. What happens? Why do you think the balls bounced differently in the different places?

Did You Know?

When a ball is falling it still maintains the energy it starts with. When it hits a soft surface like carpet, some of the ball's energy is absorbed into the carpet because it is spongier. When a ball hits a hard surface it only loses a very small amount of its energy.

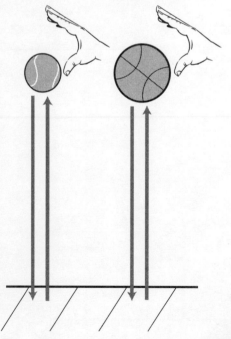
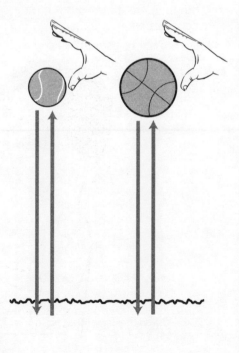

Bounce!

AIM

To see how energy is transferred by bouncing different balls.

MATERIALS

- basketball
- tennis ball
- friend
- outside space

Did You Know?

The tennis ball bounces much higher than the basketball. This is because energy from the basketball is transferred to the tennis ball. A ball loses energy from the moment it is released.

STEPS

1. Bounce the basketball and take note of how high it bounces.
2. Bounce the tennis ball from the same height as the basketball and take note of how high it bounces.
3. Now hold tennis ball on top of the basketball. What do you think will happen when you drop them? Which one will bounce the highest?
4. Ask your friend to watch and then drop the balls. What happens?

EXPERIMENT
498

Bend 'Em, Don't Break 'Em

AIM

To show how light refracted through water changes how an object looks.

MATERIALS

- deep bowl
- ruler

STEPS

1. Fill up the bowl with water.

2. Slowly put the ruler into the bowl of water. Only put the ruler in up to halfway.

3. What do you see? Is it real?

4. Slowly pull the ruler out. Has the ruler changed?

5. Put the ruler back into the bowl and observe again.

Did You Know?

You bent the ruler but you didn't break it. This is possible because light refracts in water – this means that the light changes direction slightly. This is why objects look different in water.

Balloon Static

AIM

To make static electricity.

MATERIALS

- balloons
- water tap
- jumper (preferably wool)
- paper

STEPS

1. Tear the paper into small pieces and put them on the table.

2. Blow up the balloon and tie the end.

3. Rub the balloon on the jumper.

4. What happens when you hold the balloon on the wall in a warm dry room?

5. What happens when you hold the balloon near running water?

6. What happens when you hold the balloon over the torn pieces of paper?

Did You Know?

Everything around us is made up of tiny little parts called atoms, and atoms are made of even smaller parts, which are called protons, electrons and neutrons. The protons, electrons and neutrons are very different. Protons have a positive (+) charge. Electrons have a negative (–) charge. Neutrons have no charge. Usually, atoms have the same amount of electrons and protons. When the atom has no charge, it is 'neutral'. If you rub things together, electrons can move from one atom to another, then some atoms get extra electrons and the other atoms might have a negative charge or no charge at all. When charges are separated like this, it is called static electricity.

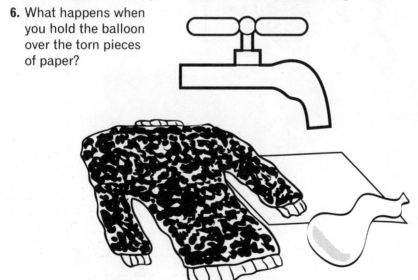

EXPERIMENT 500

Attractive Stars

AIM

To demonstrate the electric field surrounding charged objects.

MATERIALS

- balloon
- jumper (preferably wool)
- coloured markers
- scissors
- strong paper

Did You Know?

There is an electrical field surrounding charged objects. The balloon became the charged object and it could then attract the stars. Once the stars had touched the balloon, they were repelled and fell to the ground.

STEPS

1. Blow up the balloon and tie the end.
2. Draw some small stars on the paper and cut them out. Put them on a flat surface.
3. Rub the balloon on the jumper.
4. Place the balloon about 10 cm (4 in) above the stars. What happens?

EXPERIMENT
501

Alphabetical Index